THEIR VIEW OF NORTH CHINA

1910-1923

Robert W. and Edith G. Clack

By Norma Geraldine Clack

Robert Wood Clack and Edith (Gordon) Clack
Their wedding at the Methodist Mission
in Tientsin (now Tianjin), China.
March 21, 1911

THEIR VIEW OF NORTH CHINA, 1910 TO 1923:
Robert W. and Edith G. Clack

Compiled and edited by Norma Geraldine Clack

A portrayal of life in North China in the early twentieth century narrated through the personal letters written by Robert Wood Clack and his wife, Edith Gordon Clack, and enhanced with images of the snapshots taken in China by Robert Clack.

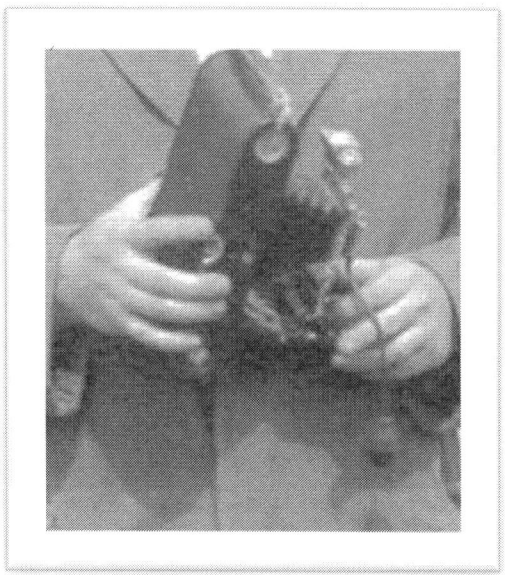

In his hands: The camera used by R.W. Clack
to take the "snapshots" reproduced in this book.

Front Cover – Images from Robert Clack collection
1. Y.M.C.A. staff in Paotingfu (photo ca. 1915 – Robert Clack front row center).
   Banner translations: "Enthusiastic in Service" and "Help Young People"
2. Porcelain Pagoda, west slope of Jade Fountain Hill (photo 1912)
3. Entrance to Li Hung Chung Memorial Hall, Paotingfu (photo 1912)
4. Chinese logograms – Robert Clack's name written by him in Chinese (see pages 8 and 312)

Additional credits for photographs are listed in the Appendix (p.321).

Copyright Pending ® 2021 by Norma Geraldine Clack
All rights reserved

Paperback ISBN-13: 978-0-578-90936-3

This is the First Edition

Book design and editing by Norma Geraldine Clack
Cover design by Christopher W. Tremblay, Ed.D.

Published by Norma Geraldine Clack

Ordering Information: Amazon.com
Printed in the United States of America

DEDICATION

On behalf of Robert W. Clack, this book is dedicated to his loving wife Edith (Gordon) Clack. She was the cherished mother of their six children, and a devoted helpmate throughout their 53 years together, including thirteen remarkable years in China.

This book is also dedicated to Wynne R. Clack, youngest son of Robert and Edith, who lovingly preserved all the Clack family letters and photographs used in this book.

Norma Geraldine Clack
daughter of Wynne R. Clack

Robert and Edith Clack, 1954

Wynne Clack receiving his Alma College diploma from his father, "Prof" Clack, 1949

The Placid Yellow Sea

(Chinese Proverb: "China is a great sea that salts all water that flows into it.")

Under sunny Eastern skies lies the placid Yellow Sea,
A briny flood: from West and North great rivers ceaselessly
Pour in their fresh rain-swollen tides, which soon are swallowed up
And vanish; all their freshness lost in the saltness of the sea.

But fierce storms come and grip both sea and land with fingers chill.
The rough winds howl and gusts of snow and sleet the heavens fill.
The sea is lashed to fury and the waves rise mountain high . . . . . .
Yet when the wintry gale has passed again the sea lies still.

Across broad plains and terraced hills is massed a patient horde,
The Chinese race: from West and North for centuries have poured
Invaders fierce to rule an hour and then be swallowed up,
All racial traits and culture lost in China's teeming horde.

Though wars may crimson China's face with many a bloody stain,
Across the fields great armies rage, battling with might and main.
The patient Chinese bides his time, in confidence supreme,
When war's grim storms have spent themselves, then peace will reign again.

by Robert Wood Clack

CONTENTS

PREFACE x

ACKNOWLEDGMENTS xi

PROLOGUE xii

INTRODUCTION xv

PART ONE: THE TEACHING YEARS, 1910–1913 (Chapters 1–12)

1	The Beginning of an Amazing Journey	1
2	First Impressions of China and Chihli Provincial College	7
3	Robert and Edith: Their Paths Unite	19
4	Dedication of Presbyterian Martyrs' Monument in Paotingfu	31
5	Summer Excursion to Japan and Settling into Their New Life	37
6	War and Pestilence and Separation (1911-1912)	43
7	The Collapse of 3,500 Years of Chinese Dynasties	55
8	First Election for the New Government (1912)	71
9	Y.M.C.A. Conference at the Sleeping Buddha Temple near Peking	93
10	Republic of China Established; Third Year of Teaching Begins	109
11	Y.M.C.A. Chinese National Convention (1912)	119
12	Final Semester at Chihli Provincial College	129

PART TWO: THE Y.M.C.A. YEARS, 1914–1923 (Chapters 13–25)

13	Establishing the Y.M.C.A. in Paotingfu	143
14	End of First Full Year with the Y.M.C.A.	155
15	Beginning of Second Fiscal Year with the Y.M.C.A.	163
16	Third Year with the Y.M.C.A.	173
17	Fourth Year with the Y.M.C.A. and Beginning of Homeland Sabbatical	185
18	Fifth Year with the Y.M.C.A. and End of Homeland Sabbatical	191
19	Sixth Year with the Y.M.C.A.	198
20	Seventh Year with the Y.M.C.A.	211
21	Warlords, Famine, and More (1920)	227
22	Tuchuns' War – July 1920: R.W. Clack Serves as Interpreter	231
23	North China Famine and National Athletic Competitions	245
24	Famine Relief Work, 1921	257
25	Under Martial Law and Return to the United States in 1923	265

PART THREE: LIFE AFTER CHINA

⌘	Transitional Year in Iowa (1923–1924)	275
⌘	Teaching at Alma College in Alma, Michigan (1924–1954)	276
⌘	Retirement Years (1954–1964)	279

EPILOGUE

⌘ Published Works: Translations of Chinese and Japanese Poetry
and a Study of Chinese Music — 283

⌘ Poems Composed by R.W. Clack: Reflections on His Experiences in China — 287

⌘ Clack Art Center at Alma College and the Chinese Artifacts Exhibit — 289

APPENDICES AND GLOSSARIES

⌘ Chinese Name Conversion Chart (Wade-Giles and Pinyin Systems) — 294

⌘ Major Political Events in China, 1911-1922 (Selected Highlights) — 295

⌘ Glossaries

   1 Descriptions of Selected Places and Organizations — 296
   2 List of Individuals Mentioned in the Clack Letters — 298
   3 Annotations for Family Members in the Clack Letters — 309

⌘ Information from Yiding Gao, Present-day Resident of China — 312

⌘ Endnotes, Bibliography, and Sources — 317

⌘ Photography Credits — 321

⌘ Compiler and Editor, Norma Geraldine Clack — 322

Notes from Norma Geraldine Clack, compiler and editor –

The letters written by R.W. Clack were mailed to his family members in Clear Lake, Iowa. He alternated addressing the letters between his parents and his three sisters. Edith Clack also wrote to her husband's family, but wrote more frequently to her mother, Elma Gordon.

The brief summaries of Chinese events that are found at the beginning of some chapters are intended to provide some historical context for the Clack letters and photographs. The letters have been edited for length by removing some of the extraneous personal material, as well as the salutations. The Clack correspondence came from two sources: first, the personal letters which were passed down through the family to Norma Clack; and second, the official records of the Kautz Family YMCA Archives located in the Andersen Library at the University of Minnesota in Minneapolis, Minnesota.

PREFACE

In a spacious hallway of the Clack Art Center at Alma College – a small private college in Alma, Michigan – there is a wall of floor-to-ceiling wooden cabinets with protective glass doors. The items displayed in approximately 30 linear feet of cabinets are Chinese in origin. Nestled within these cabinets are three colorful, embroidered Chinese robes, brass candleholders and plates, ceramic vases and bowls, an artistic watercolor scroll, and dozens of smaller items – all of which may seem somewhat out of place in the middle of Michigan.

The hallway leads to the college's art gallery and student classrooms and studios. How many students go by these display cases in the course of a day? How many take notice and wonder why these Chinese antiquities are in this building?

For me, these Chinese items are poignant reminders of my childhood visits to the home of my grandparents in Alma – just a few blocks away from Alma College, where Grandpa (Robert Clack) was a professor. I saw these treasures displayed in their china cabinet, as well as on the walls, and in all available nooks and crannies. It was more than just visiting another town – their home was a fascinating glimpse of a faraway country!

The story of my grandparents' years spent in China was so much a part of my childhood narrative that I didn't question the presence of the intriguing Chinese objects placed throughout their home.

Our branch of the family lived a little over 100 miles from my grandparents' home in Alma, and we visited them a couple of times a year. When we were there, it was like being "home" to me – imbued with the familiarity of visiting the same house throughout the years and the steadfast love of grandparents. There would always be a homemade Chinese meal made from scratch by Grandpa. It was here that, as a little girl, I learned the art of eating with chopsticks. During our family visits, the adults talked and shared their stories, and there would be an occasional tale about one or another of the family's Chinese objects.

Decades later, my father was the one who – several years after the opening of Alma College's Clack Art Center in 1971 – had the impassioned vision that the family's Chinese objects should be donated to Alma College for display. Over the years, these family treasures had been distributed throughout the family. My father packed up most of his own inherited items and convinced some of the other family members to do the same. Then he made an inventory, carefully packed the cherished items, and gave them to me to deliver to Alma. These artifacts were in storage at the college until an appropriate space could be built for their display. At long last, the attractive cabinets were installed and a student who was minoring in Art History researched and organized the collection for her Senior Practicum around the year 2000.

In 2009, some of Rob and Edith's grandchildren and their families gathered in Michigan for a family reunion. One of the reunion activities was to visit Alma College, in order to tour the Clack Art Center and view our family's Chinese artifacts in their new display area. This visit turned into a time of sharing childhood memories evoked by seeing these Chinese antiques.

For my family, this book tells the story of why our ancestors went to live in China and how their keepsakes made the journey from China to Alma College in Michigan. For others, this book is a presentation of first-hand information about one of the most strategic turning points in the history of China – from these two Americans who lived there during this tumultuous era.

Norma Geraldine Clack

ACKNOWLEDGMENTS

Wynne R. Clack, youngest son of Robert and Edith, for lovingly preserving these family letters and
    photographs and for sharing his cherished family memories with all of us.
R.W. Douglas Clack, son of Robert and Edith, for all his caring work to prepare and publish his father's
    poetry translations in a professional format. He was competently assisted by his daughter Janet.
K.D. Gordon Clack, eldest son of Robert and Edith, for facilitating the publication of his father's books,
    as well as lovingly taking care of many practical matters for his parents during their later years.
Constance (Clack) Fisher, daughter of Robert and Edith, for her loving and capable care of her mother
    during her later years after Rob passed away.
Gordon McCracken Fisher, son of Constance (Clack) and F.M. Fisher, for copyreading the manuscript.
William A. Close, my domestic partner, for meticulously transcribing all the handwritten family letters.
Yiding Gao, a native and present-day resident of China, for opening my mind to the importance of my
    grandfather's photographs; for his translations, and for sharing his contemporary photographs
    of places in China to compare to the century-old images. (Comparison below of Li Chung
    Memorial Hall in Baoding, now under renovation, to the photograph taken by R.W. Clack.)

1912 (above) and **2018** (below)

PROLOGUE

ROBERT CLACK AND EDITH GORDON
THEIR UNRELATED JOURNEYS TO CHINA

Who were Robert Clack and Edith Gordon, these two young Americans who met and married in China? What was the path that led each of them to that particular place where their two lives became intertwined? One was born and raised in Iowa; the other was born in Chicago and raised in California. They did not meet in America but were destined to come together on the other side of the Pacific Ocean in a country that was at the height of a colossal social and political revolution. Their life together began during the summer of 1910 near the shore of the Gulf of Chihli, the innermost gulf of the Yellow Sea on the eastern coast of North China.

EARLY LIFE OF ROBERT WOOD CLACK

Born in Clear Lake, Iowa in 1886, Robert Wood Clack was the second of four children of Dr. William Rollinson Clack, a dentist, and his wife Sarah Adda (Wood) Clack. The Clack family was a traditionally religious household with the additional feature of having two grandfathers who were preachers – Rev. William Clack and Rev. Reuben Richardson Wood.

As a youngster, Rob enjoyed participating in a variety of sports, including football, track, and basketball. During high school he was also a member of the Grinnell Institute Literary Society. Following graduation, Rob attended Iowa College (now Grinnell College) in Grinnell, Iowa. He was a member of their basketball team that won the state championship in 1905. While attending college, Rob signed a declaration for the Student Volunteer Movement for Foreign Missions that stated, "It is my purpose, if God permit, to become a foreign missionary." During his senior year, he competed for the Rhodes Scholarship, and was one of two finalists in the state of Iowa. He graduated Phi Beta Kappa from Iowa College in 1907, earning an A.B. degree with majors in Latin, German, Greek, and mathematics, and a minor in astronomy.

After earning his bachelor's degree, Rob was employed at Iowa College (campus in Ames, Iowa), as an assistant in mathematics. While there, he continued his post-baccalaureate education, and in 1908 received a Master of Arts degree in mathematics with a minor in physics. That same year, he accepted a position at Grinnell High School as a teacher of physics and math, and athletics coach. Under his coaching, the football team won the Iowa state championship in 1909. Later that year, he attended summer classes at the University of Chicago. During the summer of 1909, he joined Company K of the 54th Infantry of the Iowa National Guard as a cook. He was honorably discharged in February 1910 by reason of "permanent removal from the state" because he was going to China! This decision would lead him on an amazing and life-changing journey.

EARLY LIFE OF EDITH (GORDON) CLACK

Georgia Edith Gordon was born in 1888 in Chicago, Illinois. Her father, William Thomas Gordon, a former ordained United Brethren minister, was a gifted musician. Her mother, Elma (Butler) Gordon, was trained as a music teacher. Edith was their fourth child and only daughter. In the spring of 1891, while the family was living in Chicago, Edith's father deserted his wife and children. Seeking refuge, her mother took their four children, aged 2 through 10, to California, and stayed at the home of her brother for three years.

When Edith was about five years old, her mother decided to dedicate herself fully to God's work, and moved her family to Selma, California, to study to become a missionary. She belonged to the Quaker Church and went out to work in city missions from 1894 to 1896. Her commitment involved a great deal of training and working in a variety of locations, so she needed to find stable homes for her children. She boarded Edith (6) and Moore (7) with a family in Selma, California, for about two years. Karl (12) and Clark (10) each were left with a different farming family in the same region. In 1896, she moved Edith with her to Los Angeles and stayed there two years. Then, from 1898 to 1899, they moved from one mission to another in Pasadena, Long Beach, San Bernardino, Santa Barbara, and Glendora, staying only a short time at each mission. In 1900, they moved to Truckee, Nevada, where Edith's mother opened and operated a mission for five years. After leaving Truckee, they moved to a series of missions in Sacramento, Berkeley, and San Francisco for her mother's missionary training.

In 1904, Edith's brother Karl, now age 22, went to China for missionary work. In the spring of 1905, when Edith was 17, she and her mother joined Karl in T'zu Chou, China. In the fall, second-oldest son Moore (age 18) joined them in China to seek missionary work. Edith and her mother returned to the U.S. in 1906, staying in Huntington Park, California, where her mother taught at a Friends Bible School for three years.

ROBERT AND EDITH MEET IN CHINA

In 1909 her mother returned to China, but Edith stayed in California for another year at school, after which she joined her mother in China. It was common, during the hot summer months, for many of the non-Chinese residents to leave the cities for cooler seaside locations. One of these places was Peitaiho (now Beidaihe) on the northeast side of the Gulf of Chihli (now called the Bohai Sea), an inlet of the Yellow Sea. This area is about 160 miles northeast of Tientsin where Edith and her mother lived.

Mrs. Gordon and Edith spent the summer of 1910 with friends in Peitaiho. That same summer, Robert Clack went with some fellow teachers to the same summer resort area. Edith and Rob met at a dinner party, and there was an immediate attraction between them, which continued after they returned to their lives in separate cities in the fall. They stayed in touch through letters, and Rob also made frequent visits to the Gordon household in Tientsin. Their relationship continued and they were married in Tientsin, China, on March 21, 1911.

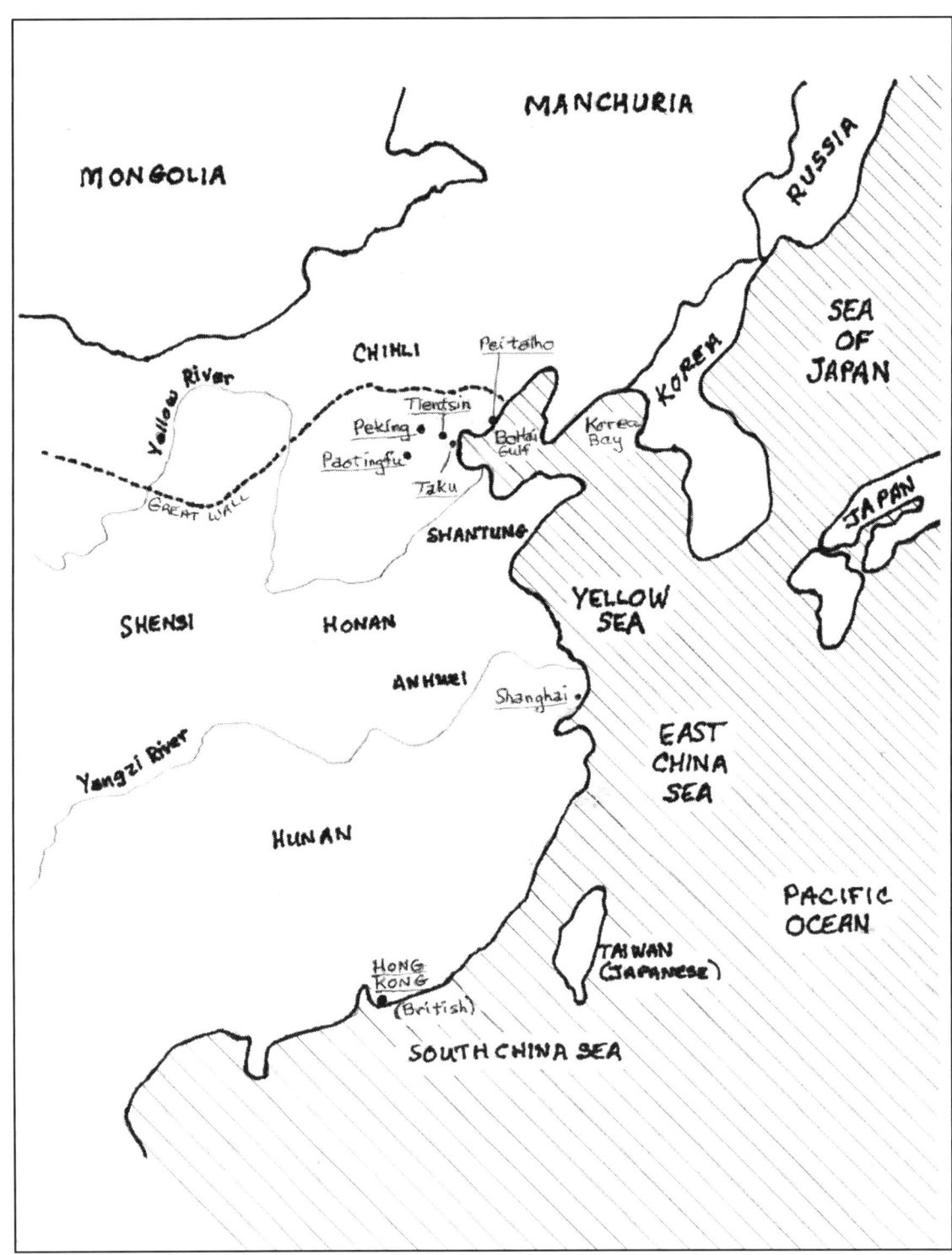

Map depicting an area of China in about 1910, including places where the Clack family lived and visited from 1910 to 1923. They lived in Paotingfu and spent summers in Peitaiho.
(Illustration by Norma Geraldine Clack in 2020)

INTRODUCTION

The creator of this book hopes it will be of interest, as well as historical value, to general readers and researchers. It is based on the letters that Robert and Edith Clack wrote to family members while living in China from 1910 to 1923 and is interspersed with many snapshots taken by Robert Clack. Some of those images are of places that no longer exist, and of events that were unique to that era. This is a story of China during this period – in Robert and Edith's words and through their eyes.

CHINA: A COUNTRY IN TRANSITION
In the late 1800s and early 1900s, China was a nation in constant turmoil. This ancient country had been ruled by Imperial dynasties since about 1600 BCE (or possibly earlier), a total of at least 3,500 years. By 1900, the Qing Dynasty, of Manchu ethnicity, had been in power for 264 years. One of the most notable revolutionary efforts of this time, the Boxer Rebellion, was an anti-imperialist uprising of peasants in northern China from 1899 to 1901. (The term "Boxer" refers to Chinese martial arts.) This rebellion was aimed at expelling foreign interlopers from China. Some 100,000 people were killed during this horrendous two-year struggle. A majority of those were civilians, including thousands of Chinese Christians and more than 200 foreigners – most of whom were Christian missionaries. This was the setting for the troubled political environment that Robert Clack (by himself) and Edith Gordon (joining her mother and brother) encountered when they arrived in China in 1910.

A Preview of Robert and Edith Clack's Years Together in China

- 1911   Robert Clack married Edith Gordon in China and continued to teach at Chihli Provincial College in Paotingfu.
- 1913   Robert was hired by the newly formed Paotingfu Y.M.C.A. at the end of his 3-year teaching contract.
- 1913   Their first child, K.D. Gordon Clack, was born.
- 1915   Their second child, Constance Elizabeth Clack, was born.
- 1916   The family of four went on a 15-month furlough to the U.S. for Rob's YMCA training.
- 1917   The family returned to Paotingfu.
- 1918   Their third child, R.W. Douglas Clack, was born.
- 1920   Robert briefly traveled as an interpreter for the military negotiators during the "Tuchun's War" at Chochou, an ancient walled city halfway between Peking and Paotingfu.
- 1920   Robert was one of the leaders who coordinated providing food to nearly one million people during the Great Famine in China.
- 1920   Robert served as China's representative to the International Olympic Federation.
- 1921   Their fourth child, Hugh Llywelyn Clack, was born.
- 1923   The Clack family left China and returned permanently to the United States.

Image of one section of a four-dragon silk needlework (photo by Norma Clack, 2019)

This silk needlework was displayed for decades in the Clack family home in Alma, Michigan.

The Chinese dragon symbolizes auspicious powers. It is a symbol of strength and good luck for people who are worthy of it. During the days of Imperial China, the Emperor usually displayed the dragon as a symbol of his imperial power. Beginning with the Yuan Dynasty (1271-1368) the five-clawed dragons became reserved for use by the emperor, while the princes used four-clawed dragons. [1] The dragons represented on the Clacks' needlework wall hanging are four-clawed.

1   *The Beginning of an Amazing Journey*

⌘ In early 1910 Robert ("Rob") Wood Clack was teaching and coaching at Grinnell High School in Iowa when he received information about a mathematics professorship at a college in China. He went to Chicago to interview with a representative of the Chinese government about this opportunity and shortly afterward was offered a three-year teaching contract. Travel plans were made quickly and, by March 9, he was on his way to China.

⌘ He began the trip by train across the country to San Francisco, then by ship across the Pacific Ocean to Japan, with a stop in Honolulu. After arriving in Japan, he traveled by boat across Korea Bay, then on a river to arrive in Tientsin (now Tianjin), China. From Tientsin he traveled by train to his new home, Paotingfu (now Baoding) in North China.

⌘ After this one-month journey of nearly 10,000 miles, he began teaching at Chihli Provincial College on April 25, 1910. He was 23 years old.

LETTERS WRITTEN EN ROUTE

Written by Rob to his family in Clear Lake, Iowa

February 5, 1910 / Grinnell, Iowa

    I had a letter from Ernest Jaqua several weeks ago about a mathematics professorship in the government college at Paotingfu, China. It is a position which will pay 200 Taels ($120) a month till Sept. 1st after which it pays 300 Taels ($180). There is also 800 dollars (*Mexican) traveling expenses (about $350 in our money) salary of course paid by the Chinese government. I have been writing the secretary about it and he says he will let me know definitely by the end of the week. He will be in Chicago then and I may go on from Davenport Saturday to see him. If I take the place I'll have to sign a three-year contract and go as soon as I can get someone to take my place. I'll let you know about it as soon as I hear definitely.

February 15, 1910 / Grinnell, Iowa

    Made the trip to Chicago safely and was successful according to a telegram I received this morning from New York. The appointment is of course subject to confirmation from China. I will go as soon as I can get someone to take my place which will probably be a couple of weeks and, of course, will come home for a day or two first.

> *Editor's note: Mexican dollar coins (sometimes referred to in the Clack letters as "Mex") were one of the foreign trade currencies in China during this time. The "Mex" comprised approximately one-quarter of the total Chinese currency in circulation.*

GOLDEN STATE LIMITED / CHICAGO – ST. LOUIS – KANSAS CITY
CALIFORNIA / VIA ROCK ISLAND LINES
EL PASO & SOUTHWESTERN SYSTEM / SOUTHERN PACIFIC COMPANY

EN ROUTE: Los Tanos, N.M.
March 11, 1910, Friday, 8:15 A.M.M.T.

"All right so far", as the man who dropped off the twelve-story building said when he passed the sixth story. Just had my breakfast and set my watch back an hour so I'm prepared for the day. We've been running all morning up a steep grade and are about two hours and a half behind time, but they say we will make it all up when we start down on the other side.

Saw Klein and Paul in Kansas City. That certainly is a bustling town. It would remind you of Chicago if it wasn't for the hills. It certainly is rugged. When you go up town from the depot, you go up to a two-story elevated road, then start off on a steep grade and the first thing you know you're in a subway.

We get to El Paso about four this P.M. then start across the desert and get into California early tomorrow (Sunday morning). Get into Los Angeles 3:30 in the afternoon, leave there at 7:30 and get to San Francisco, 500 miles north, at 11:40 Monday.

Haven't struck any mountains yet, but I guess we will about noon when we get to the top of this grade. We'll be up about 7,000 feet then. Well, I guess I'll stop and go out on the observation platform a while and get some fresh air.

EN ROUTE: just out of Yuma, Arizona
March 13, 1910, Sunday 9 A.M.

I thought I saw some desolate country yesterday morning, but you ought to see this. Sand, sand, sand. Some places it is powdered as fine as flour and drifts just like snow. Then again it hardens into a sort of rock and scattered all over it are large rocks and in the crevices of these the sagebrush and cactus shoot up. The low mountains look just like burnt out cinders. The ones we saw yesterday in eastern New Mexico were pretty. They had pines on them and the tops were snow covered, but these –

You ought to have seen us make up forty-five minutes yesterday P.M. between Alamogordo, N.M. and El Paso. It is eight-six miles, and we ran the first eight in ninety minutes. Lots of times when we hit a downgrade we'd go a mile in fifty seconds. Almost as good as an ice boat. El Paso is a pretty place. Mountains on one side, the Rio Grande on the other. Across that is Juarez, Mexico. Its buildings are mostly white, Mexican style and they look beautiful in the sunlight. I guess when you get close they are awfully dirty.

We just left Yuma, came across the Colorado and are now in the Southern Calif. Desert, a couple of hundred feet below sea level. It is pretty hot but not uncomfortable. The dust is the worst. In about an hour we get to the Salton Sea and in an hour more we begin to leave the desert. Yuma is a beautiful place. Right in the heart of the desert but they have water for irrigation, so they have palms, oranges, oleander, etc. Small boys were at the train offering oranges as big as their heads, three for a nickel.

We get into Los Angeles about 4 o'clock this afternoon, and I expect I'll get about three hours there with Glenn. Get to Frisco tomorrow about noon.

Toyo　Kisen　K'aisha
Oriental Steamship Company

Ten　yo Maru
Heavenly Ocean Boat

TOYO KISEN K'AISHA

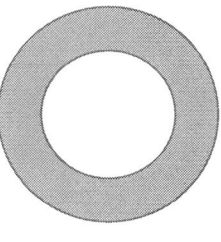

S.S. TENYO MARU

Lat 27°47'N
Long 147°22'W
Saturday, March 19, 1910
12 o'clock M

Onboard the Tenyo Maru (Heavenly Ocean Boat), Chefoo Harbor in Korea Bay, 1910

Rob on right. Mr. George Collingwood (left), an American from New Orleans,
"who has been out here for nineteen years". Manager of the Tientsin "Press".
Also on board were Mrs. Collingwood and her sister, Lady Betty.

Shanghai, 1910 / Sunday, April 10

Finally arrived in China and though it is raining, I like the country. It's way ahead of Japan. Japan is a beautiful country but the people and everything they have seem so small. It seems almost like being in a toy land.

Impressions of Japan

We landed in Yokohama in the rain but in spite of that took jinrickshas in the afternoon and went all over the city. The jinricksha men are the curse of the city. They meet you in droves at the wharf and about all you hear is "rickshaw, rickshaw" and the only way to get rid of them is to hire one. Sunday we walked over to the railway station from the wharf. There were four of us and I guess there must have been about fifty of them who followed us all the way trying to tell us how much they'd take us over to the station for.

We spent Sunday in Tokyo and left Yokohama Monday. Passed very close to an island volcano which has been active for over a thousand years continuously. And just at sunset, way off to the south, had a good view of the snow cap of Fuji.

Kobe, Japan

Arrived in Kobe Tuesday and spent the afternoon there. I like it the best of the four Japanese cities we visited. Just outside the city are some waterfalls which are beautiful beyond description. We also spent some time looking through the Japanese shops. I wish you girls could have seen some of the bargains they offered in silk kimonos.

Inland Sea of Japan

Wednesday we sailed all day through the famous inland Sea of Japan, with the island of Hondo [another name for Honshu] on the north and Shikoku and Kiushiu on the south. It was like being on a big river varying in width from a few hundred feet to several miles. On both sides the mountains rise to several thousand feet and are terraced in most places to the very top, while little villages snuggle up to the foot. And the whole thing is dotted with little wooded islets, on many of which are temples. It is a wonderful sight.

Nagasaki, Japan

Thursday we spent in Nagasaki and you would never guess how we saw the city. We went to a shop and hired some bicycles and talk about fun. Would go scooting through the little narrow streets shouting and ringing our bells. The four were Abdul, Tom Irwin, who is going into engineering work at Manila, George Stewart, from Simpson, whose father is president of Nanking University, and myself.

Shanghai, China

This city is a queer mixture of foreigners and Chinese. It is supposed to be governed by a council of all nationalities, but practically is under control of the British. There are about twelve hundred Americans here. Along the waterfront it is almost like a European city except for the Chinese running around, but back a ways it is very Chinese.

I ate tiffin (lunch) yesterday with the Brockmans and Lyons, the Y.M.C.A. secretaries here. Mr. Lyon just came back from America on the "Tenyo Maru" with his wife and four children. Mr. Brockman has two small boys in his family, so he had a good lively time. Mr. Charles Harvey from Tientsin was also there.

Last night I went to the American University Club banquet in honor of Mr. Calhoun. The club is made up of American College men and there were about ninety present at the banquet which lasted from eight till one. We sang the old familiar college song between courses and the speeches were fine. Mr. Calhoun is a great hit out here so far, except with the newspaper reporters. Mr. Wilder, the toastmaster, is American Consul-General, and is one of the best after dinner speakers in the country.

Northwest corner of Paotingfu wall, viewed from the West (photo ca. 1910)

Paotingfu is located in the west-central portion of Hebei Province on the North China Plain, with the Taihang Mountains to the west. Like most cities in China, it was a "walled city" with towers and gates. These walls, which surrounded the entire city were defensive systems. Crops were grown outside of the city walls. [1]

Rob noted in his 1913 Y.M.C.A. Report that *"... the population of Paotingfu was perhaps 100,000. It is about ninety miles southwest of Peking, and about one hundred miles west of Tientsin, so that the three cities form an equilateral triangle. Mission work was begun in Paotingfu by the American Mission Board in 1873. During the Boxer uprising in 1900 a number of American missionaries and Chinese Christians gave up their lives here ..."*.

Chihli Provincial College.

Department of Mathematics.

R. W. Clack.   Paotingfu, North China.

....191

Letterhead from Chihli Provincial College

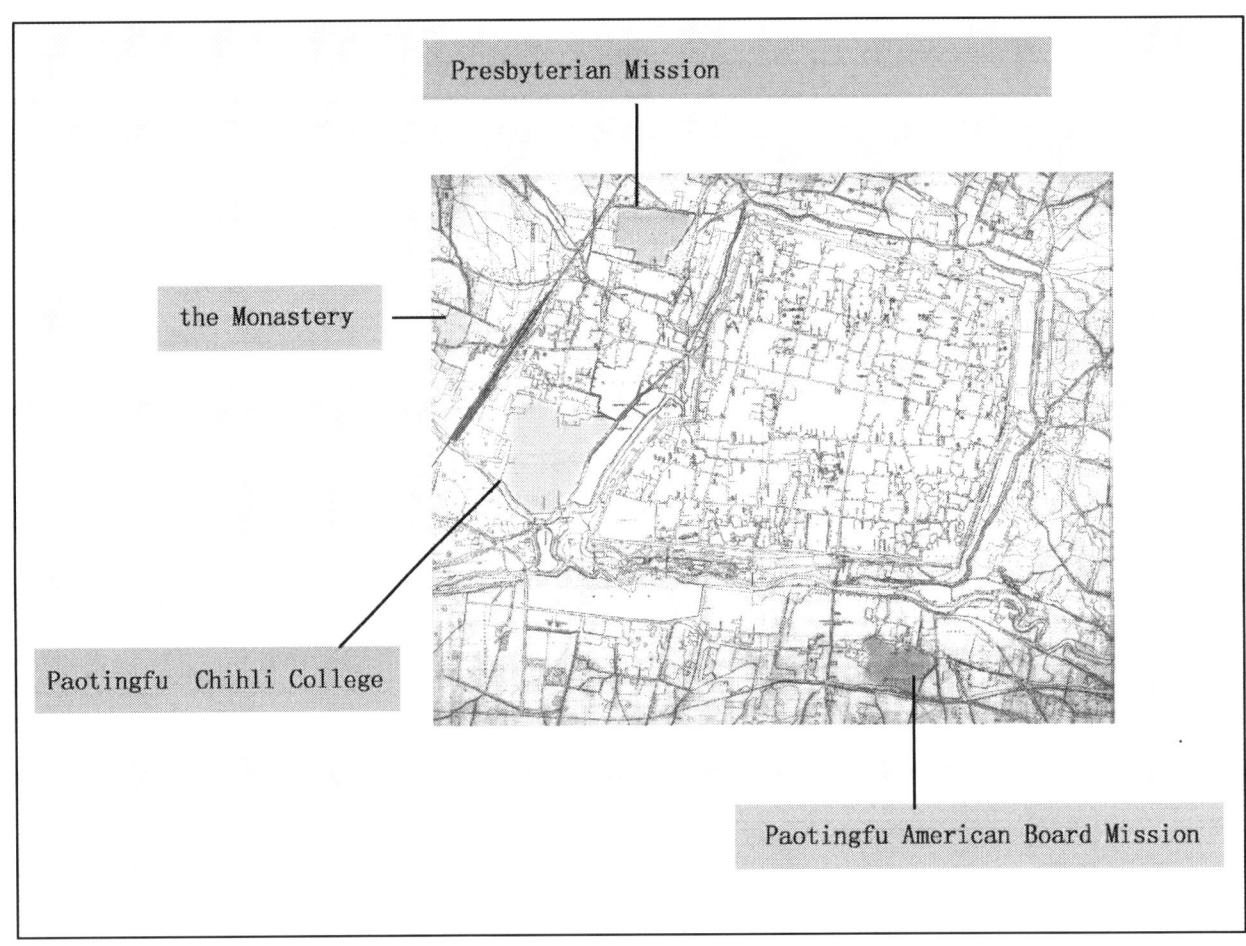

In 1910, the Presbyterian hospital and church were not far from the college
(and both were outside of the wall on the west side of Paotingfu).
The college was in the southwest, and the hospital and church
were in the northwest. (Map and notations courtesy of Yiding Gao.)

2   *First Impressions of China and Chihli Provincial College*

⌘ Robert Clack arrived in the port of Shanghai, China, on April 10, 1910, and in a letter dated May 1st he wrote to his family, "Finally here and have taught for a week." During his first week of teaching, he secured a private Chinese teacher and began studying the Chinese language.

⌘ Chihli Provincial College was established in 1902 and began to offer some western courses, such as English and physical chemistry. In 1913, the college was merged into another school, but the land and school buildings were still utilized.

THE LETTERS

Letters written by Rob to his family in Iowa

Paotingfu / May 1, 1910 (Sunday)

Finally here and have taught for a week. I would have written sooner, but you can imagine how busy I have been getting settled down. I'll tell you this time something about my trip from Shanghai here and my work and next time I'll tell you about the people.

Travel notes

I left Shanghai two weeks ago last Tuesday [i.e. April 12] on the "Hsin Ming" (hs is pronounced almost exactly like sh). There were only three other foreign passengers, George Collingwood, an American from New Orleans, who has been out here for nineteen years. First came as a war correspondent for Chino-Jap war, also went through Spanish-American in Philippines and Russo-Jap war. Now he is manager of the Tientsin "Press". With him were his wife and her sister, Rumanians, tho' they speak English fluently. Both are quite pretty, in fact, you would have to describe Mrs. Collingwood as beautiful. We had a delightful time, as the weather was beautiful.

We arrived at Taku at the mouth of the river Friday morning and then went up the river six hours to Tientsin. The river is very narrow, hardly as wide as the boat is long, but it is fifteen feet deep, so that very large steamers can go up it. Both sides are lined with little mud villages and graves, about six graves for a half a dozen huts. They occur in clusters in the fields or anywhere.

I stayed overnight in Tientsin with Mr. Hersey, one of the Y.M.C.A. secretaries. He is from Syracuse U. and his wife knows Betty Hawks. Next day I went up to Peking, about three hours trip by rail and stayed there till the next Tuesday with the Gaileys. Then I came down here with Mr. Edwards, who has been taking my place till I should come. We arrived about ten in the morning, so I had my first sight of Paotingfu (which by the way is pronounced Baodingfu) at a good time.

Right here, let me give you a guide for pronouncing Chinese names:

a = a as in father	p = b	p' = p
ê = e as in her (often just written e)	t = d	t' = t
ie = ye as in yet	k = g	k' = k
o = o as in hole	ch = j	ch' = ch
u = oo as in root	hs = sh	ts = ds
ü = German ü	j = zh	ts' = ts
ŭ = hardly pronounced		
u (before a vowel) = w	h is very, very slightly guttural, a cross	
ao = ou as in foul	between the English h and the German	
iu = you	ch.	
ai = ai as in aisle	After consonants as in English	
i = i as in police	Li hung Chang = Lee (c)hung Jang	

Of course you understand that these are not exact, because it is almost impossible to reproduce the Chinese sounds with English letters, but this is the system of Romanization that is used almost universally and is about as nearly correct as it is possible to make it. My Chinese name is Romanized K'ê Lan K'ê, which is something like this ---------

The first K'ê which is of course my surname and is one of the "hundred names" is pronounced in a very high tone of voice and is very short. It means "ax handle". The last two names of course are given names. Lan pronounced in a rather high, long, drawn-out tone means "orchid" (Long [Rob's housemate] says "awkward") and the last K'ê is pronounced with falling inflection and means "guest".

The College
I arrived here at a very opportune time as they were just in the midst of quarterly exams, so that I had a little chance to get on to the ropes before I went to work. They use the English system here. No marks on daily work, only on the four exams. The year starts in August, runs about eight weeks then they have a week of exams, then they go on eight weeks more (about), have a week of no classes in order to plug up and then another week of exams. Then comes about six weeks of vacation for the Chinese New Year festivities, and school starts again for the second half-year in February and goes through the same process again ending up the latter part of June for another six weeks vacation.

One bad feature is that a student is not passed on by subjects but on a general average, as in graded schools. For instance, if I give a student a mark of say 15 in math and he does well in everything else, then he does not have to take his math over but goes on to take advanced work. Mr. Fei, the president, is trying to remedy this but, of course, that has been the system since the time the Romans invaded Briton, so why should it be changed?

Another thing, they do not have the elective system, but two courses of study, so that every student in the class has the same work regardless of his natural talents or lack of talents. Our school is the most advanced in China so that I don't know what other archaic rules they have in the other schools. Another thing, these students carry 36 hours of work a week, 6 recitations every day but Sunday. At Grinnell, you know, they have a rule that no student should carry over 18, though it is sometimes violated. I once took the unheard of amount of 21 hours. Besides that, you must remember that half of the 36 hours is done in English, which of course makes it much harder for them. Do you wonder that they are much more serious minded than the average American student?

They have one pretty little kuei chê (custom). When the teacher enters the room, every pupil rises and stands till he steps onto the platform. A teacher is held in much greater respect here than in America. In fact we are quite the elite of the land, only the nobility is as high in social rank. In fact we are even allowed to have *green* sedan chairs. What could be a greater honor?

My start was particularly hard because of what had gone before. Mr. Fei, the head of the teaching department, though only twenty-eight, is the only survivor of a Christian family which was wiped out by the Boxers in 1900. His wife was killed (though I guess he has never seen her) and he himself barely escaped. He was the one who brought the news of the slaughter of the foreigners in Shansi (where he was in school) to Peking and he went through the siege there. He went to America and graduated from Oberlin, and took graduate work at Yale. When he came back he was called to this school, the only native Christian, so far, to obtain official recognition. At first being young, he tried to force Christianity on the students too much and he became very unpopular for a time. However, he had gradually begun to win the students back when a teacher was needed to build up the mathematics department. He sent to Oberlin for a man, and they, with the ideas that most foreigners have of Chinese schools, sent out a man who, though he was a very fine fellow and a brilliant student in other lines, knew absolutely nothing of advanced mathematics. This was last fall. Of course he made an awful fizzle of it and was obliged to resign last December and consequently Mr. Fei, though it was not his fault, was blamed for it and "lost a great deal of face."

So that this time he put the matter into the hands of the Y.M.C.A. and you can very easily see how much depends on my making good. If I do, the Y.M.C.A. will get a chance to fill almost all the positions in the rapidly growing colleges of North China. If I don't, Mr. Fei will be obliged to resign, the new president will, of course, not be a Christian, and the Y.M.C.A. will have so much ground to gain back again.

Of course I had the chance of playing safe and taking things just as I found them, to attempt no advance but let the blame or praise for the failure or success of the mathematics department rest on the shoulders of the general educational board of the Province and Mr. Fei, while I forced them to hold to their contract for three years.

However, I crossed the Rubicon and burned my bridges so I'm in for a big splurge or a big fizzle. I took the whole department into my own hands. Of course for this year (eight weeks more), I'll have to patch up, as best I may, the results of the past (or rather the lack of results of the past). Mr. Fei seems to think that the whole thing depends on that, because everything out here depends on the attitude of the student body. They are really the governing body of the school, and he says that if I can show them that I can teach them mathematics, I win. Well, I think that is done already, but I'm not going to stop there. I've added an extra year to the course, which has been allowed by the board of education but has never been taught because of the fact that the way they made out the course made it an impossibility. I've taken the liberty to change it so that it can be taught and though it is the same as telling them that they know nothing at all about mathematics (which is the absolute truth) the director of the school, one of the old order of things, has allowed it if I am willing to take the responsibility.

Then I've thoroughly revised the first two years work, kicked out some of the archaic English textbooks which were written for infant prodigies and not for normal beings and put in some good systematic American textbooks in their places. The English textbooks on Coordinate (Analytical) Geometry I kept because they are better than the American.

Housing

I'm fixed up very comfortably here. In fact, we almost live in luxury. There are very few things we have to do without. The thing I miss most is a modern bathroom, but then we are just as well fixed, as we were at home before the city water was put in. I am living with Mr. Long in a house which was built especially for two bachelor profs. I'll send the plan of the house for Ida to study, also a plan of our part of the college compound. The whole compound takes up thirty or forty acres, so that the plan takes up about one tenth of it. It is located just west of the southwest corner of the city wall, where the city moat joins the river and is a very pretty place. I'll send you some views taken around the city and the college as soon as I can get some. Long teaches Drawing and French and is 28. He is an Englishman and I like him very much. I'll tell you about him and the rest of the foreigners (which means in China, "English and Americans") next time.

We have three servants: Li Chên, who is table boy and laundryman, and withal the handsomest Chinaman I ever saw; Tze Tsung, the coolie and man of all work, and P'ei Lin, the tai sha fu, or cook. We also have a younger brother of Li Chên coming to learn the servant trade. We pay the servants very high wages, higher than anyone else, but I guess it won't bankrupt us. Li Chên gets $11 Mex. a month, P'ei Lin $10.50 and Lao Tsung $10 and the new boy will get $3. A Mexican dollar equals about 45 cents American gold, so you see our servants cost us about $15.00 gold for the two of us. Our other living expenses amount to $25 or $30 gold apiece.

Finances and Chinese money

I get more salary than I thought. It is 300 Taels per Chinese month (29 days) and is paid every month in the year so that it amounts to about $2600 dollars a year at the present rate of exchange (1 Tael =$.68). The Tael is not a coin but a weight of silver, and the Mexican dollar is the unit. However, there are even there three systems of dollars. The ordinary Mexican dollar itself is the lowest, then comes the dragon dollar, worth a few cents more, and finally the "standing man" or Hong Kong dollar which is the one generally used here. For fractional money we have twenty cent pieces, which are really worth about 18 cents, dimes of which it takes eleven plus one or two copper coins to make a dollar, copper coins worth about 130 to the standing man dollar, and the little round "cash" which are generally handled in strings. The copper coins say on them "10 cash" but they are really worth 20 so you can see what a beautifully simple system we have. Then, as to paper money, it is never used except in the cities and if I try to use a Tientsin bill in Peking they will discount it several percent and vice versa.

Native banks are only places for money changing, so that if you desire to send money you must go to Peking to get a draft. I'll have to tell you about my first experience with getting money cashed. I had an order for 200 Taels which I wanted to get cashed to pay for a lot of furniture I am buying to furnish my side of the house (it will cost about $100 Mex.) so I sent Li Chên into the city to cash it. I had visions, of course, of a nice roll of crisp bank notes. Imagine my feelings when I saw him come back staggering under a load of about three hundred silver dollars.

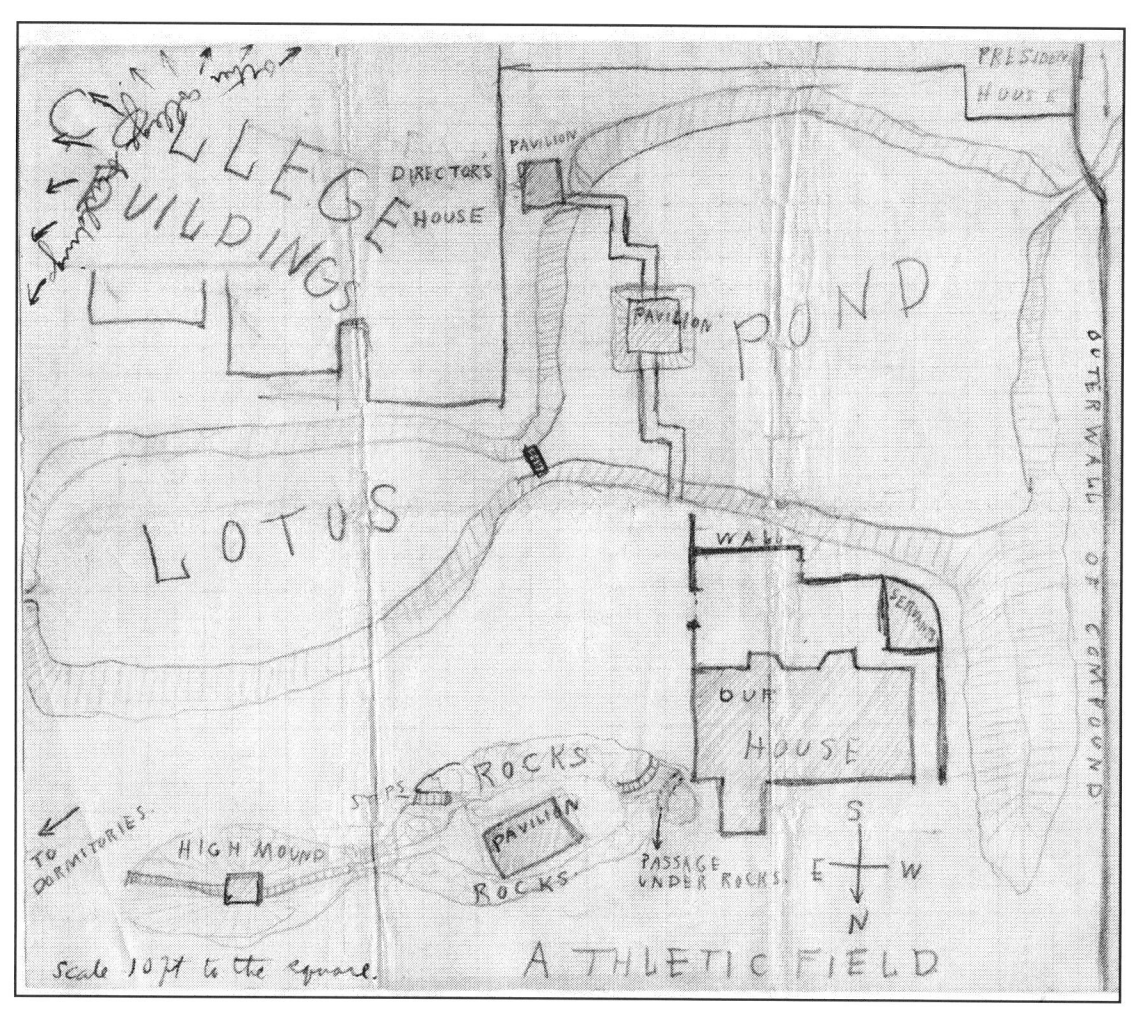

Drawing by Robert Clack in 1910
showing the general vicinity where he lived and taught
(part of the College compound).

Chihli Provincial College – Recitation Hall (photo 1910)

**Chihli Provincial College, one of the College buildings -
the student is Yü Ching Chien** (photo 1910)

Paotingfu houses from North wall (photo 1910)

(L) **Paotingfu old South Gate in West Suburb** (R) **Inside the West Gate** (photos 1910)

Paotingfu / May 8, 1910

Another week has gone by very quietly and I feel as if I were beginning to get the work well in hand. The students have gotten over their timidity and stiffness in class and I can begin to get something out of them and feel as if I had begun to get a hold on them. Tomorrow we start training and that will help still more. I don't know how many will come out, but a number have promised to get out at six in the morning and some others will come out at four thirty P.M. I guess I will have track team work in the morning and baseball in the afternoon.

Individuals at the College

I'll tell you this week about the people. Edward R. Long, with whom I live, is an Englishman, twenty-seven years of age and teaches French and Drawing. He is a genius at drawing and like most genii is rather eccentric, but we get along together in great shape. He always has a great many irons in the fire, and has no system about looking after them, so he is generally late everywhere, but he is very good hearted and I happen to know that he always has three or four cripples in the Presbyterian Mission hospital whom he is supporting.

The oldest foreign teacher is Mr. Lattimore. He is about forty I should judge, and he teaches English, Philosophy and French. He is an atheist, they say, but he is a very pleasant man, and evidently he believes in keeping his religious views to himself and not trying to force them on other people. He is an American by birth and has been here for seven years. He is married and has five children who are all very much superior to the average American children in every way. They are all great pals of mine already. Katherine is ten, Owen is nine, Isabel is seven, Eleanor is five and Richmond or "Dixie" is a curly-headed youngster of four. Mrs. Lattimore is a very pleasant woman of thirty-five. They live on the American Board compound.

Mr. Henderson, the science teacher, is about thirty-five. He is Scotch and is quite deaf, and also is rather inclined to be quick tempered and impatient with the students and others, so that his contract will not be renewed when it expires next winter. However, he has been very pleasant to me so far. Mrs. Henderson is going home next week. She is just as Scotch as she can be, and is very sweet. They have one child, a little girl, of one year.

Mr. Pitman who teaches English and History is the other teacher. He is also a Y.M.C.A. man, from Tennessee. His wife is a dear too. They are between thirty and thirty-five years of age. Mr. Pitman is tall and rather lanky, and has a keen sense of humor and is a good American college man. He has only been here one term, but lived several years in ShanTung Province to learn the language. The Pitman's people are missionaries there. I like them very much, as I always feel that they think just like I do. Mrs. Pitman, however, says she will never quite forgive me for not bringing a wife, for after Mrs. Henderson leaves she will be the only foreign woman on the compound.

Mr. Fei, the president, is a very fine man. He is only about thirty. His wife is pretty but little Chinese lady who speaks a little English. She is only nineteen.

Mr. Li is the only other Chinese teacher who has been in America. He is a Harvard graduate, but is rather quiet and shy. The other Chinese teachers in the English department are Chêng, Chang, and T'ang.

Individuals at the American Board Mission

At the American Board mission besides the Lattimore family there are only two families, as their church is now almost entirely run by the Chinese. There is Dr. Aiken, who is supported by the Grinnell church. He is about fifty. I have only just met him, as he is generally gone. Mrs. Aiken is only about twenty-five and works so hard with the Chinese that she neglects her own little girl of six. Mr. Aiken has two sons by a former wife, but they are in America in school. Mr. Perkins, the other man there, is just going home. He is very badly crippled with rheumatism and his wife is also a cripple having lost both feet in a railway accident, so I suppose they will not come back. They have a sixteen-year-old daughter who seems to be a very bright girl. Then there are two maiden ladies who have charge of the girls' school, Miss Jones and Miss Chapin. Miss Chapin went through the siege at Peking in 1900. She was the only Paotingfu missionary who escaped, as she happened to be in Peking on a visit when the missionaries were butchered.

Dr. Lowrie, the head of the Presbyterian mission is an old bachelor who reminds me in many ways of Professor Rusk. He has a great stand in with the Chinese people because he came here immediately after the massacre in 1900 and when the Germans took the city and were going to destroy the city wall, he intervened and saved it.

Other Individuals

Dr. Lewis is at the head of the hospital. He is a dandy. Has a twinkle in his eye and a square jaw and is a regular fiend for work. What would an American physician think if he performed eight operations in which an anesthetic was needed in one morning and then examined and prescribed for a hundred people in the afternoon? Well, that is Dr. Lewis's average day's work, three hundred and sixty-five days in the year. His wife is a very nice woman.

Dr. Mackay, a maiden lady is at the head of the women's hospital. The other missionaries are Mr. and Mrs. Mather and Mrs. and Mr. Keilly who are generally in the country. Then there are two other ladies there studying the language who are very pleasant. Miss Gumbrell is about thirty and Miss Keyes, about twenty. There also is a young Siamese whose name is Carr who is there studying. So much for the foreigners.

Our servants are now four. The cook, who is an old fat fellow and claims to be a Christian though the missionaries say he doesn't work at it. The table boy, Li Chên, is the best-looking Chinaman I've seen and is a wonder. He even uses the copying machine to copy work to give to the classes. His brother, Li Chang, a youngster of sixteen, in now helping him while he learns the trade. We pay him 3 dollars mex. a month, which pays for his board, (that is about $1.30 gold). The other servant who does odd jobs, runs errands, etc. is Lao Tsêng which means the Old Everlasting, so I call him the "Great I am". He is a very willing fellow but makes lots of funny mistakes.

Well, I must stop now and go to the west suburb to church. I am going to lead today. I'm going to read from VanDyke's "Other Wise Man". The foreigners have service at 4:30 every Sunday, alternating between the west and south suburbs and they all take turns leading.

Letterhead – Grand Hotel des Wagons-Lits, Limited **Letter June 16, 1910**

Peking, June 16, 1910

My dear Dad:—

I'm sending you a little remembrance for your birthday. I'm having the carpenter also make you a walking stick like the one I use myself, which I will send when he gets it finished. I have the money now to send back to the bank, but as it will be two months before I can get back to Paotingfu to draw my summer's salary, I guess I better keep this by me to carry me thru the summer. I can get practically the same interest from the bank here as I am paying, so I won't lose anything by waiting. I have finished buying up my clothes, a horse, and half the furnishings for our house besides, so I feel as if I were extremely well fixed financially, and as soon as I send that money to the bank I will be ready to save about a hundred dollars a month.

Well, I must stop as Henderson is here to take me to call on some of the legation people.

With love
Rob.

T'ung Chou / June 19, 1910

When I came home from Tientsin last Tuesday night I found out that the students were so badly frightened by the typhus that they had all left and the director was compelled to put off exams until school starts again the 12th of August, so I immediately packed up and came up here. This is the largest and most beautiful missionary compound in China and besides the A.B.C.F.M. mission they have the Union College of the American, Presbyterian and London Mission Boards. We are having a Y.M.C.A. conference similar to the one at Lake Geneva and I am helping Mr. Porter, the athletic director of this college, with the athletics. I attend a good many of the meetings though they are in Chinese, in order to get more accustomed to the tones and rhythm of the language.

Among the missionaries here are Mr. and Mrs. Galt from Tabor [Iowa] who are very well acquainted with the McCormicks and William Gleysteen, one of Cynthia Meyer's uncles from Alton [Iowa]. Also, I saw Bennie DeHaan and his wife at Peking last Sunday and we had a dandy visit. I like Mrs. Bennie very much. They were feeling quite delighted as they had just seen Pres. King of Oberlin [Oberlin College in Ohio], who is on a world tour. He gave a very fine speech here Friday morning.

The meeting here will be over Thursday and then I will go to Tientsin Friday and get my clothes which I ordered and then on to Peitaiho Saturday. I will stay with Mr. Harvey, one of the Y.M.C.A. secretaries from Tientsin.

T'ung Chou

The city here is very interesting. It was once very important being the nearest river port to Peking but the railroad had killed it, as there is now almost no river traffic. The population has gone from over 100,000 to less than 20,000 in the last ten years. The city formerly was much disturbed by floods. The people asked the gods through one of the temples how to fight the floods and they replied, "Through that which is least afraid of water." They decided that must be a boat, so the city wall was built in the shape of a boat and a very high pagoda was erected as a mast.

Also, there are still remains of an immense stone chain at one of the gates and several miles down the river is a large rock which the people say is T'ung chou's anchor. Needless to say there have been no more floods, but the people are very careful about never allowing a man whose name is Hsin (sail) to be dao t'ai (head man) for, of course, anyone knows that if the boat had a sail it would sail off and what would become of the people then?

Presbyterian Church, Paotingfu (photo 1910-11)

Coming through the mud on the road from the city to the college. (photo 1911)

3   Robert and Edith: Their Paths Unite

⌘ In order to escape the heat in the city during the summer, foreigners living in northern China vacationed at Peitaiho, a coastal resort town on northeast China's Bohai Sea. During the summer of 1910 Rob went along with some colleagues to stay at Peitaiho for several weeks.

⌘ At a dinner given on July 20 by a mutual friend, Rob was introduced to Miss Edith Gordon, whose mother, Elma Butler Gordon, was a missionary worker in Tientsin, China.

⌘ In a letter sent to his family in Clear Lake, Iowa, on July 24 Rob wrote: "I've met a dandy girl over at East Cliff [part of Peitaiho]. Her name is Edith Gordon and she is a Quakeress, but doesn't seem to be afraid to laugh, anyway. Her home is in Tientsin where her brother is business agent for a number of the mission stations. I see where I have to make lots of business trips to Tientsin this coming year."

Peitaiho, view toward West from Rocky Point (photo 1910-11)

THE LETTERS

Letters written by Rob to his family in Iowa

Peitaiho / July 3, 1910

Have had a good time this last week. Have been in bathing at least once every day and have been spending the rest of the time playing baseball or tennis or studying math. I'm going let the Chinese [language study] rest this summer though of course I pick it up all the time.

Most of the people not already here arrived this last week and there are now about six hundred of us scattered along four or five miles of beach. Here at Rocky Point is the center and most densely populated part.

The railway station is 5 miles north of Rocky Point and the Post office is here at Rocky Point. Over at West End at the foot of the Lotus Hills is the Minister's house. All along the beach the cliffs rise up forty or fifty feet and then there are low hills back ten miles or so to the mountains. The highest one is Pei Tien straight north about twenty miles. Chin-wang-tao is about fifteen miles east, and Shan-hai-kwan where the great wall runs into the sea is about ten miles further east. All the way along the coast here are fine little bathing beaches and the waves are seldom very bad for this is just an arm of the sea so is fairly well sheltered.

(The coast is something like this here)

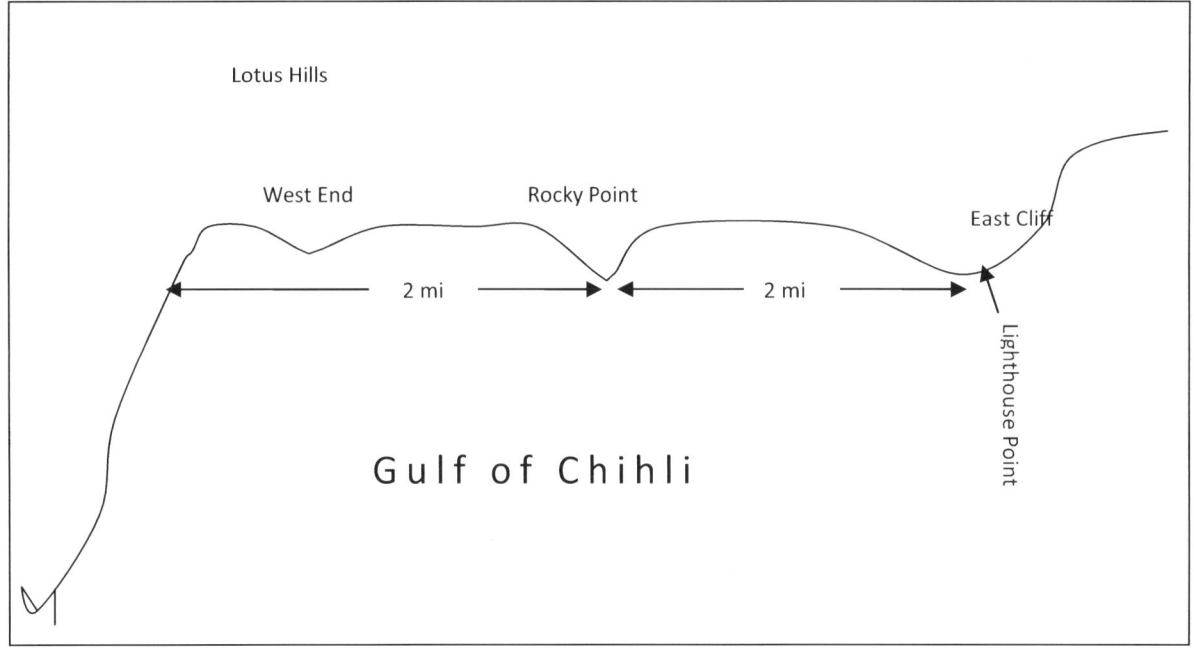

Re-created drawing of original sketch by R.W. Clack

Peitaiho, Fish Hook Point (lighthouse in the distance) (photo 1910-11)

Peitaiho, the Lighthouse, East Cliff (photo 1910-11)

Tomorrow is the glorious fourth. We are planning to have a big celebration, though no fireworks to speak of. In the morning at nine we have a baseball game between teams consisting of Y.M.C.A. and legation students vs. the missionaries. I am going to play third base for the Y.M.C.A. to start with, tho' there's no telling how we'll change the teams around. At eleven we have water sports in "Black Leg Bay". It was originally known as American Bay as opposed to English Bay, but as the American ladies all wear stockings when they go bathing and the English do not it has gradually acquired the present name.

These legation students I speak of are fellows who are sent to the American legation at Peking, after having passed the civil services exams at home, to study Chinese with a view to giving them consular positions out here. They are also required to act as secretaries to the legation while they study. There are generally eight or ten at a time. Next week the Y.M.C.A. conference starts.

Peitaiho / August 7, 1910

Well, my last week at Peitaiho this summer is up. Start back Tuesday morning. Will go to Tientsin and stay till Wednesday P.M. Mr. S.B. Harvey, our new man, will go with me. Then we'll go to Peking Wednesday P.M., meeting Long and Lattimore on the train and we'll all go to Paotingfu together Thursday morning. I expect Pittman and Henderson will be there before us. The rest of the Lattimore family will not go back for a month yet because of the heat.

Had a mighty busy time this last week. I'll give you a brief of it, just to show you what we do for amusement. Monday morning the English had water sports but they were not a howling success (from their standpoint) as the Americans were invited to compete and the two star events of the day, the 50 yd. swim and the 300 were won by Whit Chambers, of the Peking Y.M.C.A. staff, a Princetonian, by overwhelming margins, while in the shorter swim, both second and third were taken by Americans from the Peking legation. In the afternoon the ladies of the Tientsin Union Church had a bazaar similar to what we have at home. I took Edith Gordon and did the customary amount of spending for ice cream, candy, etc., etc. In the evening I was invited over to Burgess's for dinner with Gertrude Chaney, an American Board girl from Northfield, Minnesota.

Tuesday afternoon I played cricket on the World team against the English and they beat us 33 to 30. In the evening I went over to East Cliff and called on the Gordon family.

Wednesday morning we had a meeting of the Y.M.C.A. force to make plans for the next year. We had almost all North China people present, four secretaries and one teacher from Tientsin, four secretaries from Peking, two from Paotingfu and one from Taiyuanfu. In the afternoon we had a ball game between the Hill and the Shore. I pitched for the Hill and after running an extra inning we won by a score of 21 to 20.

Thursday evening we had a picnic on the rocks, in honor of Hubbard, physical director of Tientsin Y.M.C.A. who is just going home to take a seminary course, coming back in three years under the American Board.

Friday evening the Paotingfu faculty with a few others had another picnic on the rocks. Yesterday I went over to the Lotus Hills for tiffin with some of the Chinese students. Came back home and then went right back to the Lotus Hills again, this time with a picnic party consisting of the C.W. Harvey family, the Thwing family (he is head of the Chinese Reform League), Mr. Long, S. B. Harvey, Miss Reyes, of the Pres. Miss. at Paofu., Moore Gordon, Edith Gordon and myself. We had supper and watched sunset from the top of the hills and then I went clear over to East Cliff and back again afterwards making thirteen miles donkey-back yesterday.

I am invited over to the Gordon's for dinner. Altogether I must say that these vacations are not half bad. I've done quite a lot of work, too, mornings and afternoons while other people were sleeping because they thought it too hot to do something else. The Chinese stand it all right.

Paotingfu / August 14, 1910

Well, I'm back home again. I left Peitaiho with Mr. S.B. Harvey, our new man, (the other is C.W. Harvey). Tuesday morning, went to Tientsin and stayed till Thursday morning, we picked up Henderson there on the way home from Japan and Long and Lattimore joined us at Chang Hsin Lien, just out of Peking, so the five of us came in together Thursday P.M. The Pitmans came back several days ahead of us. Mrs. Lattimore and the kiddies won't come back for a month yet. It is mighty hot now. Goes to a hundred or more every day, but it is much drier than Peitaiho. We only have to go out in the morning, too, so we don't mind it much.

We started our last spring's postponed exams Friday morning. They continue two more days, then we have the rest of the week off to mark papers and then start to work in earnest. I'm having extra heavy work on the exams, as Mr. Chêng, the middle school math teacher, isn't coming back and I'm giving his exams for him. It makes about 150 extra papers. However, I can't kick as I offered to do it myself.

Tientsin

I had a good time in Tientsin Wednesday. Went over and went all thru the native city. I don't know whether I ever told you about Tientsin or not. It is the metropolis and trade centre of North China. It is situated on the Peiho [River] about thirty or forty miles from the coast. The southern part of the city is the foreign concessions of which there are eight, [British, French, German, Russian, Japanese, Austrian, Belgian, and Italian. They are built up in foreign style with paved streets, electric lights and street cars (or tramways as they say here). America had a concession but following her general policy gave it back, and practically all the Americans live in the French and British concessions. The concessions are known as the Settlements. Population about 100,000.

The rest of the city is distinctly Chinese and has a population of about a million, though of course, that is only an estimate. However, the people are very much in advance to the rest of China and there are many beautiful streets and buildings. But, oh, the crowded business streets. As we went through them Mr. Harvey said, "Why I didn't know that as many Chinese as this existed." I told him that this was only one-four hundredth of them.

Hsi-Ku, near Tientsin, both houses, American Board Compound F.M. (photo 1910)

Tientsin - Victoria Road (photo 1910)

I've just had some new calling cards printed. I'll send you a couple. How would you like to have to carry around a stack of those when you go calling? The director wrote the characters for me and then I had wood-cuts made from them so that I can have more printed any time I run short. There are two styles you will notice. I wish you would mail me my little plate so I can have some engraved English cards.

Paotingfu / September 11, 1910

I suppose you are all getting ready to send Celia off tomorrow to Grinnell. When she finishes her nurse course she can come over here, as there is a great need for them. Not mission nurses, but nurses to take care of foreigners, for, for some reason, the foreigners out here will persist in having babies and being sick otherwise, the same as at home. Carrie Lewis is practically the only qualified nurse in North China now and they keep her on the jump continually.

We had a holiday day before yesterday to worship Confucius and Long took yesterday off, also, and has gone to Peking, but will be home again tonight. I guess I told you, did I not, that he was going to leave? I will hate very much to have him go, as I like him very much, but I really believe it will be better off for him, as he has exceptional talent, and owing to his poor start he would never get along well here, while if he goes somewhere else, his experiences here will be the making of him. That will leave me with this house on my hands, all my own. I suppose I'll have to rustle around and get someone to take care of it for me. With Long and Henderson gone, the whole staff here will be Americans, and all but one Y.M.C.A. men, for I suppose the new men will be American Y.M.C.A. men. Though the English had the start of us, the Chinese now seem to prefer Americans, on account of their much gentler adaptability.

Did I tell you that Mr. Henderson's father is here visiting him? He is an old sea captain and is quite delightful, with his broad Scotch dialect and his nautical slang. Mrs. Henderson and the baby are still in Scotland but will start back in a couple of weeks.

I guess I told you last spring about our boats. We go out on the river almost every day for a little row. They are just like our rowboats at home, only they are hand painted. Just think of it, hand painted boats. I mean that literally, as all painting here is not done with a brush but with a small rag held in the fist and the man only uses that to thin the paint down after he has applied it with his hands.

Tientsin / December 25, 1910

I left Paofu, Thursday afternoon, went up to Peking and spent the night at the Y.M.C.A. and came down here Friday morning. I did intend to go back tomorrow, but I got a telegram from Eddie Long today, saying that school had closed temporarily, and that he would write, so I expect I'll find out all about it tomorrow. I think I know what's the trouble anyway.

Political situation and the students

On account of the encroachments of Japan and Russia in Manchuria, the students in the government schools here and at Peking struck the other day and demanded that a Parliament be called immediately. They have an idea, you know, that as soon as a Parliament is called, the millennium will come, Japan will be driven out, the opium traffic will be stopped, squeeze will become unknown, etc. etc. They sent telegrams to all the other schools asking them to join in, and I suppose the telegram has just reached Paofu. I expect the disturbance will only last a day or so, as it has been checked here and in Peking already. The Viceroy has been ordered to use the soldiers to stop it if necessary. Chang Po Lin, a Christian, the head of the Private Middle School in Tientsin, was forced to head the movement, and he told the students he'd take charge only if they would give him life and death authority. They finally consented and he told them that the first order would be that they should all return to school and send only one representative from each school to act as the committee with him, to see what was best. He is a man especially noted for his conscientiousness and wisdom, so everyone feels that things are in safe hands. He is also very much in favor of the present plan of educating the people up to self-government, so I guess he'll try to head off the agitation for the immediate Parliament.

Paotingfu, North China / January 8, 1911

Classes closed last Tuesday and we had three days of t'ing k'ê or review for exams, and started exams yesterday. We are having ours mornings and the Chinese teachers theirs in the afternoons, so we won't be through till Friday.

Politics in China
The political situation as far as the school is concerned has calmed down completely. The agricultural school has finished its examinations and the students have gone home, and just at the present our students are more concerned in saving themselves from flunking in their exams than in saving Manchuria from the Japanese. At Peking, however, the situation is growing more tense. The Lucheng Yuan have impeached the Grand Council and are trying to force the Regent to take several steps for which the country is not ready. However, he stood firm so far, and if he'll only stick it out he can save the situation. If he does he'll make himself exceedingly unpopular for a while, but someday he'll be regarded as one of China's greatest statesmen.

The last week has been colder, which is very proper, as according to the Chinese calendar last week and this week are the coldest of the winter. It is very funny to see how they change clothes according to Imperial Edict. The Emperor, or rather the Regent, issues a proclamation, "For the next seven weeks wear fur caps and five coats," and they all do it.

Tientsin, North China / January 15, 1911

Vacation again for almost six weeks. I am now comfortably settled in the Queen's Hotel, on the British Bund, Tientsin, that is to say on the river bank. Out here they always call the waterfront street the Bund. I got here yesterday noon and of course spent all the afternoon and evening with Edith Gordon.

The Plague

I'm afraid I won't get to see Edith Parker this vacation. I could get up there all right, but I'm afraid I couldn't get back. It's on account of the plague up there. They are trying to keep it from coming down here. All second and third class traffic has been stopped, and first class passengers have to stop and go through five days of quarantine at Shan-hai-kwan, and there is considerable talk of even stopping first class passage. It was reported yesterday that there were three cases in Peking, people who slipped through before the quarantine, but they have them thoroughly isolated and it is not thought it will spread unless it gets through from Manchuria. At Harbin it is very bad. The lower class Chinese and Russians are dying like flies, so fast they can hardly bury them. At Mukden it is not quite so bad. So far, the better class people have been fairly free from it (except doctors). A hundred and fifty Chinese doctors from Peking and Tientsin went up two weeks ago. There are about fifty of them left. A large number of the foreign doctors have also gone, but so far only one, a Frenchman, has succumbed.

They think the plague is the same as the Black Plague which wiped out about half the population of Europe in 1350 or thereabouts. It seems to be a sort of concentrated consumption. They know very little about the bacteria yet, except that it seems to thrive best in the cold and is carried by dust particles like the tuberculosis bacilli. It attacks the lungs; the fever goes up to about 120, and by the next day it is all over. So far, only one person in 25 has recovered. It has done one good thing, however. It has almost put the quietus on political agitation out here, which is a good thing, as they have been trying to change things too rapidly the last month or so.

P.S. I'm sending you a picture the cook gave me to hang in your room. A p'eng-yiu (friend) of his made one for both Long and I because we let him off for a few days. The picture is of the "lao ho" (old tiger) just sneaking down from the "hsi shan" (western mountains).

Clack-Gordon Wedding in Tientsin, March 21, 1911 (Tuesday)

List of friends and family in the Clack-Gordon wedding photo
(from a letter written by R.W. Clack on Wednesday, March 22, 1911)

Front Row:
>E.R. Long, Elma Butler Gordon (mother of bride), Robert Clack (groom),
>Edith Gordon Clack (bride), Karl Gordon (brother of bride)

Second Row:
>Miss MacGown ("she is to live with Mrs. Gordon"), Moore Gordon (brother of bride),
>Mr. Ewing ("head of the Tientsin American Board Mission"), R.R. Gailey, Mrs. Hall

Third Row:
>Frances Harvey, Miss Davis ("the new young lady who just came to the mission;
>formerly YWCA secretary in Des Moines"), Emma Steel ("lived with the Gordons
>at Peitaiho last summer"), Mr. S.S. Knabenshue (the American Consul), Mrs. Hersey,
>Mr. Hersey

Fourth Row:
>Frank Beal ("of the Tientsin Y.M.C.A."), Mr. Carritt ("one of Moore's colleagues"),
>Mr. Hayes, Miss Winterbotham ("a very sweet old lady who has a little school next door
>to where the Gordons lived")

Our house, west suburb, Paotingfu (photo 1911)

Presbyterian Martyrs' Monument, Paotingfu, from the southeast (photo 1911)

4 Dedication of Presbyterian Martyrs' Monument in Paotingfu

Background – The Boxer Rebellion
The Presbyterian Martyrs' Monument – built in Paotingfu and dedicated in 1911 – was associated with the Boxer Rebellion, a violent outbreak against foreigners and Chinese Christians, that took place in Northern China between 1899 and 1901. Chinese anti-foreign and anti-Christian rebels were encouraged by those (including a number of Manchu and Chinese officials) who opposed Western colonialism and Christian missionary activity. It is estimated that a total of 136 Protestant missionaries and 53 children were killed, and 47 Catholic priests and nuns; 30,000 Chinese Catholics, 2,000 Chinese Protestants, and 200 to 400 of the 700 Russian Orthodox Christians in Beijing. [2]

Following is an excerpt from a letter written by Edith (Mrs. Robert) Clack to her mother about the dedication of the Presbyterian Martyrs' Monument in Paotingfu (now Baoding), China:
  "Sat. [April 22] we had the dedication of a Monument to the Missionaries of the Presbyterian Mission who perished here in 1900. There were a number of friends from Peking and Shuntehfu here. Mr. and Mrs. Miller among others. Yesterday [Sunday, April 23] we had two services, one at five and the other at eight. Mr. Miller led the first one and Dr. Lowrie the other. The meetings were as a memorial to those who had been killed - eight [Presbyterian] foreigners: Dr. Taylor, Mr. and Mrs. Simcox and three children and Dr. and Mrs. Hodge. That all took place in the old Presbyterian Compound two miles north of the city [Paotingfu]. It is there where the graves are. The Boxers set their houses on fire and they stayed in them and were all burned to death."

Crowd at the Dedication, April 22, 1911

Rev. Mather at the dedication of the Martyrs' Monument, April 1911
L-R: "Killie, Mather, and Edith Clack" (from back of photo)

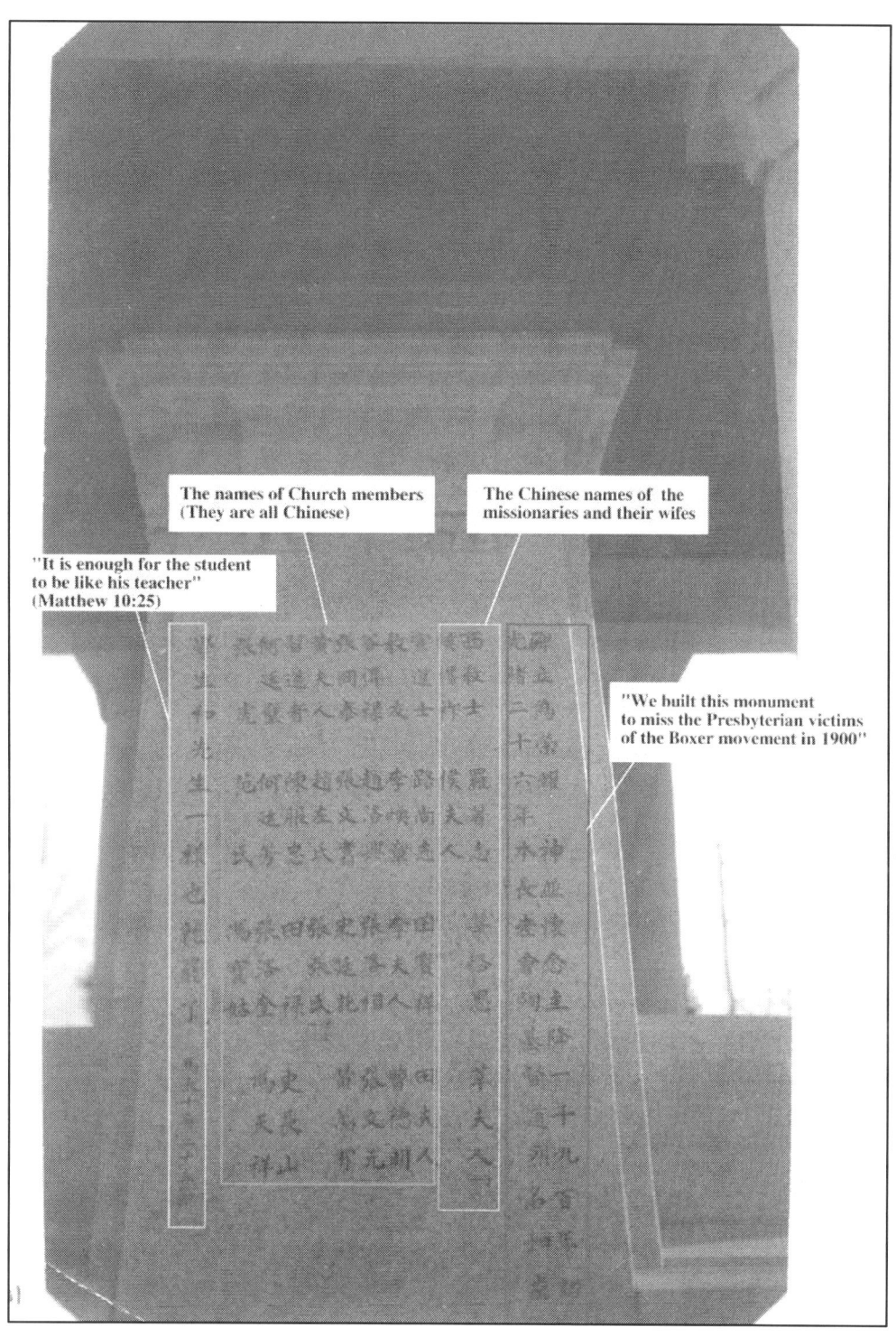

This image (based on a photograph taken by R.W. Clack) was sent to Norma Clack in 2018 by Yiding Gao from China. It contains a partial translation of the Chinese script on the northside of the Memorial Tablet inside of the Presbyterian Martyrs' Monument.

CONGREGATIONAL MARTYRS WHO DIED IN PAOTINGFU

During the Boxer Rebellion in 1900, the missionary compound in Baoding was overrun by anti-missionary and anti-foreign Chinese Boxers. Horace Tracy Pitkin was killed and the other missionaries serving in the city were also killed or later executed. Pitkin was a Congregational missionary who was a leader in the Christian missionary movement that sprang from Yale College during the last decade of the 1800s. In all, fourteen Presbyterian, Congregational, and China Inland Mission missionaries were killed at Paotingfu.

Photo taken 1912
Martyrs' graves, Congregational Church-yard.
The grave marker for Horace Tracy Pitkin is second from left.

Listed here are the Presbyterian missionaries and their family members who died in Paotingfu during the Boxer Rebellion in 1900. [3]

- Dr. Cortlandt V. and Mrs. Elsie (Sinclair) Hodge, died June 30, 1900.
- The Rev. Frank and Mary Simcox and their three children all died June 30, 1900.
- Dr. George Y. Taylor, medical missionary, led the establishment of the Paotingfu Presbyterian Hospital; died June 30, 1900.

The following two photographs are not related to the Boxer Rebellion, but are memorials to two women who were in missionary work in Paotingfu.

Mrs. Lowrie's Monument given by the citizens of Paotingfu, located just east of the Martyrs' Monument (photo ca. 1911)

Note – Mrs. Amelia (Tuttle) Lowrie, born 1833; died in 1907. She was the mother of Rev. James Lowrie.

Mrs. Lewis' Well, Presbyterian Mission, Paotingfu (photo ca. 1911)

Note –
Cora (Savage) Lewis (1873-1957), was a nurse who spent 32 years in missionary work in China. Her husband, Charles Lewis (1865-1932), was a Presbyterian medical missionary who established and was head of the Paotingfu Hospital. They are buried in Pennsylvania, U.S.A. [4]

5 Summer Excursion to Japan and Settling into Their New Life

⌘ **Rob's Textbook for Political Science**
During his first year of teaching (1910-1911) Rob wrote a 150-page textbook, *Political Science for Chinese Students*, for Geography-Political Science classes. In a letter dated June 4, 1911 he wrote: "I'm getting along famously with my book. Can't get it copyrighted out here as they have no copyright laws." In a June 25 letter he wrote: "I finished my book Saturday night … 150 closely typewritten pages."

⌘ **Trip to Japan**
In July 1911 Rob and Edith traveled to Japan for a summer vacation and tour with their friends Roy and Lynne Woodward.

⌘ **They become "Refugees" during the Chinese Revolution of 1911**
In October 1911 provincial rebellions broke out against the Manchu Dynasty that was ruling China; these rebellions turned into a revolution that resulted in the abdication of the Manchu Emperor. During these events, the college was closed for several months. Rob and Edith left Paotingfu and took refuge in the British Concession in Tientsin.

THE LETTERS

Letter written by Rob to his father in Iowa

Paofu. / May 20, 1911

Chinese Government and the Banking Trust
　　Everything seems to be going along smoothly except that the government and the Banking Trust cannot agree about their loan. The trust wants to force the government to take the loan at 6% and refuse to borrow of anyone else, while the Belgians and Austrians are offering them money at 5%. The trust is making a great splurge in the papers about the reason for a non-agreement being because the Chinese refuse to give them any control over the spending of the money to see that it is not misappropriated, but that is merely a blind to hide the fact that they want to get a monopoly on the loan at an excessive interest rate. I don't know how it will finally come out, but I'm afraid the Chinese will have to give in, as they cannot afford to antagonize the Powers, who are backing the Money Trust.

Letter written by Rob to Edith's mother in China

June 10, 1911

　　Mr. Fei went to Taiyuanfu Friday to interpret for Mr. Eddy. They will be here Tuesday. Did you know that Mr. Fei had resigned? He really has done well to keep his position for three years when there are so many returned students who have high Chinese degrees (which Mr. Fei has not) who were after the place. Up to now it has been uphill work for Mr. Fei and they have not been after it so hard, because of the work, but much of the work is now done, so Mr. Fei thought he would not be able to hold the place for another year against so many who have influential friends, so he thought it would be better to resign. He has had a number of positions offered him already, but said he did not intend to accept any before the end of the summer. We hate very much to have him go, but it will perhaps be for the best, as he may be able to open up a new field. He has succeeded in getting in a majority of Christian men here as teachers, so perhaps he can now be more useful in some other place.

I suppose you also know that Chang Po Lin has been appointed head of the new American Preparatory School, and that all restrictions against Christian teaching in the school have been removed. It ought to be a great opportunity for those people.

Letter from Rob to his sister Celia

June 18, 1911

Mr. Eddy of the national Y.M.C.A. visits Paotingfu

Our guests have all left us, and we are alone again. Miss Taylor and Miss Larsen left Monday, and Tuesday Mr. and Mrs. Eddy came and stayed till Friday. They are very nice. He is national Y.M.C.A. secretary for India, and he is on his way home for a furlough, giving lectures to the Chinese students on the way. He was a chum of Mr. Pitkin (who was killed here in 1900) both in college and in the theological seminary, and Mr. Luce, who is a missionary at Weihsien in Shantung, and who was also with them in college and seminary, met him here so that they could go to Mr. Pitkin's grave together. Mrs. Eddy is English.

Wednesday night he spoke to 3000 students at Li Hung Chang temple in the city on China's needs; and Thursday night he spoke to 600 in the Presbyterian Church on Christianity, almost half of them signed pledges to read the New Testament through and to live as best they could in accordance with whatever truths they found in it. There were six from college, and next fall will try to get them together into a Bible class.

We've had no school work this week so I've managed to get quite a bit of typewriting done in spite of the company. I think I can have my book just about finished in another week. Examinations start tomorrow for a week and then we're through for about seven weeks.

Letter written by Rob (from the ship) to his sister Ida

Nearing Japan / July 10, 1911

I expect we will arrive at Moji where we leave the ship in about four hours, so I'll write this letter in order to mail it as soon as we land. We are now out about fifteen miles southeast of the place where the Russian fleet was destroyed in 1904.

We left Tientsin Wednesday noon, and have had quite a checkered voyage. We were due in Moji yesterday morning, and, as the coast of Japan is dimly visible I guess we'll get there D.V. [*Deo volente*] tonight. First Wednesday afternoon we ran aground for several hours in the river. We finally got free and came out across the bar just at dark. Then everything went well till Friday morning when we broke a tube in the engine. After several hours, we got that fixed and were soon just off Weihaiwei. There they had up storm signals, and the captain found out there was a typhoon outside the Shantung promontory, so he returned to Chefoo for further particulars. We lay there for several hours during a severe wind and rain storm, and then came across to the Korean coast. There we laid up for twelve hours in a fog, finally starting up again yesterday noon, and playing hide-and-seek with the fog all afternoon. Today has been glorious, however. The sky is clear and the sea is almost calm. I imagine it's most almighty hot on shore, but out here it's delightful.

We'll land at Moji tonight, then on to Kobe tomorrow, and then on to Yokohama. We want to spend a day or two up at Nikko which is about 100 miles north of Tokyo, but we must be back to Yokohama by Saturday, as Roy and Lynne are due there Sunday.

Letter written by Edith to her mother, Elma Gordon, in China

The Club Hotel, Limited
Yokohama, Japan / July 17, 1911

We take the "Persia" in about two hours for Kobe. We met Lynne and Roy yesterday morning and a Miss Hodges also met them. She lives here, in the same mission as Mr. Heininger of Kalgan. She took us to a Japanese S.S. and afterwards we came up to our room and talked till it was church time. We had such a good sermon about "God is in heaven and all's well with the world." He brought out that there was a divine providence over all even if sometimes it did not look so. After church Miss Hodges took us to her home for Tiffin. She is very much like Miss Gumbrell. A Miss Gross is with her. We stayed there till after four when we came back to the room and visited till it was time for Lynne and Roy to return to the boat.

We went up to Nikko and Oh! Mama, if you ever have the chance don't miss going there. The trees are almost like our large pines in California and altogether it is most beautiful. We also went to see the big Buddha.

Letter written by Rob to his sister Celia

Shimonoseki, Japan / July 25, 1911

We are just getting ready to leave for Dairen where we will arrive day after tomorrow. Dairen is about 30 miles from Port Arthur. It is generally known by its Russian name "Dalny". We leave there Thursday night, arrive at Shanhaikwan 20 miles from Peitaiho, and go on to Paotingfu the next morning. We were just counting up and we have slept in 15 different beds so far since we left home.

After we left Kobe last Thursday we went on to Miyajima where we stayed two days. That is an island in the Inland Sea and is one of the three great sights of Japan. It certainly is a very pretty place. I think it is prettier than Nikko, but it lacks the grandeur. Friday morning we climbed the mountain on the island Miyama, which is about 1400 ft. There are steps all the way up, 2353 in all. I counted them. Edith and Lynne have hardly been able to walk since, but are getting along all right now. There is also a famous temple there built over an inlet of the sea which is covered with water when the tide is in. We came on to here Sunday morning, and have been taking a couple of day's rest.

Letter written by Rob to his father

Peitaiho, North China / July 31, 1911

Experiencing Japan

We left Shimonoseki last Tuesday on the Kagi Maru. Had a dandy trip, the sea was just like glass all the way, and we all felt fine. Arrived in Dairen (Dalny) Thursday afternoon, and left there that evening at 8. We went on the Japanese railroad as far as Tashihchiao arriving there at 3 A.M. We waited there till 5:30 and then rode 13 miles over to Yingk'ou (Newchwang). We had quite an experience there. We thought from the railway guides that the Japanese and Chinese railway stations were both on the banks of the river directly opposite of each other so we just merely had to ferry across, but when we arrived we found the Japanese station was five miles from the city. We had to ride over in little Russian carriages, and oh, such roads. Some places they had tried to repair them and had used cobble stones about the size of your head. Often we were up to the hubs in mud, but we finally got to the riverbank and from there took a sampan across. There we left about 10 a.m. on a branch line over to K'oupangtzu, leaving there about 2 o'clock. We got to Shanhaikwan, on the Great Wall at 8 and stayed there overnight.

Then we came on twenty miles further to Peitaiho station the next morning. Roy and I rode donkeys over from the station, while the girls came in sedan chairs. We are stopping at the hotel which is right on the beach only a few rods from the water's edge.

Letter written by Rob to his sister Ida

Paotingfu, North China / August 20, 1911

Well, we are home at last. We left Peitaiho last Monday and as it had rained for 24 hours before we left you should have seen the roads. It is five miles over to the station and my donkey got stuck and laid down once, but luckily there was a grassy bank close at hand, so I didn't get muddy. Other people did not get off so lucky. Mr. Thwing got rolled where the mud was knee deep and had to go into the river to wash off his clothes.

We have the opening feast at the college tomorrow and work begins the next day. Long is not back yet, so we have to start without him. I have the same work as last year except that Roy has my Latin class. The new president is named Li. He has just graduated from Pei Yang and has never been to America or England so we will have to run things ourselves. Some ways it is easier but in others it will be harder. We will miss the Feis very much indeed.

Yesterday the cook came in with some specimens of minerals which a man gave a friend of his to give to us to examine to see if they were any good. He said they came from a large piece of land over in the mountains and if they were worth anything he wanted some foreigners to go in with him on them as if he tried to develop them himself the government would take them away from him. Roy is going to examine the samples in the lab and see if they are any good. I think there is no question as to the copper and lead. The specimens seem to be exceedingly rich. There are also others which he thinks are silver and gold ore, but we can't tell without testing them. If the stuff tests well, we will go over to look at the fields and see if the ore is commercially accessible and if so we'll see what can be done about it.

Letter written by Rob to his mother Paotingfu, North China / September 17, 1911

Flood disaster

At present there are big floods on the Yangtze and I expect at least a million people have been drowned and all crops destroyed so that probably several million people more will die this winter from starvation. Up here in North China, however, though the heavy rains have done a little damage, it has not been sufficient to make a very great difference.

We are having the house at the college all fixed over again. We expect to move sometime next week. The house won't be finished yet, but enough will be done so that we can get in, and if we are there to supervise things the rest of the work will be done much better and more quickly. Some of the Y.M.C.A. girls are coming to live in this house this winter in order to have less to distract them from their Chinese study than they would have in Peking.

Roy and I developed and printed some pictures last night which he had taken with his little camera. I'm sending a few of the best. I still have a number I took which I'll send as soon as we get to it to print them.

Letter written by Rob to his mother Paotingfu, North China / October 23, 1911

I did not get time to write yesterday, as I went over to the station to take some pictures and I had to lead foreign service in the afternoon. This will catch tomorrow's Siberian mail just the same anyway.

Civil War – Rebels vs. the Imperialists

Roy came back from Tientsin Thursday. Lynne did not come as they have been having a panic in Tientsin over the revolution and she was too scared. It's awfully funny how easily scared the Peking and Tientsin people are.

It has been very hard to get any authentic news from Hank'ou as the wires aren't working and the government has shut up the newspaper. However, according to the letter Mr. Lattimore received yesterday from Mr. Tenney, First Secretary of the American Legation the rebels have defeated the imperialists and driven them back up the railroad to Hsinyangchou about 100 miles north of Hank'ou on the border of Honan. They are also in possession of not only the Wuhan cities (Hank'ou, Han yang, Wu chang) but also I Cheng up the Yangtzê, Huangchou, down the Yangtzê and Ch'angsha, the capital of Hunan. It is very likely that they will try to make the south solid before they attempt to come north. I think they will unquestionably win out in the south and very likely will in the North, also. I think we are in no danger here, certainly not from either rebels or Manchus and I think the local officials will keep the situation in hand all right even if the Manchu officials leave as, if they keep good order, they will hold their places under the new government the same as under the old. Also, our contacts will be continued under the new regime if they win out. You see the new government will be very anxious to get the recognition of the foreign powers, so will do all in its power to keep on the good side of the foreigners.

We did think somewhat last week of sending the ladies and children to Tientsin, as we were afraid train service might be cut off as most of the cars had gone south to take troops, but the cars are coming back now, so that I think regular service will soon be restored. The Minister of Communications has promised to furnish us a train in case we have to leave, though I think there is much less danger from riots here than in Tientsin. The worst of the situation is that it is so hard to get reliable news.

Letter written by Rob to his sister Ida

Paotingfu, North China / October 30, 1911

I haven't time to write a very long letter, as we are so busy getting things ready to go to Tientsin, if we need to go. I am now engaged in making a list of everything in the house with its value, so, in case we leave and anything is harmed we may recover damages. I am sending a newspaper clipping which gives the most accurate résumé of events to date of any I can find.

Sending women and children to Tientsin for safety

Mr. Lattimore just came in with a note from the American legation saying that Taiyuanfu, just across the mountains in Shansi was in the hands of the revolutionists and advising us to send the women and children to Tientsin as soon as possible. We men will not go as long as school keeps open, but as the students are getting excited and leaving, school may soon close and we will go, too. As yet, however, Paotingfu seems to be the quietest place in North China.

Street just east of the railway station, Paotingfu (photo 1911)

6   *War and Pestilence and Separation (1911-1912)*

⌘ Many foreigners fled from Paotingfu during this perilous time of battles between the Imperialists and the Revolutionaries. Chihli Provincial College in Paotingfu closed temporarily and the Clacks went to Tientsin. Tientsin (now Tianjin) is a city of northeast China near the Bohai Sea and southeast of Peking. In 1911 there were eight concessions in this city well guarded by foreign military units.

⌘ Rob occupied himself during this time of exile by teaching classes at the Anglo-Chinese College, doing some teacher training at the Y.M.C.A. with another college professor, S.B. Harvey, watching or participating in athletic competitions, and taking photographs in and around Tientsin. During this time of political upheaval, Rob also became involved with a committee that was making plans to establish a Young Men's Christian Association (Y.M.C.A.) in Paotingfu.

Clack residence while in exile in Tientsin – 35 Dickinson Road (photo 1911 or 1912)

THE LETTERS

Letter written by Rob to his sister Celia

Tientsin, North China / November 13, 1911

Well, for the first time I've let a week go by without writing home, but things have been so unsettled I just haven't been able to get at it. I'll give you the history of the past two weeks in order, as near as I can remember it.

The Revolution and its impact

Last time I wrote we had just had word of the capture of Taiyuanfu and advice to send the ladies and children away. That night just at midnight we received a telegram from the American minister that Chengtingfu (the first "fu" city south of us – 80 miles) had been captured. That, afterwards, turned out to be untrue as the revolutionists had only come down the railway line to the Niangtzekuan, the first mountain pass in Shansi, about fifty miles west of Chengting.

However, on Wednesday Roy and I brought Lynne and Edith up here, the Lattimores having gone Monday, and the Pitmans and Harveys, Tuesday. I went back Friday, and Roy Sunday and we kept on holding classes, though the students had begun to leave until we were down to about a third.

Meantime, the sixth division (Chinese) under General Wu Lu Chêng had been sent to Shihchiachuang just south of the Chengtingfu where the railroad branches off into Shansi, and also the first division (Manchu) had been sent down from Peking. They had a number of brawls in the ensue and last Monday night Gen. Wu went over to the Manchu headquarters to try to get affairs patched up, but he was stabbed in the back and beheaded by the Manchu officers.

Immediately his men heard of it, they broke loose, attacked the Manchus and defeated them after a fight lasting nearly all day Tuesday. The Manchus were scattered and fled in all directions. Some of them tried to come to Paotingfu but about 500 men of the sixth division who still remained there met just south of the city, and the last we heard of them they had urgent business elsewhere with the sixth division after them. Some of them did ultimately get into Paotingfu and took the train for Peking. During all this trouble there were no trains south of Paotingfu, and as we daily expected the whole city to go over to the revolutionists we expected trains to stop at any time.

College temporarily closed

This trouble frightened away most of the remainder of our students and finally Thursday with less than twenty left the director closed school temporarily, so we all left Friday morning at ten, arriving in Tientsin at 2 o'clock Saturday morning, being delayed by troop trains, etc.

You ought to see the people coming out of Peking Friday; in less than an hour I think we passed over 25,000 coming along the railway track on foot. You see the Manchus are afraid of the Chinese and the Chinese fear the Manchus so both are leaving.

Meantime the government has become thoroughly frightened and has granted the people a Constitution and a Parliament, have made Yüan Shih K'ai Premier and are giving in to every demand made on them; but I fear it is too late. The revolutionists control over three fourths of the empire and nothing will satisfy them but the absolute expulsion of the Manchus and a republic.

Tientsin was supposed to be taken over last week, but the revolutionists tipped off the consuls so as to let them get their nationals who were in the native city in a place of safety, and the fool consuls tipped it off to the Viceroy who immediately brought in extra troops, so that the city cannot be taken now without a battle, which the revolutionists wish to avoid here as they fear foreign property might be damaged, and they wish to avoid all foreign complications. Why can't the consuls mind their own business? The American consul here is the worst of the lot, too. I know this is true as it came from the best Chinese man in North China, who is on one of the committees. I won't write his name here as it might cause him trouble.

All the Foreigners have now left Paotingfu except Mr. McCann and Miss Chapin at the ABCFM Mission and Dr. Lowrie, Mr. Cunningham, Dr. Mackey, Chas. Lewis and Elizabeth Lewis at the Presbyterian Mission. However, I really think there is no danger, as the city will go over peacefully to the revolutionists at the first opportunity, and they are extremely careful to protect all foreigners and their property.

Long and Palmer left a week ago Friday for Shansi. They wanted to get down where there was some fighting to get some pictures and have some excitement. Haven't heard from them since Thursday but suppose they are all right.

Mr. H.H. Kung, "a descendant of Kung-fu-tzu (Confucius), a graduate of Oberlin, now in the A.B.C.F.M. (American Board of Commissioners for Foreign missions) at Taku, and Chief of Police in the city during the Revolution" (photos Nov. 1911)

Letter written by Edith to Rob's father   **Tientsin, N. China / November 26, 1911**

    Everything had been so upset the past few weeks that I have been unable to write, but now we are safely settled here in Tientsin and I am going to try to write each week as Rob does.

    We are living in a new role for us; we are now refugees. But we are a lot better off than some I have seen. We have one family (a man, his wife and two babies), in one room and this week we're expecting three ladies and three children to come into two other rooms. Everything in Tientsin is so full. Lots of the people from inland are crowding in here. Some of the foreigners inland have been killed and some have been attacked by robbers and one lady who came this last week was badly cut and bruised; her husband also was badly mistreated in trying to protect her. We are very glad that we are at the coast. Some of the people are still in Paofu, but I do wish they would come away. So far, they are safe but the trouble in this country is you never can tell what is going to happen next.

    It would be very nice if we could go home on a visit now, because we will have more time now for a visit than we may have again soon. But there are two reasons why we can't come. The first is we haven't any money, and the second is that China is too interesting a place in which to live right at the present moment. And then there are many other reasons, such as: I don't like to leave Mama here alone, etc.

    Rob is writing to you now. He is going to send his letter by the Pacific and I am sending mine by Siberia. Please tell us which one gets there first and how much difference there is between them. My! how odd to send two letters from the same place, one going one way and one the other and have them meet on the other side of the world. Strange things do happen in this old world.

    I don't believe I have written you at all since we had to "flee for our lives". The last week in Oct. we had been thinking it might be necessary for us women to come down here and stay until the trouble was over. On the strength of that I went ahead and packed all of our winter clothes etc. on Monday. That night, just at midnight, we received a telegram saying that the first largest place south of there had been taken by the rebels. Up until that time I had kept my nerve very well, but to be awakened from a sound sleep with that news and then to have the clock strike 12 right on top of it was more than I could stand. I didn't go into hysterics or even cry, but I had a severe nervous chill. But you can see how calmly we took it when you know we went to sleep and slept good till four o'clock when we received another note, but it was only from Mr. McCann asking what we were going to do. After answering that we slept until morning. We didn't tell Roy and Lynne about the notes until morning.

    Mother had rented two five-roomed houses [in Tientsin]. We three are living in one and we have rented the other one to three different parties. Mother has all her furniture here, so we are fixed very nicely. We brought our own bedsprings and mattress and bedding, our winter clothes and all the small wedding presents, silver, etc. and my great-grandmother's Bible and hymn book, also our wedding clothes. Those chairs you sent us we had not unpacked yet so we could bring them too. We had left them packed until we got the house straightened up. I don't know now when we will ever see them. We are stranded here indefinitely. My how I hate to leave our pretty home. We were just putting on the finishing touches. All the new furniture we had made in the Mission Style. If we ever do get to go back and the property is unharmed we will have a lovely little home.

Letter written by Rob to his mother

Tientsin, North China / December 3, 1911

The weather has moderated a little this week after the cold of a week ago, and it has been fine outside, just cold enough to be bracing. Edith is now taking a nap as she is rather tired. We walked down to the Anglo-Chinese Church (two miles) and back this morning. Mother Gordon has three young Chinese whom she is teaching English here by singing hymns.

The people from Taiyuanfu all came into Tientsin this last week. The rebels gave them a train down to the Niangtzukuan tunnel on the boundary of this province and then the Imperialists brought them on from there. The trip would not have been so hard but for the fact that there were nine babies in the party. One Chinese officer tried to come through with them, but he was taken from the train at Shihchiachuang and shot as a spy.

A telegram came from Sianfu last week asking for help, so a party of young men was made up, and they have started from Taiyuanfu with a large escort of soldiers to bring the foreigners out. That is where the foreigners were reported killed, though it is still uncertain whether the report is true or not. Long and Palmer and five or six others are in the relief party. I would have liked to go but as they may have to fight their way through, of course a married man has no business going.

Thanksgiving was a wet, rainy day. We had Miss Winterbotham to dinner with us. There was a reception at the American consulate in the afternoon but as Edith had a headache, we didn't go. I went over to the Chinese City railroad station, the other side of the native city, in the evening to meet some people we expected up from Shantung, but they didn't come. It is about seven miles from here and the roads were just a sea of mud, so I had a great trip.

Vacating their home in Paotingfu

Tomorrow I am going back to Paotingfu to get some more things. I will be back Wednesday. Mr. Pitman and Mr. Harvey are also going. This will probably be our last trip back until school opens again in the spring (or the next).

Also, I think I've got hold of a big news item, and I want to get it verified at the hospital. There are a lot of wounded soldiers from Hank'ou there and they can give me the straight of it, if there is something to it. If it's true it's one more great crime the Manchus have got to answer for in this world or the next. I'll tell you about it next week and give you freedom to publish it.

False newspaper reports

According to reports the Imperialists have retaken Hangyang and the revolutionists at Wuch'ang are anxious to treat *[sic]* for peace. But some of the Chinese say that the government knowing that the truth cannot be known for several weeks, have deliberately falsified reports and hired newspapers to publish their reports, so that their cause will look better and give them a chance to get a loan from some foreign nation. What makes this seem plausible is the fact that the fighting is still going on at Nanking and the city will probably be taken by the rebels today. If the rebels had been defeated at Hankow they would probably have sent some of the troops back to hold things there instead of throwing such a large force against Nanking.

Meantime, things here remain about the same. The Provincial Assembly had demanded the abdication of the Manchus and has declared that they will declare themselves independent as soon as Honan does. That gives another reason why the government should falsify the Hankow reports. Also a large body of troops has been stationed at Langfang between here and Peking, which looks as if they feared after the fall of Nanking the rebels will come up the railroad across Shantung and attack Peking from this side. But, of course, the real facts are hard to get at.

Letter written by Rob to his sister Ida

Tientsin, North China / December 12, 1911

Well, I went to Paofu last Monday as I had planned and returned on Wednesday. I brought out all the things we are going to bring. We have most of our stuff except the books and furniture. I really don't think there is any danger of losing it, anyway.

Everything is very quiet at Paofu now. The people think it will stay quiet unless the Imperialists, who are advancing from Shihchiachuang into Shansi, are defeated and I don't see how they can be, as they are much superior to the revolutionists in numbers and equipment. Also, other armies are coming into Shansi from both North and South, so it seems that the revolutionists there must surely be defeated.

15-day truce

Meanwhile a fifteen days truce has been declared at Wuch'ang while the representatives of both sides try to come to an agreement. I do not think the rebels would treat [sic] at all were it not for the fact that their leaders have been quarrelling among themselves. The main question is whether the government shall be a republic or a constitutional monarchy. I think the republicans would be satisfied all right with a monarchy provided the emperor were Chinese, but they may be enabled to effect a compromise whereby the present baby emperor [5-year-old Puyi] may be still kept on the throne, but entirely removed from all Manchu influence. At least, that's what we're all hoping and praying for, as the country certainly is not ready for a republic. The Regent has resigned but his power seems to have been taken over by the Empress Dowager, who seems to have a desire to emulate her illustrious predecessor. If that happens, about the best thing we foreigners can do is to stand from under as quick as possible, as something will drop and drop hard.

Burning and slaughter in Hankow

I found out at Paofu the cause of the burning of Hankow by the Imperialists and the reason they killed so many innocent women and children. They were kept practically without food for two days, then filled up on whiskey and sent into the city. It does seem as if the Imperialists ought to have an awful beating due them for that, doesn't it? I found that out from the wounded soldiers, many of whom are in the hospital at the American Board Mission, and Roy has gone down today to take charge of it. It will be under Dr. Lewis's supervision. There are a great many foreigners going into the Red Cross work now. Perhaps I shall go to Paofu myself to help if there is any real need.

Letter written by Edith to Rob's sister Ida

Tientsin / December 12, 1911

Just think, in eleven more days I shall be twenty-three years old. My! how old we are all getting to be. Karl will be thirty his next birthday. Still our Mother seems so young, she will be fifty-three her next birthday. We are so glad that we could be with her this winter. I don't see how she could ever have gotten along without us. We got a good cook last week which is a great relief to us all. My old cook wanted to wait a while longer before he came, and I don't blame him.

We are cozily fixed here now, and I think we are as happy as two mortals could be in this old world. My! if Rob were my brother I most certainly would be proud of him. Whenever we go calling together, people always listen when he speaks, and they ask his opinion etc. on certain subjects, and his answers show such care and thought. I tell you, dear sister, I am proud to be the wife of such a dear, noble man.

We are having lots of fun pasting our Kodak pictures into books. We have one book just full of our wedding trip pictures. Last night we were pasting our Chinese pictures in one book, while we have another book for personal pictures. We do get so much pleasure from our Kodak. We got it back from Mr. Long this week.

Letter written by Rob to his sister Celia

Tientsin, North China / December 26, 1911

Well, Christmas has come and gone. We had a very good time. Mr. and Mrs. Taylor and three children, Mrs. Troxell and Miss Winterbotham were here for dinner and stayed most of the afternoon. We had a beautiful day. The temperature got up above freezing point part of the day and the sun shone all day.

The war news these days is mostly conspicuous by its absence. The armistice has been extended till Jan. 1st, as the delegates had just gotten together when it was to have expired, and had had no chance to really do anything. We are all hoping that they will be able to arrange terms satisfactorily, though I would much rather have the war gone on now, than have merely a temporary peace patched up.

Last Thursday night we went to hear the Messiah at Gordon Hall. It was our Christmas present to each other, as we did not feel that we could afford to spend much till we find out whether we are going to get any more or not. It was very well given and we enjoyed it very much.

At the entrance to the athletic field on Ku I Chieh Street, Tientsin (photo 1912)

Letter written by Rob to his father   **Tientsin, North China / December 31, 1911**

    Just received Mamma's letter of Nov. 29th with the newspaper clippings. You tell the Mason City paper if they are going to print things about China they want to get a little closer to the truth. They said Edith was a native of China, which she decidedly is not. Also, that story about the rebels eating the hearts of their victims is absurd. The Chinese wouldn't dream of such a thing, not any more than Americans. The Chinese are really the most peaceable people on the face of the earth, and the rebels have shown great moderation, and such stories as that ought to be vigorously suppressed.

    The Peace Commission has at last arrived at a decision, such as it is. The question of the future government is to be left to a National Assembly to be elected as soon as possible. However, that is going to be an awfully big undertaking, and it will be several months, at least, before the Assembly can be convened. Even then, I am not sure that all the provinces will abide by the decision, and though things will perhaps quiet down enough so that we can go back to work, it will probably be a long time before everything is settled.

    Most of the missionaries from Sianfu, where the foreigners were killed, have now come out, so there are very few women and children left anywhere in the interior. There are still quite a large number of men, but they, of course, are better able to care of themselves. It is not like 1900. They are in no danger from the ordinary people, but it is only the robbers they need to fear, and the foreigners are perhaps even less in danger than the Chinese. The party of which Long and Palmer are members got almost to Sianfu in safety when they were last heard from. Don't expect any more news from them, though, until they return, unless they are unreasonably delayed.

Victoria Park and Gordon Hall in winter (photo 1912)

Stacked arms of Inniskillings [Irish line infantry regiment of the British Army] **in Victoria Park. The men are attending service in Gordon Hall.** (photo 1912)

Stanley House, A.B.C.F.M., Hsiku (photo 1912)

Russian Monument from across the Peiho, Tientsin (photo 1912)

Elgin Avenue, Tientsin from the "old mud wall" (photo 1912)

German Consulate and Monument to the German soldiers killed in 1900, Tientsin (photo 1912)

The German Club, Tientsin (photo 1912)

The Tientsin Club (photo 1912)

7   *The Collapse of 3,500 Years of Chinese Dynasties*

Highlights: January-March 1912

⌘ The rule of the Qing [Manchu] Dynasty came to an end in 1912 and was replaced by the Republic of China [a government which was superseded by the People's Republic of China in 1949].

⌘ Within a few months after the fall of the Qing dynasty, Empress Dowager Longyu died at age 45 of an illness. She was the only Chinese empress whose coffin was transported by train from the Forbidden City to her burial place, the Chongling tomb of the Western Qing tombs. [5]

⌘ Chihli Provincial College reopened in the early spring of 1912 under the auspices of the Republic of China. The College had been closed for about six months.

⌘ On February 18, 1912, Rob wrote: "… abdication announced; Yüan Shih K'ai elected President of the United Provinces of China". This was a temporary name used by the Shanghai Military Government.

⌘ After nearly six months of exile in Tientsin, Rob returned to Paotingfu the first week of April for college classes to begin on April 11. Wives of the faculty members remained away because of the continuing threat of uprisings. Edith returned to Paotingfu in early May.

THE LETTERS

Letter written by Rob to his mother   **Tientsin / January 9, 1912**

      We were shut off from the outside world for several days last week. The troops at Lanchou, this side of Peitaiho, mutinied and held up the railroad for three or four days, so we had no connection with either Chinwangtao or the Trans-Siberian, but the mutiny has now been put down and trains are running as usual. To insure against any further interruption the powers have taken control of the railway, each nation being responsible for a section. The Americans and British and Germans will do most of it. There are no American troops here now but 1200 will be here next week and relieve the British who are subbing for them till they get here.

      The time of armistice has expired, but fighting has not begun again, as Wu Ting Hang and Yuan Shih K'ai are still negotiating by wire, though they don't seem to be getting anywhere. T'ang Shao I, who is acting as Imperial representative, practically turned traitor when he got to Shanghai and was forced to resign, so negotiations since then have had to be done by telegraph. I'm afraid there won't be any settlement for a long time. The revolutionists seem to be acting like a bunch of fanatics, they are impractical, while Yuan Shih K'ai, who seems to be the only practical one here, seems to be losing his power.

      I think the revolutionists will probably win out and get the republic founded, but pity the poor people. I'm afraid there will be a long period of anarchy, and perhaps the country will split up into several parts.

A "Republican" Post Office, Lake Road, Tientsin (photo 1912)

Taku Road, Tientsin (photo 1912)

Letter written by Rob to his sister Ida

Tientsin / January 15, 1912

There is not very much news this week, but expect there soon will be. The armistice expires today and I think both sides are anxious to fight the thing out. If the Imperial troops remain loyal, it is going to be almost impossible for the rebels to force their way very far north, as the Imperialists are better equipped, trained and general-ed, but it is not at all certain that they will fight if they can avoid it, and many of them would mutiny if they had a real good chance. No one is rash enough to venture any prophecy as to what the outcome will be, but we are all hoping it won't be long in being settled. Most people seem to think that a try at a Republic is inevitable, but we all have grave doubts as to its success. However, time will tell.

Word has been received that the party of which Mr. Long is a member reached Sianfu in safety two weeks ago and are coming out with the party they went to reinforce by the southern route through Honan. If all goes well they ought to be back within two weeks. They certainly have had a great experience, something they can talk about all the rest of their lives.

I guess I told you how sick Mr. C.W. Harvey, of the Y.M.C.A., had been. Everybody thought he'd have to be sent home sure, but he's now up and around again. Has been down to see me twice, and made a trip up to Peking to see about their new building up there. They are worried now for fear that the capital will be transferred to Nanking and are wishing they were putting some of this money into the Nanking work. However, I think it will be all right, as most of the work in Peking is with the students, and it isn't likely that the schools will be moved, even if the capital is.

I guess I told you that 1200 American soldiers are coming here from the Philippines this week. Mamma said she did not think Tientsin was much safer than Paofu, but you tell her she needn't worry about us here. It is against the treaties for the Chinese troops to come within ten miles of Tientsin and we have about 10,000 foreign soldiers with more coming.

Letter written by Rob to his sister Nan

Tientsin / January 24, 1912

American soldiers arrive

Well, this has been quite an eventful week. The American soldiers have at last arrived. They arrived at Ch'inwangtao (the winter port of Tientsin) Saturday. The machine gun squad of 24 men arrived in Tientsin Sunday and are camped in a warehouse just across the street from us. They also have the horses and the mules over there. The mules are real mules, about twice the size of the Chinese mules, and are a great source of wonder to the Chinese. But the greatest wonder of all are the three negroes in the squad. There has been a gang of coolies and youngsters hanging around the place over there, ever since they came to get a look at the negroes and mules. Our boy said last night he'd been over to look at the soldiers. I asked him if he saw the negroes. "Huh!" he said, "Hei Tê hên" (awfully black).

The majority of the troops came in Monday afternoon. There are 4 companies in all (a battalion) and they are on a war footing, making about 500 men. About a third were left along the line to patrol the railroad between Lanchou and T'angshan, and the rest came down here. They got about the biggest reception ever given to any troops arriving in Tientsin. Of course, all the Americans were there, with a good sprinkling of the other nationalities, especially the English! The Inniskilling (Irish) Band was there and I guess all the British soldiers who were not on duty. It was fine to see how the British and American soldiers mixed. When the Americans got ready to leave the station the Inniskilling Band headed the procession and the British soldiers fell right in besides the Americans and marched with them to their quarters. They are camped in a large godown [warehouse] in the French concession in the same block in which Roy is staying. I guess they sent us the pick of their men from the Philippines, as these are surely a fine-looking bunch. I think they average two or three inches taller than the soldiers of any other nationality in Tientsin. They came for business and they look it. Didn't even bring their dress uniforms along.

Government

The political situation becomes more tense, if possible, every day. It looked for certain last week as if the abdication of the Manchus would be announced before now, but owing to the opposition of some of the younger Princes they are still holding on. Most of the older ones are in favor of giving up (especially Prince Ch'ing and Prince Ch'un, the ex-regent) and accepting the very liberal terms of the revolutionists, but the younger ones want to fight it out. If they attempt it, Yuan Shih K'ai and the rest of those favoring a Constitutional monarchy will certainly desert them, and I don't see how they can hold out for long, and then what a slaughter there will be. I do hope the older ones will finally prevail, as it will save lots of bloodshed. There may be lots more trouble after they get their republic, but they seem to be bound to have it, and we can only hope it will succeed, even though we can't see how it can.

Written by Rob to his sister Celia

Tientsin / February 1, 1912

I finished up my work at the Anglo-Chinese College yesterday with the last exam. These fellows were much more stupid than my Paotingfu pupils as they have only been taught by the English method, which is to work out all the examples yourself and let the pupils copy them and memorize them. The passing mark at the A.C.C. is only 30 but even then I flunked 17 out of 23. At Paotingfu I generally can pass over half of them on a passing mark of 50.

Bombings

There has been quite a bit of bomb throwing in Peking and Tientsin lately. A couple of weeks ago one was thrown at Yüan Shih K'ai, but killed one of his officers instead. Saturday Liang Pi, one of the Manchus, was fatally hurt by one in Peking, and one was thrown at a general at the Chinese railway station here. Monday there were two exploded near the Viceroy's yamen, but luckily only the throwers themselves were hurt.

Yesterday we heard a number of explosions while we were in the French Concession and everybody was quite excited, but it afterwards turned out that the French police had roughed up a bunch of Chinese with bombs in their possession, and in order to get rid of the bombs they took them out to a large open field and exploded them by having one of the soldiers shoot at them.

The Manchus

Last Sunday the Generals of the Army put quite a crimp in the Manchus by sending them a notice that they were all agreed that further fighting was out of the question and that they better abdicate at once and accept the terms of the revolutionists. As this was signed by all but one of the fifty highest officers in the Imperial Army it was quite a blow, as it was the same as saying they wouldn't fight if ordered.

The rumor today is that the Manchus have abdicated. I expect we'll know for certain tomorrow. If so, now comes the big job of getting together an efficient provisional government. I fear there will be trouble between the Nanking government and Yuan Shih K'ai, but I hope not. I don't think the foreign nations will recognize any provisional government which does not have Yuan Shih K'ai at the head, as he is the only one in whom they have much confidence as being able to handle the situation. The Nanking government is too much a bunch of amateurs.

I see in some of the magazines that they don't understand anything at all about the cause of the rebellion. They all seem to think that the railway trouble in Ssŭch'uan brought it on, but that had about as much to do with it as John Brown's raid did with the Civil War in America. The whole trouble was the misrule of the Manchus, the railway policy being one of the few redeeming features of their government. The affair in Ssŭch'uan was entirely separate and was caused, not because of the Four Nations' Loan as 'The World's Work' would have it, but because the government wanted to take over a railroad already commenced by the people of Ssŭch'uan without returning to them the money they had invested.

Letter written by Rob to his father

Paotingfu / February 5, 1912

Manchu Abdication

The public edict in regard to the abdication of the Manchus has not yet been issued, but the Empress Dowager has given Yüan Shih K'ai instructions to act with the Nanking Government to provide a suitable provisional Republican government, and I suppose, as soon as that has been done, the Manchus will move out. There seems to be absolutely no question that it will only be a matter of a few days until the edict comes. The only disagreement now seems to be over the amount of the allowance to the Emperor, and that ought to be easily settled. So we are either at the end of the trouble, or else just the beginning, because with all the different factions among the revolutionists no telling what they will do when the Manchus are gone and they have no common foe to fight against. It's up to Yüan Shih K'ai. Even if he fails there he has already shown himself one of the greatest statesmen in the history of the world.

Conducting an institute for teachers

Mr. Harvey and I are conducting a sort of an Institute for the teachers of the middle schools of Tientsin, at the Y.M.C.A. this week. We have eighteen of them enrolled. It was planned by Mr. Hall and Chang Po Lin, and they plan to conduct it hereafter on a larger scale. This year it was to be an experiment, but it seems to be very successful so will be increased next year to make it more like what we have at home. We are giving the lectures at the Y.M.C.A. quarters down in the Chinese city, about four or five miles from here.

Tientsin, Anglo-Chinese College from the West (photo 1912)

Letter written by Rob to his mother

Paotingfu / February 12, 1912

Political Situation

We just got word this afternoon that the Edict of Abdication had finally been signed. They have been holding off until the provisional government had been completely arranged. Last word we had there was a split over the capital. The Revolutionists insisted on Nanking, but Yüan Shih K'ai said that was out of the question for the present, so I suppose it has been postponed until the meeting of the National Assembly. It certainly would be out of the question for Yüan Shih K'ai to leave the North at present, as he is the only one who holds things together, and if he should leave, anarchy would be the result. In fact, I don't think the foreign powers would let him.

We got word day before yesterday that the Viceroy of Hupei, Tuan Chi Jui, is encamped in the college with his body guards. They are not in our houses, however, as they have been sealed up and put under guard. He is the highest officer in the Imperial Army and is supposed to be the one who instigated the letter from the generals advising abdication.

College Remains Closed

The Board of Education is having a meeting today to decide upon the reopening of school. I think that, if possible, they will want to start about March first, but they may decide not. I think if it is postponed for any definite length of time I will go down to Anhui province to help with the famine relief work. Anhui is the province southwest of Shantung. It is crossed by the Yangtze River, which overflowed last summer and there are millions of people absolutely destitute. The war has not helped conditions any. If I go I will go to Shanghai, then to Nanking and then out to wherever I am stationed. They have to have big, strong men as the crowds at the distributing stations are so thick that the food has to be let down from the walls in baskets.

Arranged Marriages in China

Li Chang was married last week. I am enclosing the invitation we received to his wedding. Just think of being married at the age of eighteen to a girl you've never seen and probably never even heard of before. And yet that is what happens to 999 out of every thousand Chinamen. I do hope Li Chang got a good wife because he is such a dear youngster. Lien Ch'êng, Woodward's old boy, said the girl was from a very good family.

Monetary Values

Silver is certainly high out here now. Last summer a Tael was worth 60 cents U.S. but now it is worth 70 and still going up. You see at present affairs are so unsettled that everybody is afraid to ship much to China while the export trade is going on as usual, consequently all the money payments are coming this way, so the banks have run up the price of silver, so as to get as big a squeeze as possible. I'd like to have a good bunch of silver now so I could buy gold and hold it till next summer and make 10 to 15 percent on the transaction.

Kung I, Ch'ing Liang and baby (Dickinson Street, Tientsin) (photo 1912)

Letter written by Rob to his sister Ida

Tientsin / February 18, 1912

Well, this past week has been a history making one. The long-expected edict announcing the abdication came at last on Monday afternoon. The next day the Provisional Government at Nanking met, and after agreeing to leave one subject on which the two parties still disagreed (the capital) over to the National Assembly, they all resigned their offices, and the next day representatives of all the provinces met and Yüan Shih K'ai was unanimously elected President of the "United Provinces of China" [temporary name], the only president ever elected unanimously in history, except Washington.

There have been big celebrations all over the Empire, as all the majority of the people ask is peace, and apparently everything is going to quiet down, although it is not quite certain yet about Manchuria and Mongolia. I think anyway, things will be quieter until the National Assembly meets. There may be a split then, but we'll sincerely hope not. Here in Tientsin they had quite a celebration in the native city and the flag of the republic is flying everywhere. It consists of five equal horizontal stripes, the colors beginning with the top being red, yellow, blue, white and black; the five stripes being for the five races, as the Chinese say: Chinese, Manchus, Mongols, Mohammedans, and Tibetans.

The Board of Education had a meeting Wednesday to decide about the reopening of school, but were unable to set any definite date as yet, as they are still short of funds, most of their revenue having been diverted to the War Department. However, I think it will certainly begin within a month, and you can address our letters to Paotingfu again, as soon as you get this, unless of course you hear of some new trouble. I think now that it will be impossible for me to go into the famine relief work in Anhui, as just about the time I got there, I'd have to leave, so it wouldn't pay.

Chinese New Year

Today is the Chinese New Year's Day. It will probably be the last one of this sort, as the new government has adopted the Gregorian calendar. This date will still be celebrated I think, however, as Independence Day. It is something like our 4th of July, you know. We could hardly sleep last night for the firecrackers. All the Chinese houses and shops are togged out with colored lanterns (red) and paper flowers and flags etc. Edith and I were down in the native city yesterday and it reminded me of Clear Lake [Iowa] on Sunday.

I was also down Friday with one of the American soldiers named Mills. He is just a youngster. His father is a Presbyterian minister in Schenectady, New York, and his older sister is a missionary in Korea. Last year while his parents were visiting his sister out here, he left school and joined the army. His sister found out he was here and wrote Mrs. Gordon, who came over to China at the same time she did, so we looked him up. He seems to be a pretty good kid.

Tomorrow there is an English Rugby Football match between Shanghai and Tientsin. This is the fourth match, as they played before in 1907, 1908, 1909 and Shanghai won all three times. They have a good team now, however, as they have in a number of the British soldiers who are experts. One American is playing, Lucker, an old Cornell Univ. man, who has learned the English game out here. The rest of the team are Britishers.

Game between Shanghai & Tientsin: Tientsin Athletic Park, February 19, 1912

A close attempt for a goal, ball in bounding back from the post; Shanghai vs. Inniskillings, February 21, 1912

Thornton Mills, Co.D., 15th Infantry, U.S.A., stationed in Tientsin (photo 1912)

Letter written by Rob to his sister Nan   Tientsin / February 27, 1912

Well, at last we've got the long-awaited news. The college is to reopen a week from Friday, March 8th. At least that is the date of the official opening, but classes won't begin for several days after that. I don't know what day we will go back. Alas, I don't know yet what the plan is about making up the back work. We may have to stay and teach all summer. However, we can't do much kicking if we do, for we've had four months of vacation this winter. Anyway, I don't see any other possible way of finishing up my required work for the year, and even then it will crowd me considerably. I suppose the day that we go back will depend somewhat on whether we can get a boat to carry our baggage down the river (it only costs about 1/4 what it does by rail). I don't know yet whether the river is open as far as Paotingfu. From Tientsin down to the sea it has been open all winter except for ice in some of the bends. The first boat came up a week ago yesterday, the 19th of Feb. and there have been several others since.

Last week Lynne and Mrs. Harvey gave a party. It was a Spanish affair, everybody supposed to dress Spanish. There were teachers from Paotingfu, Pei Yang and Ch'ing Hua Universities, missionaries (Methodist and Presbyterian) from Tientsin, Shuntefu and Taianfu (where Perry Hanson is stationed), agents of the British American Tobacco Company, the American Vice-consul, two American soldiers, a lieutenant and a corporal, YM and YWCA secretaries and commercial people. And they all got along splendidly, too. The two tobacco men were very fittingly attired as pirates.

Letter written by Rob to his sister Celia

Tientsin / March 6, 1912

Mutiny in Peking

Well, this has been a rather exciting week, especially since Thursday night. Thursday night a number of the Imperial soldiers, dissatisfied because their pay had been cut, mutinied in Peking and started looting and burning. A large section of the northeast part of the Tartar City [Inner City] was burnt, as well as some of the Chinese City [Outer City]. Guards from the legations went out and brought all the foreign women and children into places of safety, but most of the men stayed with their buildings. However, none of the foreigners or their property were harmed. In fact, whenever the looters broke into a house and found foreigners there they immediately apologized and withdrew. Many of the police and, of course, all the riff-raff joined in with the mutineers. A great many of the soldiers, however, remained at their posts. The looters then scattered out over the country with their loot, as, of course, as soon as possible, an attempt was made to restore order in Peking, and all found looting were beheaded immediately.

Looting in Paotingfu

One squad wrecked and robbed the railway station at Fengt'ai but was finally driven from there by the British soldiers Sunday. Another squad went toward Paotingfu and I guess did some looting there, though we can't learn for certain. All we can find out is that there were some fires in the city, the Roman Catholic Cathedral was burned, but by accident, and none of the foreigners were harmed, and apparently none of our property at the college was touched. Just after these men went south the railroad engineers tore up part of a bridge on the railway so that we've had no direct communications with them, but yesterday the bridge was restored so that some of the loyal troops could go down to drive out the mutineers, so I expect we'll hear definite news today. All the American troops except sixty have gone to Peking, as well as 500 British, 300 French, 100 Germans and a lot of Japs.

Looting in Tientsin

Saturday night the troops in Tientsin native city mutinied, and were joined by the riff-raff and some of the police, until there were perhaps 10,000 looting and burning. A great share of the northern part of the city was destroyed. The police authorities appealed to the foreigners for help, but they had only enough men to protect the concessions and could not very well help. The American Board Mission was surrounded on all sides by burning buildings but they were not molested. Only one foreigner was harmed. Dr. Shreyer, a German, was out in the city when the riot was at the worst and was struck by a stray bullet and killed. The looters did lots of shooting into the air to frighten off the shopkeepers but only killed those who attacked them.

Not more than fifty of the Chinese were killed, but a great many were wounded by the flying bullets, and the Red Cross people have had their hands full. The police finally got some control over the situation as soon as daylight came Sunday, and there has been fairly good order since. They are executing looters as fast as they catch them, and sticking the heads up for a warning to others. I was all over the burned district yesterday and saw five men beheaded. Altogether about a hundred have been executed so far.

They certainly made a clean sweep where they were at it though. Several streets are absolutely cleaned out from end to end. Ku I Chieh, the famous shopping street where all the foreigners go for their curios, embroidered coats and so forth has hardly a wall left standing.

Edith and I were down there Saturday afternoon helping Mills, the American soldier, buy some curios and the street was filled with busy people and the shops were doing a rushing business but yesterday you wouldn't have recognized the place.

There are still many bodies of the mutineers scattered about the country, looting in the villages, but order is gradually being restored. It is very likely that the foreign troops will be used to help restore order, as 1500 Americans are coming from Manila, 5000 Japs from Port Arthur, 500 Germans from Tsingtao, a lot of French from Annam, and a lot more British from Hong Kong and I suppose the Russians will send some more too.

College opening postponed again

The opening of school, I suppose, will have to be postponed again, as the Province lost all of its funds, and also I don't think the consuls would allow the foreign teachers to go back till order is restored again. However, I don't think that will take but a week or two.

Letter written by Edith to Rob's father   **Tientsin / March 12, 1912**

Our hearts are very heavy this morning as we think of the awful state China is in at the present moment. From Shanghai to Hankow there is not a single large city that has not been looted and in the country districts the famine is raging. All over China thieving and looting are going on daily, while up here in the north everything is "luan ti". That word cannot be expressed in English as there isn't an equivalent, but it has the idea of confusion and all mixed up condition of affairs.

Paofu is all in ruins inside the city walls and they are carrying off women and girls to sell into slavery. It is not the common people that are causing the trouble but the armed soldiers. We don't know now when we will ever go home. We are so tired of the waiting and uncertainty of everything. It is wearing on our nerves so.

Letter written by Rob to his father   **Tientsin / March 12, 1912**

Another week had gone by. Nothing very much has happened, but we have been getting more of the details of the week before. Peking, Tientsin and Paotingfu have been quiet, but there has been considerable looting going on out among the country villages where the mutinied soldiers have scattered.

Reports (rumors) of Paotingfu fire devastation

Paotingfu was the worst sufferer, I guess. In Tientsin and Peking it was only certain sections which were burnt, but they say that at Paotingfu everything inside the wall except the Catholic property was cleaned out. Contrary to first reports none of the foreign property was touched, except that of the British-American Tobacco Company, and they had no right there, as they were violating treaty rights by carrying on business away from the treaty ports. Also, none of the foreigners were molested anyway. The looters even sent out guards to the missions to protect them. Also, they say none of the native Christians were harmed.

One of the Church of England missionaries was killed at a village southeast of Paotingfu, but I think that was unintentional. Two of them were in the village when a crowd of looters came along and commandeered their cart. They attempted to take it back, but the looters became threatening and they took refuge in the inn. The looters then fired at the inn, apparently only with the intention of frightening them but one of the bullets went through the door and killed Mr. Day.

Our property at the college was all untouched except Long's horse. His groom came over to the Presbyterian mission the day after the looting started, weeping because the horse had been taken. But the next day he came again with smiles all over his face, saying the looters had brought it back. Long's old horse always has been rather a joke, but I think that is the best yet.

I've had two or three pitiful letters from the Chinese at Paofu. Mr. T'ang, our Chinese teacher who teaches in English lost everything he had, but took refuge at the Presbyterian Mission with his family. This morning I had a letter from our carpenter that he was cleaned out. Mr. Chao, the telegraph operator was able to get his family and property to the Presbyterian mission in time to save everything.

Mr. Lattimore came down Saturday and went to see the Director about school. The Director said of course it couldn't open now, but he didn't know when it would. However, he said, he'd try to get us at least half salary until school opens, and then all would be paid up. Personally, I don't see how school can be opened up till next fall. It might be possible to open it in two months, but there would then be no chance to finish even half a year's work, so I think we won't open before August. We had done less than two months' good work last fall, so they better just drop it out and begin the years' work over again.

Military in Tientsin

Mr. Mills was just across the street from us all last week guarding the quarters of the mounted scouts who had gone to Peking, but all the soldiers came back from Peking (being relieved by 200 more Marines) so he had gone back to the French Concession. There are now 400 American Marines in Peking. We have 500 American infantry here now, besides the two machine guns; while next Sunday more are coming; 1000 infantry, 500 cavalry, and a company of field artillery, so we ought to be well protected. The Japs have brought in several thousand more men; and a lot of other foreign soldiers are on the way here from other countries. I think the foreign powers are getting ready to interfere and disarm all the soldiers who have mutinied. You see the affair is no longer political, so they can interfere all right.

Famine in Anhui (Eastern Chinese Province)

Mr. C. W. Harvey just got back from Anhui Saturday where he has been investigating the famine conditions. He says it is something awful. There are about 3,000,000 people affected and they can only get aid to about 100,000. He gave me some samples of all the food they have. He bought this out of the kettles of the people who were preparing it, so it is the real thing. He says they last about ten days after they get down to this. It seems bad to have all this looting and destruction up here when just south of us the people are starving, but, hard as it may seem, a big reduction of the population of China will be a great help to the country.

We went last night to a farewell social for Dr. and Mrs. Hart. They came to China twenty years ago and founded the Anglo-Chinese College, but are now going home to stay because of their health. They will be a great loss to Tientsin, as I fear the school won't amount to much without them.

Letter written by Rob to his sister Nan

Tientsin / March 31, 1912

College opening delayed again

I expected to go back to Paotingfu tomorrow, but now do not intend to go before Friday. We had word that college was to begin tomorrow, but Friday Mr. Li, the president called and said that there would be no attempt to hold classes for a couple of weeks, as there would not be enough students back before then; so we did not need to return just yet, but he said they would like to have us come back before long, as they thought the students would come sooner if we were there. So, I think I'll go about Friday unless something new happens.

Edith will not go back yet as the American consul will not give the ladies his permission to return yet. I think she will probably stay here till it gets too hot, and then go to Ch'ifu where I will go as soon as school closes for the summer, July 1st.

The plan is now to change our salaries over to the foreign calendar, as that has been officially established by the government. That will mean that we get T_s 310 a month instead of T_s 300, as the Chinese month was one day shorter than the foreign. Mr. Li said that we would get our salaries as usual on the fifth of every month from now on, and that our month and a half back salary would be paid before the first of May.

Roy and Lynne were planning to go to Peking yesterday morning, and Lynne was going to stay with Mrs. Lattimore and the children while Roy and Mr. Lattimore went to Paofu, but when they were waiting for the train at the station yesterday morning they got a telegram from Mr. Lattimore not to come. I suppose that some of them are sick or something, and they couldn't take them in as they are only living in two rooms.

We are certainly lucky to have as much room as we have. I don't believe there are any refugees in any of the port cities who have as many rooms as we have. Here are three of us in five rooms, while the house next door with the same number of rooms has twelve Swedish missionaries and two more coming in for meals. Luckily, there are no children, but one of the ladies is expecting one next week, so I guess we'll give up one of our rooms to three of the unmarried ladies.

Inspection of the Troops

The American consul reviewed and inspected the American troops at the Recreation Park yesterday morning. There was a large crowd there to see them. They make a mighty good showing, and they have their regimental band here now to furnish music, too.

Crowd awaiting arrival of American troops, Recreation Park, Tientsin, March 30, 1912

American officers entering Recreation Park, March 30, 1912

American Consul-General Samuel Knabenshue inspecting troops, March 30, 1912

8 First Election for the New Government (1912)

Highlights: April-June 1912

⌘ Ending their months of sanctuary in Tientsin, along with other foreigners Rob returned to Paotingfu in early April, but without Edith. He took snapshots of areas of Paotingfu that had suffered destruction at the hands of the rebels. He also took aerial view photos of the city from the top of the city wall. College classes resumed in mid-April.

⌘ On April 22, Rob went to Peking to attend a banquet for members of the American College Club. Edith travelled from Tientsin to join him for the weekend although she did not attend the banquet. They viewed the Forbidden City and Rob took snapshots of some iconic city sites. In his letter dated April 29 Rob mentioned the April 15 sinking of the Titanic.

⌘ It was finally considered safe for women to return to Paotingfu, so Edith finally returned home on May 2. They visited Tientsin in late May to see the All-British Sports competition. On Monday, May 20, a distinguished speaker, Dr. Charles W. Eliot, retired president of Harvard College, came from Peking to Paotingfu and spoke to a crowd of 2,000 students at the Li Hung Chang Hall about their duty to the newly-established Republic.

⌘ In June, Rob took photos of Paotingfu citizens voting in their first election. Premier T'ang Shao I left Peking for "parts unknown" because of an investigation of misuse of $10,000,000 borrowed from Belgium.

THE LETTERS

Letter written by Rob to his father

Paotingfu / April 14, 1912

Well, one week of our stay in Paotingfu has gone by, and everything had gone along beautifully except that it's darned lonesome without any Edith around. However, it seems so peaceful that I think perhaps she can come back all right in two or three weeks. There had been no disorder in the city for several weeks, and they are rounding up the t'u fei ("dirt vagabonds") and executing them as fast as they can. Yesterday Roy, Long and I went over to the west suburb and going around by the west gate of the city, saw two men who had just been beheaded about five minutes before.

Paotingfu Ruins

We went into the city last Tuesday to see the ruin which the looters had wrought. There was not nearly so much burned as I supposed, but absolutely everything had been looted. The big street running from the east to the west gate is the only one which was badly burned, though there was some burning on the streets to the north and south gates. From the west gate to the centre of the city, Roy and I counted only twenty shops which were still left standing along over half a mile of street. From the centre to the east gate only about half are burned.

We took a few pictures which we developed this afternoon. We also took a lot of pictures this morning from the city wall, but none of those are of the burned section. It is supposed to be against the city law to go up on the wall except on one day in the year, at New Year time. However, we six teachers from the college went over this morning and crawled through a hole in the gate to one of the ramps and went clear around the city on top of the wall. It is about six miles around. You get a fine view from there as it is about fifty feet high, so that it overtops all the trees and buildings.

Missionaries Rev. and Mrs. Killie Retiring
Yesterday they had farewell tea for the Killies at the West Suburb. They are leaving for America this week. Mr. Killie's health is so bad that the Board has ordered him home and there is absolutely no chance that he can come back, so they are feeling pretty bad about it. Mr. Killie is the man who took all the pictures which were taken of the siege of Peking in 1900. There were 25 foreigners present at the tea so you can see we are not quite alone here now.

School Resumes
School work finally started in Thursday with about two thirds of the total number of students present. We will finish up the half-year's work by the end of the term, and the year's work next winter, and hereafter the school year will end in the winter instead of the summer. The director has not yet come back. He is sick in Tientsin. I fear from what the Chinese say, that he has been living a little too fast and got stung good and plenty.

There are only seven students left now who still wear queues, and only one of the Chinese staff still wears his queue. That is Mr. Wang, my Chinese teacher, who is one of the college secretaries. He wanted to cut his off but his father wouldn't let him. Poor little boy, he is only 45, you know, and has seven children of his own; but still has to get his father's permission to get his hair cut.

Those clippings you sent were about the most accurate things I've seen yet in the American papers about China. They were no more overdrawn than the ordinary first article about any disaster at home. About the only really bad break was that about the French priests being killed here in Paofu, and we had that rumor even in Tientsin at first. I did see one bad one in the "Register & Leader" (which came regularly) the other day. It said that "K'ai had formed his Cabinet" which was just the same as if they had announced Cummins' candidacy for the presidency as "Albert seeks the Presidency", for the Chinaman's given name always comes last (which is really the sensible way) and Yüan Shih K'ai's surname is Yüan. The Chinese themselves generally do not speak of him as Yüan Shih K'ai, but as Yüan Kung Pao, the Kung Pao being an honorary title given him by the old Empress Dowager, and meaning "Guardian of the Palace."

Security
I'm glad to say that there apparently won't be any chance that we'll have to use our guns here, as you feared there might, but if there is a new outbreak and the foreigners here in Paotingfu are attacked by the riff-raff, you can just bet your bottom dollar that said "riff-raff" will know they've been in a scrap before they get us. I don't think there is one of us here that hasn't got the blood of somebody who has shouldered a musket in his veins, and we all have guns and we know how to use them.

Looking toward the West Gate of Paotingfu after the sack (photo March 1912)

Ruins in Paotingfu after the sack (photo March 1912)

Letter written by Rob to his mother

Paotingfu, North China / April 22, 1912

Well, we are getting pretty well started into our work now. Saturday we had 173 of our students back and I think two or three more came yesterday. We had 231 on the rolls last fall, and two of them died from tuberculosis during the winter, so we would have 229 if all came back. They certainly have done well; none of us expected 100 to come back. We will start right in with our regular work now and finish up the first half-year's work by the end of this term which will end in July, and then hereafter the school year will end in the winter instead of the summer.

Banquet in Peking

I went to Peking Saturday afternoon to attend the banquet of the American College Club. We had a fine affair. There were about 100 Americans and 40 Chinese present. The Chinese attendance was kept down by the fact that under the republic so many of the foreign educated Chinese are holding positions that keep them too busy to come.

Talk about hobnobbing with noted people. This is the place to live if you want to do that. Our guest of honor was Pres. Eliot of Harvard. We also had present American Minister Calhoun, S.K. Alfred Sze, the Chinese Minister of Communications, W.W. Yen, the Chinese Minister of Justice, Dr. W.A.P. Martin, who has been in China longer than any other foreigner now out here and a number of others. T'ang Shao I, the Premier, had just come back from Shanghai that day, so was unable to attend. After the banquet Dr. Wu Lien Lê, who has just returned from the Hague where he was the Chinese representative at the Opium Congress, came around with his notebook to get my autograph. So you see we get a good chance to get acquainted with the men who are now making history.

I had Edith come up from Tientsin so we had almost a whole day together. We went out in the morning (yesterday) and got a lot of pictures of the barricades etc. in the legation quarter. Since the looting, the legations have been fortified to the utmost. I tell you it would take some army to rush them now. Every possible way of approach is covered with rapid fire guns and barbed wire which can be heavily charged with electricity, and guards stationed constantly as if in time of war. Of course, now no one thinks any such thing could happen, but they are taking no chances.

Views of the "Forbidden City"

We also went up to the top of the Ch'ien Mên, the big gate between the Chinese and Manchu cities, where we got a fine view of Peking, especially the Forbidden City. The wall here is now held by the American soldiers. They have a number of guns mounted and a man up there with a telescope sweeping the city constantly for any sign of disorder.

I wanted to bring Edith back but when I spoke to Minister Calhoun about it he said that while everything was peaceful now, and very likely would remain so, still things were too unsettled yet for any people to go into the interior unless it was absolutely necessary, and while he was issuing no orders against it, he would very strongly advise against it. As far as we are concerned, of course, that practically amounts to an order, so I guess we'll have to be separated a while longer. If the minister is still of the same mind a month from now, I guess Edith will go down to Ch'ifu and wait for me there, as it will soon be too hot to stay in Tientsin.

Banquet at the American College Club (Paotingfu delegation), April 20, 1912, Peking
(photo from Clack family album)

Standing (top row):
2nd from left – S.B. Harvey, teacher at Chihli Provincial College
4th from left – David Lattimore, American Board Mission; teacher at Chihli Provincial College
6th from left – Robert W. Clack, teacher at Chihli Provincial College
7th from left – Norman Pitman, teacher at Chihli Provincial College
8th from left – possibly The Rev. A. M. Cunningham of the Presbyterian Mission

Middle row (seated):
5th from left – probably Mrs. David (Margaret) Lattimore
6th from left – Mrs. A. M. Cunningham

Bottom row (seated):
3rd from left – The Rev. James Lowrie, head of the Paotingfu Presbyterian Mission
4th from left (in center) - Edward R. (E.R.) Long, teacher at Chihli Provincial College
6th from left – Dr. Charles Lewis, Presbyterian medical missionary

The Forbidden City from the Ch'ien Mên (photo April 1912)

Entrance to the Forbidden City from the East range of the Ch'ien Mên (photo April 1912)

Note: In October 1912, this ceremonial entrance was renamed "Gate of China". In 1954 it was demolished for the expansion of what is now Tiananmen Square.[6]

Southern Gate of Imperial City (a closer view of previous two photos)

South Gate of the Ch'ien Mên. This gate is opened only once a year, when the Emperor goes to sacrifice at the Temple of Heaven. (photo 1912)

Barricade at the West end of Legation Street guarded by American soldiers (Peking)
(photo April 1912)

Editor's note –

The Legation Quarter was the area in Peking (now Beijing) where a number of foreign legations were located. This district was created in 1861 and is East of the Imperial City. The Legation Quarter was the location of the 55-day siege of the International Legations, which took place during the Boxer Rebellion of 1900. After the Boxer Rebellion, the Legation Quarter was under the jurisdiction of foreign countries with diplomatic legations (i.e. "embassies"). The foreign residents were exempt from Chinese law. The Legation Quarter attracted a large number of diplomats, soldiers, scholars, artists, and tourists. [7]

Peking, West end of Legation Street (photo 1912)

Entrance to the British Legation in Peking (photo 1912)

Inside the British Legation. Most of the civilians stayed here during the siege in 1900 [i.e. Boxer Rebellion]. (photo 1912)

American Legation from the top of the Ch'ien Mên (photo 1912)

The Water Gate through which the Sikhs entered the Legations in 1900 (photo 1912)

Southeast corner of the Forbidden City, Peking, from the Italian Legation (photo 1912)

Letter written by Rob to Edith's mother

Paotingfu / Monday night [April 29]

We have our college work running regularly now, with over three-fourths of the students present, so I guess there is no danger of our having to do our work all over again. We will finish the first half-year's work this term and then finish the school year hereafter in the winter time.

Chinese language study

I am getting along fine in my Chinese since I got back. I find I can understand more than twice as much as I could when I went away last fall. I've read over 35 pages in Hillier's Second Book and 16 chapters in the New Testament since I came back, and I've only had my teacher 9 hours, too. Also, I've learned over 100 new characters.

The Titanic

Did you read the accounts of the sinking of the *Titanic*, the largest ship in the world? She struck an iceberg off the coast of Newfoundland and went down in about four hours. They picked up another ship by wireless but it did not get there till about five hours after she went down, and 1500 of her 2300 passengers and crew went with her. Most of the women and children were saved, except for a few of the women who refused to leave their husbands when they were ordered into the boats. I read the account in a French paper and it said that the ship which brought the survivors to port had over seventy widows on board. I suppose no one will ever know just what caused the accident on what was a bright, starry night, as all the officers and crew went down with the ship.

Well, I must close, as the drums are beating for ten o'clock.

Letter written by Rob to his family

Paotingfu, North China / May 12, 1912

I'm sending some Kodak pictures. All of them but the one of the bridge I've done absolutely by myself, developed the films, printed them and all. I'm also sending a lot of stamps to distribute among the kids. You will notice a lot of them have four characters printed across the face in red. Those are Republican stamps. These stamps ought to be quite valuable in a few years as there will be no more printed. The new Republican stamps will be entirely different; this is just their method of using up the old stamps of the Empire.

There are now 202 of the students here and several more who are coming this week so I guess we'll have as big a school as ever. So far as I can find out only two of the students have been in the army at all. They are two of our best students and come from Peking province. They were stationed in one of the forts on the Woosung at Shanghai. The director came back this week, but is still too sick to get about.

Letter written by Rob to his mother

Tientsin / Sunday, May 26, 1912

Here we are in Tientsin for a day or two again. We had to have some more stores as we did not take any down before, not being certain how long we would stay, but finally used up all we had and so had to come for more.

All-British Sports in Tientsin

We chose this particular time to come because of the All-British Sports which were held yesterday and Friday. They are held every year under the auspices of the British Municipality, but, except for a few events especially for the soldiers, the events are open to all. In fact, there were a number of events which were won by other nationalities. The French soldiers won the tug-of-war. That is an event they train for all the year round, and they certainly have it down to a science. It's a revelation to see them pull, because they are not nearly so big and strong as some of the teams they defeat. Then a Chinese boy from Chang Po Lin's school won the high jump. He jumped 5 ft 5½ and I guess could have gone a little higher if he had been forced to it. I won the shot put myself.

Retired President of Harvard Visits

We had quite a treat at Paotingfu the first of the week. Dr. Eliot* of Harvard came down Monday and stayed a couple of days. Mr. Palmer and Mr. Ma of the Normal College [in Peking] are both Harvard men and they got him to come. He spoke to a crowd of about 2000 students at the Li Hung Chang Hall in the city on Tuesday afternoon [May 21]. He spoke to them on their duty to the Republic and I never saw an audience listen more attentively. Mr. Ma translated for him, but he spoke so distinctly and his choice of words was so good that even our freshmen students said they understood him in English, which was certainly a great compliment to him. I'm sure they did understand too, as I was sitting on the platform where I could watch them and I could see from their expressions that they understood.

I'm sending you a couple of pictures which I took from the city wall the other day. One is of the college and the other of the new prison. You can't see our house in the picture of the college as it is clear to the other side and is hidden in the trees.

Editor's note –
Dr. Charles W. Eliot (b.1834-d.1926) had been appointed the 21st president of Harvard College in 1869. He was the "youngest president in the history of the oldest university" and served until his retirement in 1909. He authored many articles about reforming American higher education. [8]

ALL-BRITISH SPORTS – May 1912

Baluchi Band (photo May 1912)
[The Baluchis are a regiment of the British Indian Army.]

Chinese student winning high jump (photo May 1912)
[… from Chang Po Lin's Nan K'ai Middle School]

DR. ELIOT IN PAOTINGFU, MAY 1912

Dr. Eliot [second from left] leaving his sedan chair, and about to enter the Li Hung Chang Hall at Paotingfu to address the Chinese students. (photo May 21, 1912)

Dr. Eliot surrounded by Chinese students, Paotingfu. (photo May 21, 1912)

Chihli Provincial College from the southwest corner of the city. (photo 1912)

Paotingfu Industrial Prison being built inside the southwest corner of the city. (photo 1912)

Letter written by Rob to his family

Paotingfu / June 2, 1912

Well, we are back home again after our strenuous holiday at Tientsin. Edith was pretty well tired out by it, but I have managed to go about things in the accustomed way. In fact, I have taken on two more hours a week of Political Science with the Seniors to take the place of Chinese Classics which have just been abolished from the course of study. Just think of it. It is almost as if we would abolish the study of the Constitution from American schools. Of course, the classics are slightly more out of date than the Constitution (but not very much in some ways) but on the other hand the Chinese are much more conservative than we are. Well, anyway the Classics are abolished from the course of study and modern studies put in their place.

Summer heat

College work finishes two weeks from yesterday and then after that we have the exams. I suppose we'll be all through by June 25 and then we'll have a two-month vacation. We are going to stay right here if Edith can stand the heat without getting sick. Roy and Lynne were going to stay but we had quite a hot day last Wednesday, about 100 in the shade and 120 in the sun, and they have decided to go to Peitaiho. I think they are wise for the summer heat is awfully hard out here on people who are not well acclimated. I think we'll stand it perfectly well, as this will be Edith's fourth summer here and my third and the heat doesn't faze me anyway. Also, we won't have a thing to take us out of the house except in the early morning or the evening, and it is quite easy to keep the house cool.

Lotus Pool Bridge

The College workmen have also built a new bridge across the lotus pond. The old one which you have seen in the pictures I sent you was getting so old and rotten that we were all afraid to cross it.

Chinese women's names

You know our little boy, Li Chang, was married last February. The other night Edith was asking him about his wife. I asked him what her surname had been and he told me. Then Edith asked him what her given name was. He looked quite astonished and said he didn't know. Just think, married four months and didn't know his wife's given name. Then we asked him what his mother called her. "Oh," he said, "Second Daughter-in-law".

Later I asked my teacher, Mr. Wang, if he knew his wife's name. "Yes," he said, "I know it, but I never use it." "What do you call her?" I said. "Hsi-Tien ti ma" (Hsi Tien's mother). Hsi Tien is his eldest son. "Well," Edith said, "supposing she didn't have any children what would you call her?" "T'a" (she). Just think, suppose Dad just called Mamma, "Rob's ma" all the time. The Chinese colloquial name for mother is the same as ours, "ma". But they call the father "Ba-ba" instead of "papa" or else "Dieh" instead of "dad".

Letter written by Edith to her mother **Paotingfu / June 9, 1912**

We of the College have had a sorrowful time this week. Little Louise Pitman died early Wednesday morning, from clot on the brain. The doctors do not know what caused it, hardly. Mrs. Pitman bears up very bravely, but it has been very hard on her and also for her husband. They had waited six years for the baby and it seems so hard to have it taken away. It seemed so well and strong to begin with. It was only sick about twelve hours. They buried it beside old Mrs. Lowrie in the old Presbyterian Compound. They made a little box and covered it with white satin, inside and out. We women did not go to the funeral, but all the men did. They took turns by twos of carrying the little body. The parents appreciated that more than most anything else that was done for them. The foreign men also filled the grave. I went to see Mrs. Pitman yesterday. She is very resigned and says she knows it was done in love, but Oh! how she wants her baby.

I have been pretty well this week, and it has been very cool here. The Lattimores left for Peitaiho yesterday. The Harveys and Woodwards go as soon as school is out. The Pitmans have not decided whether to go or not. The house is all divided and I have netting at all the doors and windows, so we are free from flies from the kitchen forward. It is so nice and secluded since the house is entirely divided.

Edith and the Lattimore girls in Chinese coats (photo June 1912)
L-R: Edith Clack; Lattimore daughters - Katherine, Isabel, and Eleanor

Letter written by Rob to Edith's mother

June 9, 1912

    I went into the city Thursday and saw them conduct the first Chinese election. It was a very quiet affair, as there are so few voters. Only middle school graduates and officials can vote. There was a list published outside of all the voters of this section of Chihli and there were only about three thousand in all, so I figure that the proportion must be less than one to each thousand of the population. The election was for the Provincial Assembly.

    Yesterday the Presbyterian Mission held their Sunday School picnic. Eight of our students attended. They had an enormous crowd, I should judge at least a thousand.

Editor's note: Rob took three rare Election Day photos in Paotingfu –
    (1) "List of voters for the South half of Chihli Province –
        about 1,000 voters to 10,000,000 population" (posted on a wall)
    (2) "Entrance to the Polling Place, Paotingfu"
    (3) "Voting in the first election of the Chinese Republic"

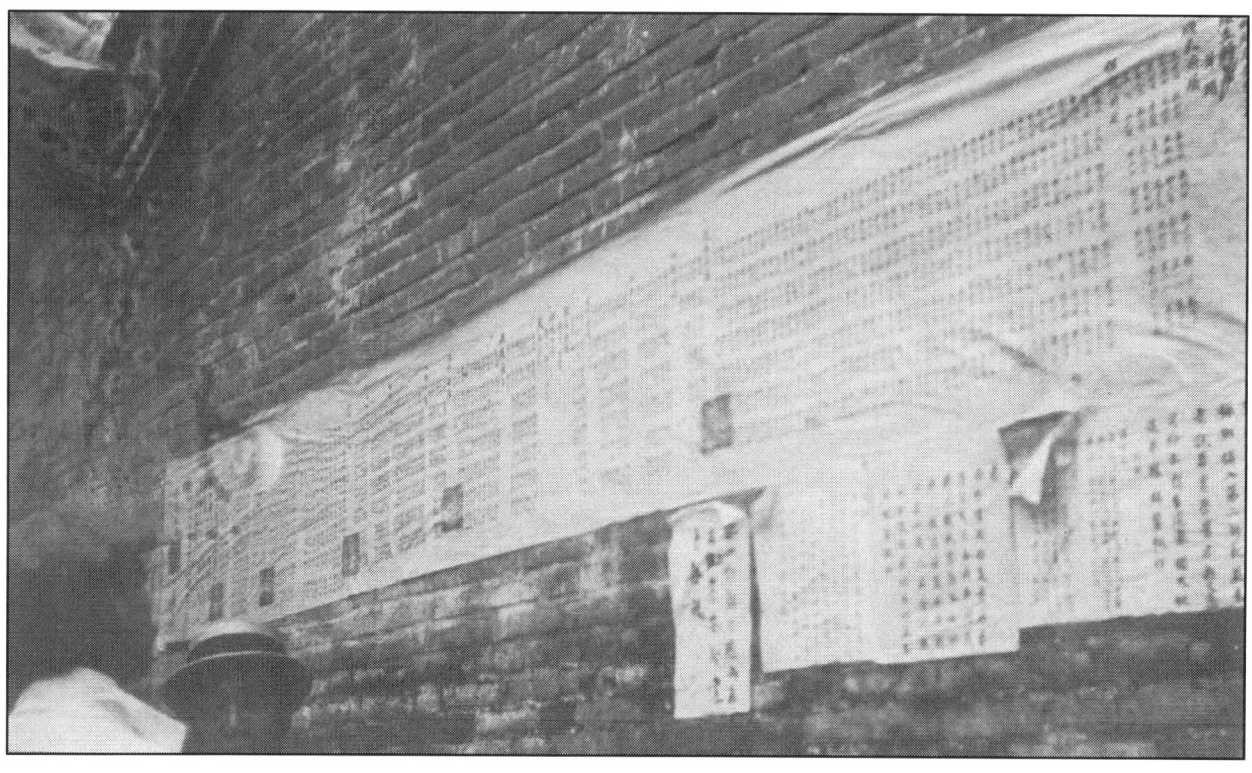

**(1) List of voters for the South half of Chihli Province;
about 1,000 voters to 10,000,000 population, Paotingfu** (photo 1912)

(2) Entrance to the Polling Place, Paotingfu (photo 1912)

(3) Voting in the first election of the Chinese Republic (photo 1912)

Letter written by Rob to his family

Paotingfu / June 16, 1912

Well, our college work is finished till the latter part of August, at least regular class work is. We start our exams next Thursday and run them for a week and then we're through for seven or eight weeks. All my exams come on one day this time, a week from Monday.

Address to Students about Good Government

Yesterday, Mr. Wilder, of the American Board of Commissioners for Foreign Missions of Peking addressed the Paotingfu students on good government. His main point was against destroying all that was good under the old system, until they had developed something to replace it. They certainly need some such advice. Just now they are engaged in trying to raise money by subscription so that they will not need to borrow from foreign countries. The only thing I fear is that only about half the money they raise will ever get to the right place, as funds seem to stick to the fingers of the Republican officials just as badly as they ever did to the Manchus'. It certainly will take years of education yet to make a real nation out of this country.

Letter written by Rob to his father

Paotingfu / June 23, 1912

Since that hot day it has been much more comfortable as it has rained a good deal. Last Thursday afternoon we had a ripsnorter of a hail storm, broke a couple of our kitchen windows, broke a lot of windows over at the college and pounded things up generally. Luckily, the storm was only local. While it was in progress I went into the kitchen and happening to look out the door I saw all the kitchen knives out on the ground. I asked the boy how they came to be there. "We threw them." "Why?" "At the mo kuei" (devils). Afterwards the cook said the Chinese always did that during a hail storm because the points of the knife would split the hail storm away.

We started our examinations Thursday and finish next Wednesday. I have all of mine at once, tomorrow morning. Then I think we will go to Tientsin next Saturday to stay over the Fourth, and then back to the Y.M.C.A. Conference at Wo Fo Ssǔ [Sleeping Buddha Temple] in the foothills near the Summer Palace Northwest of Peking. We'll probably stay there two weeks and then come back here for the rest of the summer. School will reopen about August 20th. They are planning to start in a new class then just half a year behind the present Freshman class, so I expect next fall my work will all be Mathematics, which won't make me a bit mad.

T'ang Shao I, the Premier, has left Peking for parts unknown. There are various reports as to why and where he has gone. He is generally supposed to be hiding in the foreign concessions in Tientsin. One report is that he has eloped with a foreign prostitute, but I think the real truth of the matter lies in the fact that the National Assembly had begun to make embarrassing queries as to what had become of the $10,000,000 borrowed from Belgium. There is some 5 or 6 million which is unaccounted for. I'm afraid the Chinese are beginning to find out the founding of the Republic was just a change from one set of thieves to another.

Robert Clack in Chinese robe (photo ca. 1912)

9   Y.M.C.A. Conference at the Sleeping Buddha Temple Near Peking

During a time of extraordinary political upheaval and social transition in China, Rob became involved with a committee that was seeking to establish a Young Men's Christian Association (Y.M.C.A.) in Paotingfu. In early July of 1912, he attended a conference for Y.M.C.A. associates at Wo Fo Ssŭ, a celebrated temple (Sleeping Buddha Temple) near Peking. The 150 delegates included 65 from mission schools and 85 from Government schools, plus 50 Chinese and foreign teachers and conference presenters.

THE LETTERS

Letter written by Rob to his sister Nan

Wo Fo Ssŭ / July 14, 1912

I came up here Tuesday, arrived in Peking at 2 o'clock. Left the Y.M.C.A. at 3 and took rickshaw from there. Got to the Hsi Chih Mên (West Straight Gate) at 4 and to the Summer Palace at 6 where I changed to a donkey, getting out of here at 7:15. This is certainly a great place. It is right on the foot of the mountains and in all directions there are temples and castles and palaces of the Manchu nobles. The Imperial hunting park is only two miles away on the mountain slope which faces this.

This temple is a very large one, covering perhaps two or three acres. There are a great many large empty rooms which we are using for the Conference, and there are also several scores of big idols. The biggest one (from which the temple gets its name) is an image of Buddha about eighteen feet long. He is asleep, resting his head on his arm. The image is of sandalwood covered by brass gilding. Isn't it a strange thing, holding a Y.M.C.A. conference in a Buddhist temple? There are 48 of the Chinese students here, and about fifteen foreigners, with about a dozen Chinese leaders and teachers.

We have had two fine afternoon trips. Thursday we went over to the Pi Yün Ssŭ on the mountain side about two miles west. The name means Green Cloud Temple. The temple is the biggest one in this part of China. Most of the rooms of the temple are decorated with imitation green clouds, on all projections of which are various gods. There is also one large room in which are 506 figures of Buddha, eight feet high, made of sandalwood and covered with gilding. Best of all though, at the rear is a high marble tower on which are six marble pagodas.

Friday we went over to the Yü Ch'uan Shan (Jade Fountain Hill). There is a high hill with a seven-story pagoda on the top from which there is a beautiful view of the Summer Palace. At the foot of the hill is the jade fountain. It is a spring, the water of which is a beautiful green color. It is very clear, but it makes anything on the bottom look as if it were made of green jade. The water is very cold. We all took a swim and almost froze though the temperature of the air was over 90 in the shade. This fountain supplies the water for the summer palace, and all the lakes there have this same green tint.

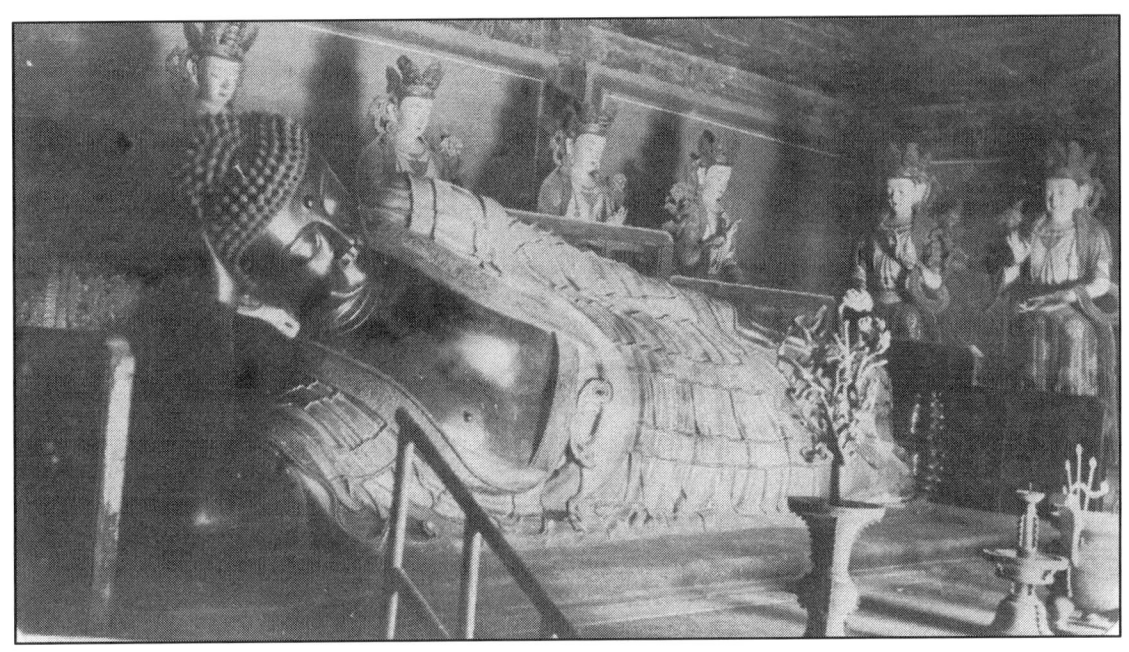

Wo Fo (Sleeping Buddha) (photo July 1912)

A god in the Pi Yün Ssŭ (photo July 1912)

Hall of the Thousand (actually 508) Buddhas, Pi Yün Ssŭ (photo July 1912)

A shrine in the Pi Yün Ssŭ (photo July 1912)

Jade Fountain, from top of the hill (photo July 1912)

**Porcelain Pagoda, west slope of Jade Fountain Hill;
Wo Fo Ssŭ in valley behind the Tower** (photo July 1912)

Precious Stone Pagoda on Jade Fountain Hill (photo July 1912)

Letter written by Rob to his father

Peitaiho / July 15, 1912

I didn't get to write last week as I was on the move. I've traveled over two thousand miles by train in the last two weeks so you see I've been going some. Last week I spent four nights in succession on the train, a different train every night. A week ago Wednesday I left for Peking, getting there in the evening. The next day I went out to Wo Fo Ssǔ, a four-hour trip by rickshaw and donkey. I stayed at the conference two days. Everything pointed to a very successful conference. There were about 150 delegates, 65 from mission schools and 85 from government schools, almost double the number of government school students from last year. There were also over fifty Chinese and foreign teachers and speakers Friday.

Description of Puk'ou
(located in the northwestern area of Nanking, between the Yangtze River and Chu River)

I got a telegram from [Mr.] Harvey asking me to meet him in Shanghai as soon as possible so I went into Peking Saturday morning in time to catch the evening train for Tientsin. I left Tientsin next morning (Sunday) over the new railroad for Puk'ou, arriving there Monday afternoon. Puk'ou is just across the Yangtze from Nanking. Had to ferry across, as the river is over half a mile wide here, and so deep and swift that they haven't ventured to bridge it. I had several hours in Nanking and went up to eat supper with Stewart [Burgess], one of the Y.M.C.A. secretaries.

Nanking is an interesting city. It gives you some idea of what an awful thing the T'ai Ping rebellion was. It has an immense wall, 22 miles long, and before the T'ai Ping rebellion it was jammed full of people, must have been much over a million. However, the other day, when I left the suburb on the riverbank and went through the city gate, I had to ride five miles before I got to the inhabited part of the city. Over all that distance there is only one street, the ruins on both sides being overgrown with bamboo thickets. The T'aipings burned and looted the city in 1850 when they captured it, and then the Imperialists repeated the dose fourteen years later when they recaptured it. Again last year the Manchu part of the city was destroyed, but it still is quite a thriving city of about 300,000, though there is practically no place where it reaches out to its walls. It's a beautiful city, filled with pagoda topped hills.

I took the night express to Shanghai arriving 7 o'clock Tuesday morning. Karl [Edith's brother], met me at the station, having just arrived from America. After I got my business with Mr. Harvey finished, Karl and I went sight-seeing. We left that night on the night express from Nanking, just getting there in time to get across the river to get the train at Puk'ou arriving in Tientsin Thursday afternoon. The new railroad is certainly a great time saver. I went to Shanghai from Tientsin, spent a day there and was back in Tientsin in four days, which couldn't have been done a year ago in less than eight.

Letter written by Rob to his sister Celia

Tientsin / July 23, 1912

Here we are back in Tientsin again together. The first of last week I spent mostly taking pictures at Wo Fo Ssŭ Wednesday and went to Paofu after some furs I had told a man I would bring to Tientsin. Then I came up here Friday. Edith had already come Wednesday.

Politics here now are rather amusing. Yüan Shih K'ai is trying to get together a Cabinet, but the National Council (who are slightly less capable of self-government than a Kindergarten) turn down every appointment he makes. The trouble is not any animosity to Yüan, but there are four or five political parties (so called) in the assembly, none of which have a majority. When anyone is appointed every party except his own votes against him, so he loses out. Yüan himself is non-partisan. I don't know how it will finally come out.

Letter written by Rob to his father

Paofu. / July 28, 1912

Well, here we are back home again. My, but it seems good to be here. We had intended to start Monday, but owing to the fact that it rained steady from Saturday till Tuesday we did not start till Wednesday. The rain was the hardest for years. Practically the whole country between here and Tientsin was afloat for several days. The crops, however, were not badly damaged as one would think as the chief crop at this time of the year is "kao liang", a sort of sorghum which grows from twelve to fifteen feet high and the water does not hurt it. Nothing could damage it now, I guess, but hail. Altogether there will be a good crop around here.

The Yangtze had overflowed again in Central China and I suppose there will be a famine even worse than last year, as last year used up every particle of reserve they had. The Chinese take it rather philosophically. They say famines and plague are a good thing as the country is too crowded now. The worst suffering caused by the rain here is that all the poor peoples' houses have fallen down. They are all built of mud, you know, and a long soaking rain just simply melts them away. It will not be quite so bad now as the weather is so warm but it is awful in cold weather.

Rumors about relocating the College

Mr. T'ang was just in. He says the Board of Education has decided to move us to Tientsin and unite the school with the Pei Yang University. I don't suppose we'll have to move before next spring, however. We've been expecting this for a long time, but it has been put off and put off until we had hopes it would never occur. None of the teachers and most of the students do not want to go, but it is really the proper thing to do as it will cut down the expense of the schools greatly, as one executive staff will be able to do the work for both schools. I think it will cost us more to live in Tientsin though. Still, it will save us lots of freight and railroad fare. The worst thing will be that it will be much harder to work there, as there are so many things to take up your time.

Problems in Korea

I don't believe I told you about the trouble in Korea, did I? Stewart Burgess, of the Peking Y.M.C.A. was over there all winter and he told me about it. It hasn't leaked out into the papers at all yet, as the Japs have bought off the Associated Press man, and they open all the outgoing and incoming mail and any letters which tell the truth don't arrive. However, Ahl, the *New York Herald* man from Peking, has just gone over there and I don't think they can buy him, so the world will probably get the facts now.

You see, Christianity has made enormous progress in Korea the last few years, until almost a third of the people are Christians. When the Japs took over the country last year without any excuse except that they were strong and Korea was weak, naturally there was great opposition. Most of the leading people who opposed them naturally were Christians and the Japs are now trying to kill them off and drive out the missionaries. They arrested a number last fall charging them with a plot to assassinate the Jap governor.

To make matters worse (and what really shows them up) they charged one of the oldest Presbyterian missionaries over there with inciting the plot and with furnishing them with guns. To give color to their story they stopped a box coming to him, took out some of the goods and replaced them by revolvers, and then several stations farther along the line they again stopped the box and searched it and of course found the revolvers. They arrested these Christian Koreans and at the preliminary trial had a large number of witnesses against them, sixty-five in all. Of these 65, 64 have since repudiated their testimony saying that it was given under torture. Now they are having the official trial. The presiding judge also acts as prosecuting attorney. The jury are all Japs and as the witnesses are mostly Korean, they give their testimony in Korean, which is then mistranslated into Japanese by a Jap interpreter.

Mrs. Burgess understands both Jap and Korean and she says there is no similarity even between the testimony and the translation. Besides, there is a strict censorship and no news is allowed to be sent out except what the Japs themselves send. The only way the truth can get out is for people to come from there to China and send it. It's one of the most disgraceful things in modern history. You can let the paper have this if you want to.

Pailou at Wo Fo Ssŭ entrance (photo 1912)

Wo Fo Ssŭ Front Gate (photo July 1912)

Amos Parker Wilder lecturing in the Liang Kiang Hui Kuan (photo July 1912)

Priest's Tomb, North of Jade Fountain Hill (photo July 1912)

Part of the Buddhas carved on the rocks below the Priest's Tomb (photo July 1912)

Summer Palace from Jade Fountain Hill (photo July 1912)

Laughing Buddha, Wo Fo Ssŭ (photo July 1912)

View of the Marco Polo Bridge at Luk'ouch'iao, 10 miles West of Peking (from a moving train). (photo 1912)

Southwest corner tower of the Tartar City, Peking (from a moving train) (photo 1912)

Kettler Monument, Hatamên Street (photo 1912)

Southern Gate of the Forbidden City (photo 1912)

One of the pillars, South Gate of the Forbidden City (photo 1912)

Peking, Emperor's Gate from the South, Ch'ien Mên (photo 1912)

Peking, camels in the street (photo 1912)

"Our sideboard and brass" (photo 1912)

10 Republic of China Established; Third Year of Teaching Begins

Highlights: August-October 1912

⌘ During the summer of 1912, Rob and Edith remained in Paotingfu for summer vacation after Rob returned from the July Wo Fo Ssŭ Conference in Peking. Y.M.C.A. leaders from larger areas came to Paotingfu to speak to student groups.

⌘ On September 17, Dr. Sun Yat Sen, provisional president of the Republic of China since December 1911, passed through Paotingfu, stopping at the train station and greeting people for one-half hour.

THE LETTERS

Letter written by Edith to Rob's mother

Paotingfu, N. China / August 1, 1912

Did we tell you about the brass pieces for $28.00 Mex? Two incense bowls, 2 vases, and a bell. One of the bowls weighs 10 lbs. and the other one about 7 lbs. The smaller one is a ball set on three little legs and the lid has a small dragon coiled on it with its head raised which forms the handle. The two vases each have three dragons carved on them in relief. The vases stand over a foot high. The bell also has a dragon carved on it and it has a very good tone. Rob got me two brass candlesticks that stand about a foot high. They are perfect beauties. We have lots of brass now. 7 trays, 12 candlesticks, 1 tea caddy, Chinese wash basin, 6 incense bowls, 2 opium dishes, 3 pencil holders and 13 little trays about three inches in diameter.

Did we tell you about the little jade cups the brass man brought to us? They are about the size of after dinner coffee cups, but each one is a different shape from any other one. Oh! they are so sweet. We had ten little brass trays made for saucers for them. If we ever go home to live we will have lots of pretty things with which to make our home pretty.

Letter written by Rob to his mother

Paotingfu / August 5, 1912

It has been very hot all week. I should judge 95 every day but one, and it has rained almost every day, and when it does not rain the air is very sticky as there is practically no breeze. However, according to the Chinese calendar we have six more days of hot weather. You know they have their calendar divided off very accurately, so that people would know what clothes to wear. The common people dress more according to the weather than according to the calendar, but the officials have formerly had to dress by the calendar. I don't know how it will be about that under the Republic.

Letter written by Rob to his sister Ida Paotingfu / August 12, 1912

Before I forget it, as soon as there is money enough to my credit from the things I have sent home, I wish you would get and send us a good cookbook and a good atlas. We haven't them, and can't get them very well out here. Everything is too English.

Man Walking Around the World
A man passed through here today who is walking around the world. He is an Austro-American named Mikeluc. He has already been all over the U.S., has signatures of governors of all states as well as Roosevelt and Taft and Yüan Shih K'ai. He has also been in South America, New Zealand, Australia, the Philippines, Japan, Manchuria and is now on his way through China toward Siam. He is quite interesting to talk to, though he is uneducated and rather coarse. He is doing it because he likes roving, and he intends to write a book after he gets back to New York in 1914.

The Chinese Economy
China has finally kicked the six nations banking group out, and will try to get funds elsewhere. She only wants some $50,000,000, but they said she must take $300,000,000 or none and it was too much like highway robbery. If they had not wanted to hog too much they could have gotten quite a neat investment, but now have lost it all. I think the Chinese will now try to get what they want in small loans. An American, Robert Dollar, will let them have several millions and they can pick up the rest easily enough. The country seems to be getting quieter all the time.

Letter written by Rob to his sister

Paotingfu / August 18, 1912 (Sunday)

Well, our vacation is about over. The Pitmans and Harveys came back yesterday afternoon, Roy and Lynne come today, and Mr. Lattimore tomorrow. Mrs. Lattimore and the children will wait for a month yet at Peitaiho. As for Mr. Long, he and Mr. Palmer are somewhere between Sianfu and Hank'ou going across country. I expect they'll be home some time this week, as they will come back from Hank'ou by rail and it's only a 36-hour trip. School is supposed to begin Tuesday, but I don't think it will begin till the next Monday as only about half of the students are here. The Director isn't even back yet.

The office of President has now been combined with that of Director, and Mr. Li, our President, has been made Director of the Normal School here, where Mr. Palmer teaches. I suppose most of the President's work here will fall on Mr. T'ang.

Mr. Wang, our Chinese teacher, told me last night that the Board of Education had refused to ratify the actions of the Provincial Educational Conference and therefore we will probably not be moved to Tientsin. I sincerely hope that is so. I think none of us want to go.

I am sending some more pictures which I printed this week. I've written the description on the back. I think making pictures is great fun. The only way is to do it yourself. If I have it done by the photographer it costs 7¢ Mex. each to develop the films and 12¢ each for the prints.

I can do it myself for about 2¢ for developing and 4¢ for the prints counting in spoiled ones and all. The only thing I don't save on is buying the films in the first place and they cost 17¢ each either way.

Letter written by Edith to her mother

Paofu. / August 20, 1912

Mr. and Mrs. Harvey and the boys, Mr. and Mrs. Pitman, Mr. and Mrs. Woodward and Mr. Lattimore and Owen are all here. Mr. Long comes today. Mrs. Lattimore and the other children will not return for three or four more weeks. School opened officially yesterday morning, but classes won't begin for a day or two at least, most likely not till next Monday. Formerly the school has reopened with the "k'e too" to Confucius, but now they have the flag crossed over the Confucian tablet and the students salute the flag.

We are very happy about our Bible class. The one student who went to the Conference with Rob has become a Christian and a worker. He has gotten five more to join the class, so we have nine in all. He said last night that he most likely could get more when all the students got back.

Letter written by Edith to her mother

Paofu. / August 27, 1912

Classes began last Wednesday, very much to our surprise. Mr. Woodward has been sick in bed ever since last Thursday so Rob is taking some of his classes. He is somewhat better today. You know he had a slight sun stroke at Peitaiho and he overdid it.

We are very badly worried about the robbers that you have been having up at Peitaiho. I do hope they haven't frightened you folks. We heard they have put the British soldiers on to police the place if that's true.

Altogether we have ten in our Bible Class. It certainly is marvelous how it has all come about with hardly an effort on our part. We certainly are thankful for it all. Most of the members of our class are beginners so if all goes well we can have them under our instruction at least three years.

Letter written by Rob to his mother

Paofu. / September 8, 1912

Our last year's president, Mr. Li, is now President and director of the normal school here, which is quite a promotion. He's a fine young man, and ought to rise pretty high, as he likes to work and isn't afraid to ask about what he doesn't understand. So many of the modern Chinese graduates are too swelled headed to amount to anything, so that he is quite a change.

The missionaries are beginning to drift in from Peitaiho. In another week I guess they will all be back. Mr. Lattimore has gone to Peitaiho to bring back the children. Mrs. Lattimore is not well and will not come for several weeks. Owen came back three weeks ago with his father and is hard at work at his studies. I am teaching him arithmetic.

Mr. Whallon left Friday to go to Kobe and will bring a bride when he comes back. She left America August 31. They will be back in about three weeks. He just came last fall. He is a fine young fellow. Was a Rhodes Scholar, and played on the Oxford tennis team. He lives in the house Mr. Killie used to have.

Letter written by Edith to her mother
Paofu. / September 16, 1912

Rob and I went over to the South Suburb to foreign service yesterday afternoon. The McCanns leave either next Sat. or Monday. They hadn't yet decided fully. Margaret is a little stronger than she was a week ago. Mr. McC. is feeling poorly. Mrs. King and Miss Chapin both told me of seeing you, and they thought you had stood your settling very well. I am so relieved.

We were very much surprised last week to receive the 109 Taels to make up the difference between the Chinese year and the foreign. That enabled us to send Moore $30 gold besides paying up all our big debts. I want Moore to pay Clark for whatever duty they had to pay on those things we sent him, and then keep the rest for himself. Clark's got the things all right, and were very pleased with them.

Last Tuesday evening we had Dr. Mackey, Mrs. Price and Miss Gumbrell, Mr. DeHaan and Mr. & Mrs. Pitman to dinner. Mr. DeHaan stayed all night. Our first guest in our home. Mr. and Mrs. Price are to be in the American Board this winter. We are so glad as we like them so much.

Letter written by Rob to his sister
Paotingfu / September 22, 1912

Another week has rolled by and I tell you your brother has been the busy kid. I've had all the Fifth Year Trigonometry in addition to my own work, as Mr. T'ang is sick. It is quite a strain to teach them, as they are only prep. students and know very little English. They never understand anything you *say*. You have to write it on the blackboard where they can *see* it. I'll have to keep them another week and perhaps two, but it won't be quite so bad as I've finished up my senior Poli Sci class which gives me two free hours. In about a month from now I'll finish up my other Poli Sci classes, however, and then I'll have only 16 hours a week instead of 29 as I had this last week.

Dr. Sun Yat Sen stopped in Paotingfu
Last Tuesday Dr. Sun Yat Sen passed through Paotingfu on his return from Peking to the South. He stopped here about half an hour. There was an immense crowd who greeted him with great enthusiasm. All the soldiers were there in force, as were the students from all the schools and all the members of the Kuo Min Tang, the political party to which he belongs. He came in a special train all decorated with Republican flags and had a large retinue with him, all dressed in

foreign clothes. There were a large number of the Paotingfu people at the station who had on foreign clothes, and you ought to have seen them. Worse than the friends from the rural districts at home on the Fourth of July. I wanted to get some pictures of them but didn't have any films to spare. Sun and Yüan were very friendly at Peking and Sun has been appointed official "Promoter and Developer" of China with 30,000 Taels a month to use for that purpose.

Initiating the idea of forming a Y.M.C.A. in Paotingfu

Well, I must close and prepare my lesson for my Bible class this evening. I have eleven in the class now. I think Saturday I will go to Peking to see the Y.M.C.A. secretaries there about organizing an Association in the school here. So far there are only two other government schools in North China which have them. Those are Ch'ing Hua (the American Preparatory School) and Nan K'ai Middle School (Chang Po Ling's school).

Editor's note –
Sun Yat-sen (1866-1925) was the founding father of the Republic of China. The first provisional president of the Republic of China, Sun was a Chinese medical doctor, writer, philosopher, and revolutionary. He played an instrumental role in the overthrow of the Qing dynasty during the years leading up to the Chinese Revolution of 1911. He was appointed to serve as Provisional President of the Republic of China when it was founded in 1912. He later co-founded the Kuomintang (Nationalist Party of China), serving as its first leader. Sun was a uniting figure in post-Imperial China. [9]

Dr. Sun Yat Sen [center, in suit] on the station platform at Paotingfu, reviewing students. (photo September 17, 1912)

Letter written by Rob to his sister   September 29, 1912

Tell Nan her story about Taft has been very much appreciated out here, as there are no "stand-patters" in China. Here at Paotingfu we are all "bull mooses" or "bull-dozers" (feminine of bull moose), though the Peking Y.M.C.A. (being Princeton men) are all for Wilson. The thing that hurts Wilson most with people who have been in foreign countries is the old moth-eaten "States' rights" plank in the Democratic Party. The sooner the U.S. forgets about States' rights the faster she will advance as a world power. That's just why the Chinese Republic is having such a time to get started. "States' rights" literally translates as "States' selfishness". The only way for a country to advance properly is to subordinate the good of any particular state to the good of the whole, and I'm hoping I'll live to see the day when "National rights" will be as dead an issue as "States' rights" ought to be. Tell Nan I can quite sympathize with her Socialistic tendencies, as I was always inclined that way myself. The only trouble is to make it *practical* instead of *theoretical*, and so far T. R.'s platform comes as near to practical Socialism as anything we've had in America.

Tell Nan that a contract in not necessary here in China for nurses, but Mrs. Burgess (who was formerly a nurse) told me yesterday that it was much better if a nurse had someone to fall back on, especially till she gets established, as there may be dull seasons when she'll want to go someplace where she won't have to pay her board up promptly but can let it run for a little. The regular rate to a nurse out here is $45 Mex in missionary families and $50 for others. Of course, she'll have us.

Misleading news published in America about China

Those clippings mamma sent about Sun Yat Sen fearing to come North etc. were quite a joke. Another example of our Japanese brethren trying to give the Chinese a black eye. It is true that two southern generals were executed by Yüan Shih K'ai, but they were sent North by Li Yüan Hung, because he had absolute proofs of the complicity in a plot to bring back the Manchus, and furthermore they had even misappropriated Republican funds to use in their plot. A number of Japanese officials were also implicated in the plot and had to leave for home. The two men who were executed were given perfectly fair trials, and the evidence against them was absolutely incontestable. And they were shot by official order the same as would have happened in any European country. The only thing which the American papers might howl about was that they were not allowed to plead insanity, or get out several writs of *habeas corpus* and appeal through half a dozen courts and then get off because somebody forgot to cross a "T" in writing the indictment. The men did belong to the T'ung Mêng Hui, as the paper said, but that is not Dr. Sun's party, which is the Kuo Min Tang. And, furthermore, the difference between the North and the South are rapidly being done away with instead of getting worse as the paper said. The aggressions of Russia and Japan, and the dictatorial attitude of the Six Powers [Germany, Austria-Hungary, Britain, France, Italy, and the U.S.] in regard to the loan are doing that much for the country.

And last and not least, China does *not* have woman suffrage and I don't think it has occurred to ninety-nine percent of the voters that such a thing was even within the remotest bounds of possibility. I don't see where the story ever originated. It is very funny to see the American papers and magazines say so much about it, when it is absolutely without foundation.

Thursday night there was a partial eclipse of the moon and the Chinese in all the villages round about were beating tin pans and gongs and making a fearful racket. We asked Li Chang why they did it and he said it was to scare away the dog who was eating it. I explained to him just what caused it but I don't suppose he believed it.

Bible classes and Y.M.C.A. planning

I went up to Peking yesterday to consult with some of the Y.M.C.A. secretaries about work among government school students in Paotingfu. Mr. Burgess is coming down this week for a couple of days to see what can be done about starting weekly meetings for them somewhere in the city. Then at the end of the month a couple of American secretaries will be here and we are going to try to start some more Bible classes. I have thirteen members in mine now.

Letter written by Edith to her mother

Paofu. / October 3, 1912

Sat. Rob went to Peking to see Mr. Burgess about coming down and helping to organize a permanent work for students here. So Mr. Burgess came down Tues. and that afternoon all the gentlemen met together and discussed ways and means. We are going to try to get things into good working order so they will simply have to send a man to take charge of it.

They are going to start a reading room in the city and every Sunday have a speaker and on weekdays have someone over there to answer questions an hour or so every afternoon.

We have 15 in the Bible class now and they keep coming. Mr. Li says many of the students are reading the Bible themselves, alone. So we want to try and start some more classes for them.

There isn't much likelihood of Rob's contract being renewed here, but he feels sure he will be able to get a [teaching] position either in Peking or Tientsin. If the contract was to be renewed he would get a raise of 50 Taels a month, but if he has to get a new position he most likely will have to begin with the same that he is getting now. But we aren't worrying about the matter.

Letter written by Rob to his father

Paotingfu / October 6, 1912

The College closing and job situation

We don't know whether our school will be continued or not after next year, or whether it will be united with Pei Yang University at Tientsin, or with Peking University, and the matter cannot very well be settled until the Loan Question is settled, so that the Board of Education knows something definite about their finances. However, it will very likely be settled early next spring and then we can make our plans. I'd much prefer to stay right here. I don't know whether I'd rather go to Peking or Tientsin if we have to move. Peking is a much more interesting place to live, but the University has a rotten organization, while Pei Yang is the best organized school in North China.

Y.M.C.A. planning

We've had a very busy week. Mr. Burgess was down Tuesday and Wednesday and we worked out plans for Y.M.C.A. work among the students here. We want to get a reading room for them in the city which will be open every day, and then plan to have lectures weekly on religions, scientific and social topics. Then we are going to try to organize a lot of Bible classes in all the schools. At present I have one of 15 members, and Mr. Palmer has one in the Normal School. We have gotten a number of other teachers now and plan to have a large number, in English where the students understand English, otherwise in Chinese. I don't know enough yet to attempt to teach in Chinese, but I'll bet I do before another year.

Tuesday afternoon Mr. Whallon returned from Japan with the new Mrs. Whallon, and Wednesday the Cunninghams had a reception for them. Mrs. Whallon will be awfully nice, I think. I told Mr. Wang, my Chinese teacher, that Mr. Whallon had a new wife (which is Chinese for bride and doesn't imply that he has had any before). He wanted to know if it was five-colored. I couldn't figure out what he meant for a second and then it dawned on me. The word *wife* and the word for *flag* are almost the same, differing only in tone, and he thought I said "flag". So you see one reason why Chinese is hard. Only a trained ear detects any difference in tone, though to a Chinaman they are entirely different sounds.

This week we have two holidays. Monday is Confucius' birthday and Thursday the first anniversary of the outbreak of the revolution. It certainly seems more than a year. The students are planning a great celebration Thursday. I'll try to get some pictures of it.

Letter written by Rob to his mother

Paotingfu / October 13, 1912

Well this has certainly been an exciting week. Monday [October 7] was Confucius' birthday, so, of course, we had no school. In the afternoon we had our picture taken, all the foreigners in the college, for the first time. We've had a number of pictures taken before but there has always been someone absent, but this time all eighteen were there. The photographer in the city took a large picture. Mr. Long's boy took a middle-sized one with his (Mr. Long's camera) and Li Chang took one with our camera, and all are good. I'll send you one as soon as I get time to print one.

Our postmaster's family

In the afternoon we had Mr. Hu, of the Post Office, and his wife and two little girls over to tea. Mr. Hu is a fine young man, educated at Boone College, Wuch'ang, and speaks English very, very well. He was up at Ch'engtu in Ssŭch'uan for several years and there was treasurer of the Ch'engtu Y.M.C.A., the strongest in China. Mrs. Hu knows just a little English. The two little girls are awfully cute. One is six and one is four. The oldest one goes to the Presbyterian Mission school. She said she knew the "English alphabet" but we couldn't get her to say it. Both of them recited dialogues and sang for us. They are about the brightest children I've ever seen.

New celebrations in China

Thursday was the anniversary of the outbreak of the revolution and we had three days holiday, Wednesday, Thursday and Friday. The students had great preparations made. They issued a newspaper three times a day during the three days. Every morning they had a football game. Thursday they had a sham battle and after that exercises in the College chapel, theatricals, games, etc. Then Thursday evening they had a lantern parade which was the prettiest thing I ever saw. Each student had a paper lantern which of course give a much softer light than our glass lanterns and they marched all over the campus and finally ended up by sending up some fire balloons. Then they adjourned to the dining room for a feast. Friday afternoon they also had a sham battle and a number of them gave some of the old Boxer drills. I took a number of pictures but I haven't developed them yet.

Martyr's graves in the South Suburb

Thursday noon the director gave a big Chinese feast, the first we've had for over a year. Wednesday afternoon Edith and I called on the people at the South Suburb. I took over the camera and took a picture of the Martyrs' graves over there. They must be very happy the advances China has made in these twelve years when they know that without their deaths it would have been impossible.

Last night the Lotus Club gave another College dinner. Mr. and Mrs. Whallon were the guests of honor. It was a progressive dinner. After, we had the soup and fish at our house, the entrée and piece de resistance at Lynne's; the salad and the ice cream at Mrs. Pitman's and the fruit and coffee at Mrs. Harvey's. All the houses were beautifully decorated and we had lanterns hung out in the front yard. All the college people were there but Mr. and Mrs. Lattimore who had gone to Peking. Mrs. Lattimore had not been well all fall, you know, and she has gone up there for several weeks rest away from the children. The children were all very much present last night, however.

P. S. I am enclosing a small Chinese flag to let you see what it really is as I have seen so many wrong pictures of it in the American magazines. The red is at the top.

Letter written by Edith to her mother

Paofu. / October 28, 1912

We were so glad to get your letter containing letters from the boys. It seems so nice to hear from you all so often. It has been two weeks since we received the last letter from Rob's mother. We miss her letters so much. We all went to foreign service yesterday. There were thirteen from this compound alone. We made up most of the audience.

Last evening three more students came to Rob and asked if he couldn't have another Bible class for them. The first class of fourteen fills our dining room, so we will have to start a new one. And so the good work goes on. We are so happy about it all. We prefer to have the classes meet here in our house because they like to come to a foreign house so much.

Chihli Provincial College faculty and families (photo October 1912)

[Rob in back row and Edith in front of him as indicated by arrows.]

11 Y.M.C.A. Chinese National Convention

Highlights: November-December 1912

⌘ From December 12 to 15 Rob attended the National Y.M.C.A. conference in Peking, which included 400 delegates from all over China. During this conference, Rob toured the buildings of the "Temple of Heaven".

⌘ First election for leadership of the newly-established the Republic of China (1912-1949) was held December 16-20. Because of this change in governance, the continued existence of Chihli Provincial College became more uncertain.

Our house in the College in the Winter (photo 1912)

THE LETTERS

Letter written by Rob to his sister Celia

November 3, 1912

    We just got the home letters written after Marjorie's wedding. I'll bet you and Melville had a great time. I suppose you two will be next. It is hard to imagine my baby sister married, but, you see, I can't realize that you are over 21. We've had a great time trying to find anything good enough to send you, but we've found something now that will do, I guess. It is very rare, even for China and I have never seen one like it before, but my Chinese teacher says that such things are sometimes given to brides among the official class. Now you have something to feed your curiosity on, as I am not going to tell you what it is; you'll find out just before you are married, when it arrives.

    Dad also asked about those characters on my letterhead. Here they are:

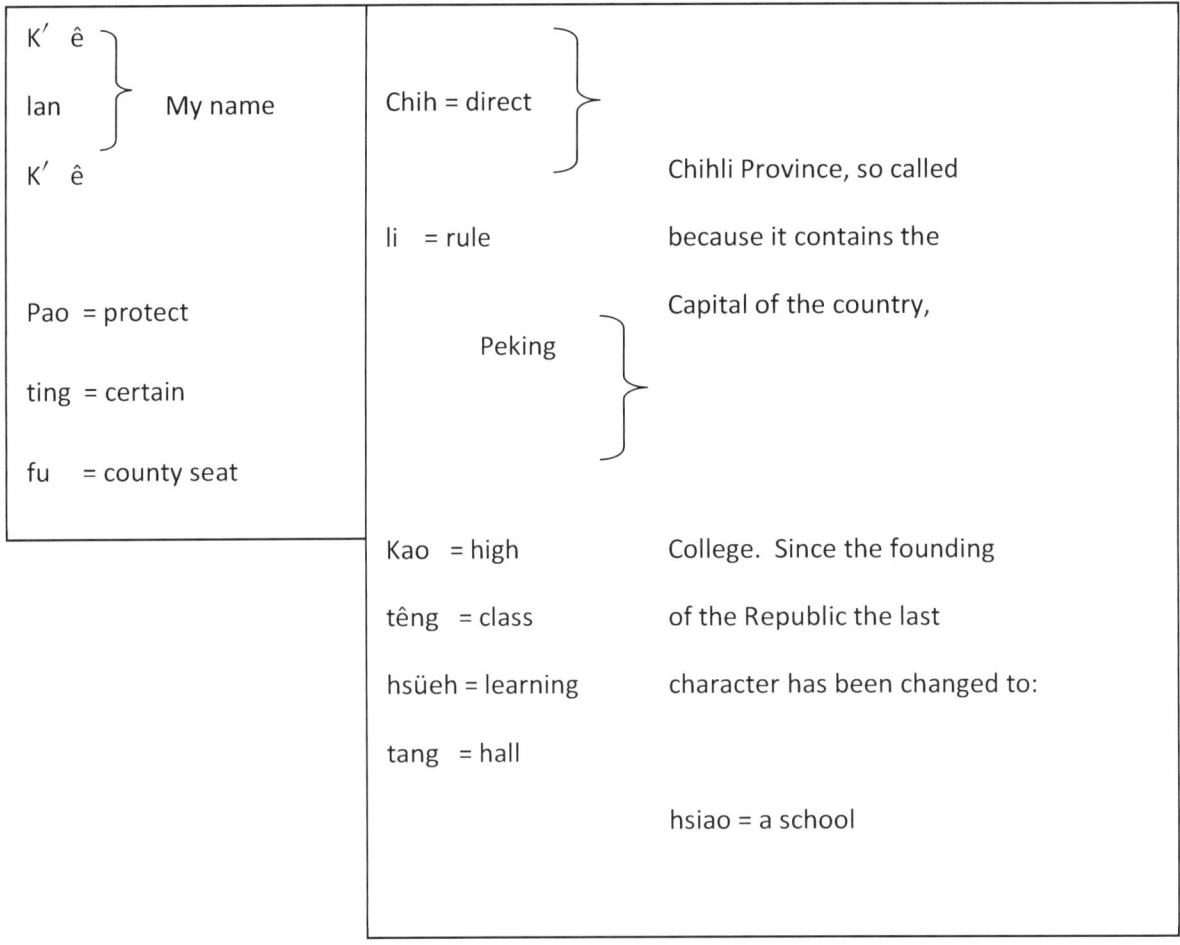

The other characters I write on the outside are:

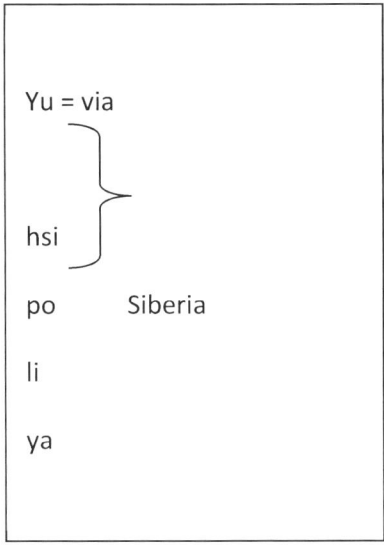

Letter written by Edith to Rob's father

Paotingfu, N. China / November 10, 1912

Teaching position uncertainty

My! I wish we could come home this year, but it seems impossible unless Rob loses his job and can't get another one out here. Maybe we can come home the next summer if Rob gets another position as good as this one. Of course, there is nothing at all certain about his losing this place, except Mr. Pitman whose contract expires this December has been told it would not be renewed and ours is the next to expire. The reason given was that they wished to combine this with either the University in Tientsin or Peking. But absolutely nothing is settled. And for that reason we can't tie our money up in lots [property] or anything else much just now.

Letter written by Rob to his father

November 10, 1912

Well, winter seems to have come on to us about a month ahead of time. All the last week has been cloudy and windy getting colder each day till yesterday it was down to about 15° and the lotus pond froze over. It has been very uncomfortable in the class rooms, but I have had a vest lined with fox legs which beats anything I ever saw for keeping warm. The Chinese are not much for fires, you know, they just pile on another layer of quilted garments and keep warm that way.

I am sending two rolls of pictures painted by a little Chinese boy, which you can give away if you wish. He is very poor, and we are practically supporting the family, so I make him paint us pictures in return. Please give Mr. Marzoff his choice of a couple of the pictures for a Chinese present.

Letter written by Rob to his sister

Paotingfu / November 24, 1912

First voting in China

We finished up our work last Tuesday for the fall. Since then the students have had four days for review, and we give exams all this week. Then, if more than half the students wish it, school will be closed till January 7th, so that they can all go home to vote as the elections are from December 16 to 20. I do not think school will begin again January 7th, for although officially the Chinese have adopted the foreign calendar, they pay practically no attention to it, and the Chinese New Year Day is February 9, so I don't imagine the old folks will let the students come back before that. Also, meantime, the school may be transferred to Peking, so we don't know yet just what will happen.

Y.M.C.A. conference in Peking and Christmas vacation

We are planning to go to Tientsin immediately after the examinations and get some clothes made. Then we'll come back via Peking, stopping there from December 12 to 15 for the National Y.M.C.A. conference. Then we'll come back home for the rest of our vacation. Mother Gordon has promised to come down for Christmas. She and Edith were in Paofu seven years ago last Thursday on their way to Taomingfu, and she hasn't been here since.

Dr. Weatherford speaks on behalf of the Y.M.C.A. and Bible studies

Last Monday Dr. Weatherford formerly of Vanderbilt University but now traveling secretary for the South for the Y.M.C.A. was here on a trip around the world he is making. He spoke to 1,200 students in the city on the importance of Bible study. Over 100 signed up for classes on the spot, while many more took cards away and have been sending them in since, so that there are about 200 altogether. They will meet today to be assigned to classes. Next Sunday Mr. Wilder of Peking will give them another lecture and another opportunity will be given them to sign up, so we hope to get at least another hundred in the classes. They seem very interested when they do get into Bible study, and very few drop out. At least, that has been Palmer's and my experience.

Letter written by Edith to her mother

Peking, N. China / December 13, 1912

I arrived here safely last evening at 6:55. Rob was at the station to meet me all right. We are to be here until Tuesday or Wednesday. Monday night is the banquet for the College men, and Tuesday night there is to be a concert by the Ching Hua and Tungchou Glee Clubs. We want very much to hear that.

I walked with Rob to the Y.M.C.A. meeting this morning. I visited Mr. Burgess while Rob was in the meeting. My! they have a lovely big baby boy. I peeked into the big hall where the speaking was going on. There was a large crowd. Several hundred, I should say. The Y.M.C.A. building is only about half finished but they are certainly going to be fine. The family's houses are all furnished. Rob has gone to the meeting now. He is to give a short address at 3:30.

Welcome Arch in front of Peking Y.M.C.A. at National Convention (photo December 1912)

Hatamên Street [Peking], new Y.M.C.A. building on the left (photo December 1912)

Interior of Y.M.C.A. Auditorium, Peking (photo December 1912)

Editor's note –
The Temple of Heaven [photos below] is an imperial complex of religious buildings in the southeastern part of central Beijing (formerly Peking). The complex was visited by the emperors of the Ming and Qing dynasties for annual ceremonies of prayer to Heaven for good harvest. With the downfall of the Qing Dynasty in 1912, the temple complex was left un-managed. This neglect led to the collapse of several halls in the following years. In 1918 the temple was turned into a park and for the first time open to the public. [10]

Looking north from the Altar of Heaven (photo December 1912)

The Temple of Heaven (photo December 1912)

Letter written by Rob to his sister Celia

                                                                                Paotingfu / December 22, 1912

The Y.M.C.A. Conference and Dr. Goodrich

     I left Tientsin and came down here two weeks ago today. I taught two days, and then so many of the students had gone home to vote that we closed up till Jan. 7. So, I went up to Peking Thursday to attend the National Y.M.C.A. Convention of China and Korea. Edith met me there. We stayed at the Hotel Des Wagons-Lits for a couple of days and then went to stay with the Goodriches.

     Dr. Goodrich is 76. He has been in China 47 years. He reminds me so much in both looks and actions of Grandpa Wood. He is so full of fun and keeps up to date so well. He is the author of a little Chinese dictionary which is probably the most used of any in North China. He is now working on the revision of the Old Testament in Chinese. Mrs. Goodrich is General Secretary for China for the W.C.T.U. [Women's Christian Temperance Union]. They have a son who was at Oberlin [College in Ohio] last year. She is a great girl, just a big unspoiled little girl. We had lots of fun with her. She sings beautifully.

     The convention lasted from Thursday till Monday. There were 400 delegates from all over China. The meetings were all held in Mandarin. We went one night and a Cantonese gentleman spoke. He didn't understand Mandarin so had to speak in English, and let a northern man translate. It certainly was strange to see one Chinese talking to other Chinese, and having to speak in English to make himself understood.

Tuesday we went out to see the Temple of Heaven. It is certainly a magnificent place. I'm enclosing pictures. The worship in this temple was to the *one* "God in Heaven" and was almost identical with the old Hebrew worship.

Tuesday evening the American College Club had a dinner, the biggest one yet. About 180 were present.

Wednesday night we went to a concert for the purpose of raising funds to send a team to Manila to the Far Eastern Olympics in Feb. It was our first musical treat for some time and we thoroughly enjoyed it. Thursday we came home, and are beginning to get rested up again. Tomorrow I am going to Peking to meet Mother Gordon who is coming down to spend Christmas with us.

Letter written by Rob to his father

Paotingfu / December 30, 1912

This has been a rather busy week. Monday I left at 6:45 and managed to keep from freezing till noon when I arrived in Peking. Met Mother Gordon there and brought her back on the afternoon train. We left Peking at 3 and were supposed to get home at 7:45 but were 2 hours late. The engineer had a lot of fun coming back. He didn't seem to want to use his air, so he'd shut off steam about four miles out of the station, and just let the train run down.

Saturday Mr. Harry Carritt, one of the teachers in the Anglo-Chinese College, Moore's special friend there, stopped off here over Sunday on a trip down to Chang-te-fu in Honan. Jack Burgess, whose parents are missionaries in South Shensi, about two months trip from here, is with him. He is a fine youngster of 13, a typical Britisher. They go on by the noon train today.

The Pitmans left Thursday for their new position in Peking. He is going to teach in a Normal School there. Our contract is the next to expire, but it will be two or three months yet before we know what will happen to the school next summer so we are making no plans until things are a little more certain.

Resting place of the Emperor, Temple of Heaven [Edith Clack on steps] (photo 1912)

Emperor's Chair, Temple of Heaven (photo December 1912)

12 Final Semester at Chihli Provincial College

Highlights: January-June 1913

⌘ In early 1913 Rob's 3-year contract with the college was nearing completion. Because of the uncertainty of a future with Chihli Provincial College under the new political regime, he explored other opportunities for employment.

⌘ Following some months of employment uncertainty, in June 1913 Rob accepted an invitation from the International Committee of Young Men's Christian Associations (Y.M.C.A.s) to become General Secretary [i.e., executive officer] of the new Y.M.C.A. in Paotingfu. The first official name was the "Chihli Provincial Capital Y.M.C.A." and it was organized on April 27, 1913, with 23 charter members – 19 Chinese and four Americans.

THE LETTERS

Letter written by Rob to his mother in Iowa   **January 7, 1913**

New Year's we had a great time. Were over at the Lattimore's for dinner and at the Woodward's for supper. Roy and Lynne have moved over to the Pitman house where they will have a larger garden, and Roy will have more room for a tool shop.

Mother *[Elma]* Gordon went home Thursday. She had to get back to her English classes. In the morning she has ten young men whom she teaches, and in the afternoon she teaches T'ang Shao I's two little girls. *[Editor's note – Tang Shaoyi briefly served as the first Premier of the Republic of China in 1912.]* [12] Then after supper she opens up her school room as a reading room for the American soldiers.

Karl [Edith's brother] may be coming back within a few months. The fight on opium is approaching crisis and Mr. [Rev. E.W.] Thwing, head of the International Reform Bureau, has offered Karl a regular missionary's salary to come out and help him, and we think Karl will surely accept.

The Chinese are celebrating two New Year's this year. They had the official celebration on our New Year, but the real big time will come a month from today on the old New Year's Day. It takes more than a year to change the customs of forty centuries.

Letter written by Rob to his sister Ida

January 14, 1913

We have our embryo Y.M.C.A. started now and are starting to use it as a headquarters to prepare for the coming of Mr. Eddy [Associate General Secretary of International Y.M.C.A.] and Mott [long-standing leader in the Y.M.C.A.] next month. The American Board have given us Mr. Ting, their best Chinese helper, to take charge of the student work, and the Presbyterians are giving us part time of several men, and perhaps later can get one of the missionaries to take complete charge. Eddy will be here Feb 26, 27 for three meetings. John R. Mott will not get down to Paotingfu, but 20 of the Paotingfu students are to be sent to Peking to meet with him and with 30 Tientsin and 50 Peking students to make sort of a student committee for student work in North China.

This week we have been having our ice crop harvested, that is, the company which supplies it has been harvesting it. It is great fun to watch them with their primitive methods after watching the harvesting as it is done at Clear Lake. Here they have no tools except very rough picks, ropes, and sticks. They break the chunks of ice off with picks, lift it out with sticks and then hand it off by tying a rope around it, one or two coolies pulling according to the size of the piece. You also ought to see the little Chinese boys skate. They, of course, can't afford skates as we use, so each little youngster gets a round hardwood stick about as long as his foot and perhaps half an inch through, then he puts his right foot on that and slides on it pushing himself with the left foot. They really get up quite a decent amount of speed that way.

Paotingfu city moat - harvesting ice (photo 1913)

Letter written by Rob to his sister Celia

January 26, 1913

Speaking of age, I asked my Chinese teacher the other day how long he had lived in the village where he now lives, and he said he didn't know exactly but it was "a good many hundred years." How's that for age? I thought I'd investigate a little further, so I asked Li Chang, our boy, how long he had lived in the house where he does now. He also was not sure but he had heard people say that it was at least since the time of his grandfather's grandfather; how much longer he didn't dare say. And yet he only claims to be 21 years old and doesn't look that.

Leaving all joking aside however, your English Lords and Earls don't really know what a true "old family" means. The best of them can't lay claim to having occupied the same place more than 300 or 400 years, but here we have just the average Chinaman living on in his ancestral mansion for "A good many hundred years." Of course, said mansion has probably been washed down by the summer rains every two or three years during that time, but at any rate, it is still the same old mud.

Letter written by Rob to his father

Paotingfu / February 2, 1913

The Director came back this week after several weeks electioneering. He certainly had hard luck. On the first count he was declared elected to the provincial assembly, but on a recount, one of his ballots was declared defective which tied him with two other men. In case of a tie the matter is decided by lot and he lost! The provincial assembly must now elect ten Senators for the national Senate, five from their own number and five from outside, and the Director still has hopes of getting in as one of these.

The Board of Education has taken no action yet about this school, except to make a few minor changes in the course of study. We are still in doubt as to what will be our ultimate fate. They cannot very well decide till the permanent government is organized next month and finances are in a more settled condition.

Letter written by Rob to his mother

February 9, 1913

Last Thursday was the old Chinese New Year, and in spite of the fact that it no longer officially exists, most of the people celebrated it as usual. It was as bad as Fourth of July used to be in America. For several days before there was a great deal of shooting firecrackers, but Wednesday night there was a continual roar all night. All the shops were closed Thursday and Friday and only a few open yesterday, but I suppose all will be open today or tomorrow, so you see really the government had made quite a change, for formerly they were all closed for a week or longer.

I am going to hear a lecture this afternoon on Abraham Lincoln in Chinese. Mr. Ewing of the American Board at Tientsin is to give it. The Chinese are very much interested in Lincoln and Washington so I imagine there will be quite a crowd.

Letter written by Rob to his sister Ida

February 16, 1913

I'm mighty busy just now getting plans laid for Mr. Eddy's meeting a week from Wednesday. There are so many little things to see about, and the hardest work of all is keeping the other fellows poked up. If only I knew enough Chinese I could do most of the work easier myself. We have to have short preliminary lectures given in all the schools this week to arouse a little more interest, and I had to write the lecture myself, but got Mr. Hu to translate it, and Mr. Cunningham, and three of the Chinese Christians are going to deliver it. I don't know how we would get along if it wasn't for Mr. Hu. He is the Postal Inspector for this district, and was the treasurer of the Y.M.C.A. at Chengtu in Ssǔch'uan for two years, so knows all about Y.M.C.A. methods.

We had a holiday on Lincoln's birthday. You didn't know that the Chinese celebrated that, did you? But they do. You see, it happens to be also the day on which the Manchus abdicated and therefore is the anniversary of the founding of the Republic. There was no special celebration, however. Too soon after the Chinese New Year, and the celebrations of that have not ended yet. They generally keep it up for a couple of weeks. There is a temple across the river where they have been drumming and pounding cymbals every day since the New Year. Just simply for the sake of making a noise. They are a lot of peasants who don't have any work to do now so do that for amusement. When the wind is in the right direction it is perfectly deafening and sounds just over the wall.

Letter written by Edith to her mother

Paotingfu / Saturday evening, March 2, 1913

Well, Mr. Eddy has come and gone and has left great blessings behind. Over 250 students signed up, wishing to join the Bible classes, and many who have been in classes want to join the church. They are organizing classes for them all. The difficulty is to get good teachers enough for them. We have started another class here in this school. Mr. Harvey teaches it. Rob has a Bible class for English speaking teachers which meets every Monday afternoon in the reading room in the city. Also on Thurs. and Sat. afternoons he has a class in English at the same place. All that besides the four evenings a week of Bible classes and his regular work keeps him very busy.

We are both well and so happy in the work the Lord has found for us to do, even in a Government school. Mr. Eddy says that the people at home want to build a Y.M.C.A. building here in memory of Mr. Pitkin who was killed here in 1900. If the city here will give the land and the Y.M.C.A. supply a man, they will supply the building. Maybe within another year we will have a regular established Y.M.C.A. here. We certainly would be happy if it might be so.

**Ch'eng Hu, District Postal Inspector and
one of the founders of the Paotingfu Y.M.C.A.** (photo 1913)

Letter written by Rob to his mother

March 16, 1913

Our ultimate fate is more up in the air than ever. Last week we thought the college was to be immediately moved to Peking and that we were to close up our work last week and give exams this week. Then we heard that the Province had not yet given over the school, but that the Director had gone to Peking to consult with the National authorities about the school, as all they wanted was the funds, without taking the students or teachers. Evidently they did not come to any agreement, as Mr. T'ang, the Director's assistant told me last night that he had received orders to come to Tientsin to make arrangements for moving our scientific students to Pei Yang University, and that we were to go on with our work as usual for two weeks more, spring vacation time. So I don't know what will happen. We will very likely be moved to Tientsin along with the students.

Li T'ien Lu, our pet student who went to Wo Fo Ssŭ with me last summer, has the scarlet fever. He seems to be getting along very well, however. I'm afraid it is likely to start an epidemic among the students, as they don't know what quarantine means. They have moved him off away from the rest, which is better than they did three years ago when some had it, but his friends go to see him as they wish.

Letter written by Edith to Rob's sister Ida

Paotingfu, N. China / March 24, 1913

Friday evening (March 21st) we had Mr. and Mrs. Harvey, Mr. and Mrs. Woodward and Mr. Long to dinner. We had twenty-three candles lit in our dining room, sitting room and hall. It did look so pretty. Have I ever told you that my "fad" is collecting brass, especially candle sticks? I have a few very nice one and lots of plain ordinary ones. I have about thirty altogether, two silver ones but the rest are brass.

Letter written by Rob to his sister Nan

April 1, 1913

Status of Chihli Provincial College
College closed up yesterday for a week's vacation. It will, however, contrary to previous rumors, open again next week and run on till June, and then the plan is to transfer the whole school to Pei Yang University at Tientsin next fall. Some of the teachers will be taken, but I am not expecting to be, as my contract expires and they have a bunch of engineering teachers at Pei Yang University who are only teaching about half time and can just as well teach math as not. At least that would be the logical thing, though you can never tell whether the Chinese will do the logical thing or not.

We have as yet received no notification (officially) of what will be done, as the whole scheme may be overturned again by the National Assembly, who are supposed to meet next week. They probably will not take up school matters for several weeks, either, as they are too busy playing politics to pay much attention to serious business for a while.

Politics of the new Republic
You'd think in a country in as shaky a condition as this the people would develop an unselfish patriotism and leave their party quarrels until they had at least partly set the country on its feet, but there isn't one in a hundred of these big talking Republican leaders who really care one whoop about the country as long as he can satisfy his personal ambitions. The only three I can think of are, luckily for the country, the three with the greatest influence, that is Yüan Shih K'ai, the only man who has any chance to control things whatever, Li Yüan Hung, the Vice-President, and Sun Yat Sen, who contrary to all expectation showed his bigness by resigning and joining Yüan's party. To paraphrase Shakespeare, "Nothing in his official life became him like the leaving of it."

Letter written by Rob to his sister Celia   **April 6, 1913**

Preparations for funeral of the Empress Dowager
    There was big excitement in Peking, preparing for the Empress Dowager's funeral on Thursday and the opening of the National Assembly next Tuesday. They had a big time with the funeral. Made almost as much of it as if the Manchus were still in power. She was the niece of the Old Empress Dowager who died five years ago, it was chiefly through her influence that the Manchu princes were finally brought to consent to the abdication last year. She was buried at the Imperial Tombs in the Western Hills about half way between here and Peking, the body being taken on a railway train (shades of the departed ancestors!).

National Assembly and more politics
    This week witnesses the opening of the National Assembly, and Peking is fuller of politics than Washington ever thought of being. I don't suppose any real business will be done for several weeks, until at least the various parties try out their strength. They will have to elect a president very soon, but it is only possible to elect Yüan Shih K'ai. I think if they elect anybody else, we foreigners will move to Tientsin as quickly as possible. The only other man who has any ability at all is Li Yüan Hung, and he will not accept it while Yüan lives, as he is Yüan's staunchest supporter. I think the best thing they could do would be to make Yüan Emperor with the privilege of electing his successor, as I haven't much faith in these Republicans. All they are looking for is a chance to feather their own nests. They don't care a hang for the country, that is, the majority don't. However, the few really patriotic ones may be able to save the day yet.

Railway station (in Peking) – matshed built for funeral of Empress Dowager, Lung Yu (she died February 22, 1913)

Letter written by Rob to his father   **April 13, 1913**

Our vacation was supposed to be over Tuesday, but they sent around word early Tuesday morning that we would have an extra day off because of the opening of the National Assembly. Then yesterday we had another day off because of the first recognition of the Republic officially. It came from Brazil, so all the public buildings are flying the Brazilian flag with the Chinese. I was hoping Uncle Sam would get the prestige of being first, but he let the Brazilians slip one over on him.

The opening of the Assembly passed off quietly. There was a good deal of apprehension beforehand, but the Cantonese party (who are the trouble makers), the Kuo Min Tang turned out to be in a minority in both Houses, so trouble from that direction seems improbable. That also means that it is practically certain that Yüan will be elected President again.

The papers say that John R. Mott has been offered the position of American minister. He certainly would make a fine one, as he has been all over the world and understands conditions here in the Far East very well, besides being a man of such strong principles. I'm afraid, however, that he'd never consent to take it. He would feel that his present work is much bigger. So far Bryan [William Jennings Bryan] has certainly justified his appointment as Secretary of State, as least as far as dealing with the situation out here is concerned. Of course, he has been out here which helps a lot. This idea of trying to run foreign affairs by a man who has never been outside his home state belongs back in the dark ages. England is still doing it, though.

Mr. Wang, President of Pei Yang University, is coming tomorrow to look over the school, so I suppose we'll know pretty soon what they are going to do about us teachers. I don't think they need me up there, as they have a lot of engineers doing very light work, who ought to be able to teach their math. At any rate, we'll be notified so we'll be free to find other positions if they don't want us there.

Letter written by Rob to his father   **April 20, 1913**

Well, President Wang of Pei Yang University has come, made his arrangements for the transfer of the college and departed. We are not to go, as we were quite certain beforehand, as my contract expires and they already have two mathematics teachers in the Engineering Department of the University. But, at any rate, we are now free to look up another place. Mr. Lattimore will go to Pei Yang as professor of languages, a permanent position. Roy will go for a year to finish out his contract; Mr. Harvey will also go for a year. Mr. Long will be let go, although his contract is not up.

I don't know yet just what I will do. They want me to come to the Anglo-Chinese College in Tientsin, but I don't think I will take it unless I can get a position in some other school also, as they don't pay enough. I may possibly stay here in Paotingfu as Y.M.C.A. secretary, though nothing has been decided yet. They haven't said anything to me about it yet, but Dr. Lewis told me yesterday that they were discussing doing it if I did not go to Pei Yang. I think if they offer it, I'll accept it, as I like the Y.M.C.A. work very much.

This has been rather a strenuous week. The Director had a big feast for President Wang Tuesday. Then Wednesday he had us make out reports as to our work with suggestions etc. Then Thursday President Wang came over to tiffin to discuss a revision of the mathematics course, so as to make it more suitable for the engineering students. The course as at present ordered by the Board of Education is very poorly arranged, but I have a new arrangement all worked out, with text books ready and all, which I think President Wang will work through the Board and adopt at Pei Yang.

Yesterday we were over at Dr. Lewis' for tiffin, and last night Edith surprised me by having the Lattimores over for dinner in honor of the third anniversary of my arrival in Paotingfu. Well, I must stop and prepare a sermon for this afternoon, as I have to lead the foreign service.

(Note written later by Edith to her mother):

Rob led foreign service yesterday. He read the last chapter of "Many Infallible Proofs", and it certainly was good. Service was here in this compound, so I could go.

Letter written by Edith Clack to her mother Paotingfu / April 27, 1913

As for the time of our leaving here, we can't say exactly as we don't know when the examinations are to be. The teachers always have a week's vacation just before exams and it would be best if Rob could take me up then. We are hoping that the exams may be early this spring. In that case Rob wouldn't have to come back at all. We will plan to go up as soon after you do as possible. It will only be a matter of two or three days later at the most.

We are not sorry that we are not going to Pei Yang to live, altho' it would be a fine school to teach in, but neither one of us have liked the thought of living there.

Rob has gone into the city today to organize a Y.M.C.A. here. We feel so joyful over it. Just think, it is less than a year since Rob started his first Bible class among the students here, and now Paofu is to have its Y.M.C.A. We are still praying that – if for the best – Rob may be made secretary here.

Letter written by Rob to his mother April 28, 1913

Formal establishment of the Chihli Provincial Capital Y.M.C.A.

Yesterday the "Chihli Provincial Capital Y.M.C.A." was organized with 23 charter members, 4 Americans and 19 Chinese. There are about ten more who want to join immediately but were unable to attend yesterday. Dr. Chêng, the head of the Paotingfu Military Hospital is president, Mr. Cunningham is vice-president; Mr. Sun, the Chinese pastor of the Congregational church is recording secretary; I am corresponding secretary, Mr. Hu, the district Postal Inspector is treasurer, and Mr. Ting, formerly head of the American Board Boy's school, has been asked to become regular secretary giving all his time to the work. We also ought to have a regular foreign secretary, but I don't know whether the International Committee will give us one, as they are so short of men. I think I'll offer myself for the position, as I sort of feel that the work belongs specially to me.

The Y.M.C.A. will occupy a building inside the West gate which was formerly used by the Presbyterians as a street chapel but has been much enlarged since the looting of the city. That ought to do until we get the $25,000 building which Mr. Eddy promised us. The work which our committee has been carrying on under the name of the "General Learning Society" will be turned over to the Y.M.C.A. We had 14 Bible classes with about 250 members, one English class of 12, a good reading room and a lecture course. The Y.M.C.A. will try to increase the English and Bible classes and to do some work in Physical Training in cooperation with the National Educational Society. Altogether the prospect looks very bright. The Associate membership (for non-Christians) has not been opened up yet, but I know there will be a large number want to join.

The National Assembly which met first 3 weeks ago are still quarreling about parties and have done nothing, which is probably just as well, as Yüan has had more time to strengthen his power and thus that of the government. The Kuo Min Tang, the Cantonese party, which was opposed to Yüan, seems to show signs of going to pieces, so we may have a good strong government yet.

Y.M.C.A. first building (photo 1913)

Letter written by Rob to his sister Ida

May 4, 1913

The Lattimores finally left Thursday for Europe. Mr. Lattimore went as far as Tsingtao with them where they take the big steamer. The friends will meet them in Rome (probably Mr. Lattimore's sister, who lives in Soochow) so they will be well taken care of. Mrs. Lattimore is feeling ever so much better now, and the children are all over their whooping cough. We will miss them dreadfully. They left us their graphophone till summer and as they have some good records, we are having a regular orgy of music. That's the one thing you miss the most out here.

Photo on left, **Lattimore children (five) and Marin Harvey**

Photo on right, **David and Margaret Lattimore** (photos 1913)

Letter written by Edith to her mother

Paotingfu, N. China / May 13, 1913

Rob has been to Peking to talk over with the Y.M.C.A. about our taking up the work here. They have to write home and it will be decided in New York and they will cable the answer. So it will be about a month before we know for sure.

Mr. Taylor of the T.A.C.C. has written Rob about helping there six months. If we don't get this position and they pay enough to live on we most likely will take that, as it would give us a little time in which to look around.

Letter written by Rob to his father

June 1, 1913

Wednesday night the Galts invited us all over to a farewell dinner in honor of Abbie Chapin, who is going home for her furlough this month. We had the nearest perfect attendance of the foreign community we have ever had at any affair here, only Mrs. Mather and Roy and Lynne were absent, and we had two visitors from outside who partly made up for it. One of them, Mr. Knight from Pingyangfu in Shansi was over here for tiffin yesterday. He is a great friend of Karl & Moore Gordon, and they have visited him at his home in Shansi. He is an Englishman, belongs to the China Inland Mission, but spends all his time traveling around and training Bible teachers. He was pastor of a church in New York for four or five years and married a Canadian woman, so he is quite cosmopolitan.

Dr. Hall, of the Presbyterian mission in Peking, died this week of typhus contracted while taking care of some patients in his hospital. It was very sudden, as I saw him only two weeks before in Peking and had a long visit with him and he was apparently in the best of health. He is the fourth mission doctor to die from typhus during the last three months.

Letter written by Rob to his mother

June 8, 1913

Twelve students out of our Y.M.C.A. Bible classes are to be baptized today, among them Li T'ien Lu, our special pet. It makes you feel as if all the hard work of the last year had not been in vain when you begin to see the results come in. And better yet there are perhaps 25 or 30 more who are practically ready for baptism, but were advised to wait till they had studied a little more.

I teach my last class Friday morning, and have my first examination the same afternoon, June 13. My other two exams don't come till the 23rd and 24th, so I'll take advantage of that time to take Edith to Peitaiho. We'll probably leave here Tuesday, the 17th, and go to Peking, then to Tientsin Wednesday and Peitaiho Thursday. It's barely possible, however, that we'll take a boat with Roy and Lynne from here to Tientsin, leaving Saturday and getting to Tientsin Wednesday. It will be a much easier trip on the girls if the weather is good, as they won't have to stand any jolting.

Letter written by Rob to his sister Ida   **June 23, 1913**

Y.M.C.A. appointment confirmed

      Received my appointment today as Secretary of the International Committee of the Y.M.C.A. and will be stationed here at Paotingfu for the next year or two at least. For the next year I'll have half time for language study. The salary is not so much as I've been getting. $1200 a year (gold) plus house rent and summer vacation expenses, about $400 more in all. But then the demands are not nearly so great, as you don't have to give up several hundred dollars a year in "squeeze". Besides, it's a life job if I want it and we get a year's vacation in America every six years with full salary, and all traveling expenses paid. It's lots harder work than teaching, as you have so much more responsibility and it requires so much more versatility, but I never mind how much work you give me if it's the kind I like, brain work. I expect we'll probably live here in the same house, taking the whole of it this time. It is by far the prettiest place in Paotingfu, and will be very conveniently located, especially as another school of 400 students will be transferred to the college grounds when our students leave.

      Do you remember Marion Frank [Grinnell College, Iowa]? Just had a letter from Edith [in Peitaiho] saying Marion has just been to call on her. She is in the Methodist Mission at Hankow, but as this was her first summer in China, they thought it best for her to come clear up north out of the heat till she gets a little more acclimated. Well, I must close, as I have a lot of other letters to write.

Letter written by Rob to his sister Nan

                                                                                     Peitaiho / June 30, 1913

      I left Paotingfu Wednesday, spent Thursday shopping in Tientsin and came up here Friday. I rather thought when I came up here I could stay on till September, but just got word that they need me to take some of the classes at the Wo Fo Ssǔ Y.M.C.A. conference, so I'm expecting to go day after tomorrow and will get back two weeks from today.

      I guess from Dad's letter that he doesn't understand what a Y.M.C.A. secretary means. The word is not used with our American colloquial meaning (equivalent to the English "clerk") but in its proper meaning "an executive officer" as we use it in Secretary of State, etc. The secretaries are the Y.M.C.A. ministers except that they also have the additional powers of the "Board of Trustees." In many cases they are ordained ministers, and they are supposed to have had a number of year's special training before they are sent out.

      It is really a very exceptional case for me to get the appointment without the special training. As for the pay, it is about what an ordinary college professor gets in America, with the sixth year's vacation and all traveling expenses paid in addition, besides being a life job, and your family looked after if anything happens to you. And there is always the chance to work up into John R. Mott's place when he leaves it. He is only a Y.M.C.A. secretary but thinks enough of his place so that when Wilson and Bryan repeatedly begged him to take the position of Minister to China he wouldn't even consider it. I've also heard Gailey, the Peking senior secretary mentioned for the place, but I'm sure he wouldn't accept either.

Industrial School Bible Class in Paotingfu (photo 1913)

"Foreign" (non-Chinese) Teachers at Chihli Provincial College (photo 1913)
Standing: E.R. Long, R.W. Clack, N.H. Pitman, S.B. Harvey
Seated: J.A.R. Henderson [and his father, Capt. Henderson] (dog, Ch'isai)

13 Establishing the Y.M.C.A. in Paotingfu

Highlights: July-December 1913

⌘ On August 21, 1913, Robert and Edith's first child, Karl David Gordon Clack, was born at Peitaiho, the resort area where the Clacks normally stayed during the summer.
⌘ In September, Rob began his new career as head of the newly established Y.M.C.A. in Paotingfu.

"History of Y.M.C.A. International Work in China"
(Y.M.C.A. Archives, University of Minnesota Library)
(excerpts)

"Although the Y.M.C.A. movement had been active in China as early as the 1870s, the first North American Y.M.C.A. work in China dates from 1889.... 1895 was the beginning of fifty-five years of North American Y.M.C.A. involvement in China. Over the years approximately 150 secretaries served in about forty associations throughout the country. ... Part of the appeal of the Y.M.C.A. was the International Committee's policy of stressing indigenous leadership, support, and control, which appealed to the burgeoning nationalism of the Chinese. ... The Boxer Rebellion [1899-1901] briefly halted the Y.M.C.A.'s activities in China, but recovery and advance followed rapidly. ...

While the Y.M.C.A.'s foreign work was rooted in the missionary movement and Bible classes were among the first activities offered by the fledgling association, the program included a variety of other educational programs, including English classes, lectures, and vocational training. Physical training, public health education (a national health campaign organized by the Y.M.C.A. in the 1920s virtually ended typhus in China), and other fields of work were soon added as the Y.M.C.A. responded to local needs. The Y.M.C.A. introduced many Western sports and Western-style sports competitions, and can also take credit for the early organization of the Olympic movement in China. ... the Y.M.C.A. organized the Far Eastern Games, the first international competitions in the far east." [1]

Background for a New Y.M.C.A. in Paotingfu

Prior to the establishment of the Y.M.C.A. in Paotingfu, Rob started teaching a Bible Study class in 1911 at the request of two students at Chihli Provincial College. This grew into two classes, and an "Educational Society" was organized among the missionaries, teachers, and leading Chinese Christians. This organization opened up a reading room, started an English class, began a series of fortnightly lectures on scientific, religious and popular subjects, and took general supervision of the Bible study classes. This effort brought the total number of Chinese students up to more than a hundred.

When Rob's 3-year teaching contract with Chihli Provincial College expired in June, he accepted an invitation from the International Committee of Young Men's Christian Associations to become General Secretary [i.e., Executive Officer] of the new Y.M.C.A. in Paotingfu. While teaching at Chihli Provincial College, Rob had been a member of the committee that laid the groundwork for this new Y.M.C.A. In his new role at the Y.M.C.A. Rob trained a Chinese staff and taught English language and Bible classes. He also helped with athletic programs in a number of local schools, and was involved with regional and international student athletic meets.

Y.M.C.A. – R.W. Clack's First Year

One of the requirements of the General Secretary of a local Y.M.C.A. was to write an Annual Report. As the first executive of a new association, he faced many challenges, including raising money, finding a satisfactory location for a new building, determining the primary needs of the community, acquiring and retaining members, and hiring and training staff. These same challenges continued throughout his tenure, with the primary problems being financial shortfalls and the need for building space.

Y.M.C.A. ANNUAL REPORT, PAOTINGFU
Year ended September 30, 1913
Written by Robert W. Clack, General Secretary (following are excerpts from the Report)

"As this is the first time there has been an Association report from Paotingfu, it might be well to first give a few facts about the place. Paotingfu is a walled city, with a population of perhaps one hundred thousand. The city is about ninety miles southwest of Peking, and about one hundred miles west of Tientsin, so that the three cities form an equilateral triangle.

Mission work was begun in Paotingfu by the American Mission Board in 1873. … During the Boxer uprising in 1900 a number of American missionaries and Chinese Christians gave up their lives here, so that we feel that the place has been especially consecrated to Christian work. Among the Americans who thus died for their belief was Horace Tracy Pitkin, formerly widely known throughout Student Associations in America.

However, until the past year, the student field has been almost untouched. This has been partly due to the extreme prejudice of the educated class against anything Christian, and partly due to a lack of appreciation on the part of the missionaries of the great importance of this field and the special methods needed.

… When the Provincial College (and teachers) was moved to Tientsin [in early 1913], it was decided that in order to conserve the results already obtained, a broader organization was necessary; so, with the help of the Peking Y.M.C.A. secretaries, the Chihli Provincial Capital Young Men's Christian Association was organized with twenty-five charter members. Upon the expiration of my contract with the Provincial College, I accepted a call from the International Committee to help in this work.

… They are awaiting the arrival of Hugh W. Hubbard, formerly physical director of the Tientsin Association, who was set aside by the American Board Mission for student work. … One of the most encouraging features of our work has been the cooperation of the missionaries. The membership grew to eighty and the Bible classes are growing rapidly.

… The first and greatest of the hindrances is the lack of a trained Chinese secretary. Another lack is the shortage of Chinese helpers who can teach Bible classes and the like.

Of course, personally, I am at a great disadvantage because of my lack of a sufficient knowledge of the language. During my three years at the Provincial College I used English entirely with the students, and though I read quite readily, I have had very little practice with the spoken language." [2]

THE LETTERS

Letter written by Edith to Rob's sister, Nan, in Iowa

Peitaiho, East Cliff / Aug. 3, 1913

We had a most interesting time last Wed. afternoon July 30. We were invited to a farewell tea given in honor of an old couple, Dr. and Mrs. Davis of the Methodist Mission, who have been out here thirty-two years. Besides their son and his wife, Rob and I were the only young couple there. We felt greatly honored to be allowed to be present at such a gathering. Most of those present had been out ten- fifteen- twenty- thirty- and even forty-eight years. When we think back over the history of each it makes us feel like a babe in arms. Dr. Goodrich, who has been out here forty-eight years, was six months in getting here the first time, and Oh! it is thrilling to hear him tell of things he has gone thru. Dr. Gamewell did more at the time of the Peking siege than any other one man in protecting themselves. He had charge of the fortifications. Mr. Goforth and his family had a most terrible time to get to the coast from Honan in 1900. And so it goes thru the entire company of veterans.

Letter written by Rob to his sister Celia

Peitaiho / Aug. 13, 1913

This week has been a rainy one and cool, but today is hot and dry. There have been big rains all over this province, Shantung and Honan. Both the Peking-Hankow and the Tientsin-Nanking railways are closed because of washouts. It is reported that the big Yellow River Bridge which was over a year in building and over 50 miles of track were washed out south of Paotingfu, but I think that's probably exaggerated as it came from Chinese sources. They had three or four days straight of rain at Paofu and washed out the porch of our house in the college, but that will not bother us as we are going to live in the house in the Presbyterian Mission where we had lived the first six months after we were married. The mission has given it to us rent free as their contribution to the Y.M.C.A. Hugh Hubbard, who was formerly physical director of the Tientsin Y.M.C.A. and has been home the last three years in theological seminary, has also been set aside by the American Board Mission for Y.M.C.A. work at Paotingfu, so I'll have some help.

Marion Frank ('10, Grinnell) was over for supper the other night. She is in the Methodist Mission at Nanking, but is up here spending the summer with her uncle, Bishop Bashford. Ida Lewis, of the Methodist mission of Tientsin was over with her. She is the daughter of Bishop Lewis, who founded Morningside College [Iowa].

Letter written by Rob to his father in Iowa

Sunday, Aug. 17, 1913

The rebellion finally petered out this week when the Woosung forts at Shanghai surrendered to the Northern troops. Sun Yat Sen, Huang Hsing and the others have fled to Japan. Poor Dr. Sun, he is finding out that "evil communications corrupt good morals." Huang Hsing and the other self-seekers have used him as a cat's paw to get his followers on their side.

I suppose he'll be pardoned and allowed to come back, but I'm afraid the rest of the rebel leaders are likely to die of throat trouble if they venture back. I suppose it will take some time to bring the province where the fighting has been taking place back to order, but all organized resistance has been put down.

Mr. Killie whom Aunt Fannie Carpenter saw in Chicago used to live in the Presbyterian Mission at Paotingfu but had to go home on account of his health. He was one of the "Six Fighting Parsons" of the Peking Siege in 1900, so called, not because they fought, but because they had charge of keeping the fortifications built up and were really under fire more than the soldiers. In fact, I believe Mr. Killie has a medal for going out and bringing in a wounded soldier from the wall under heavy fire. He is a very dear friend of ours.

Letter written by Rob to his mother (Baby arrives!)

Peitaiho / Aug. 22, 1913

Karl David Gordon Clack arrived yesterday morning at 10:45 just nicely in time to be a birthday present to his grandmother [Rob's mother, Adda Clack]. He is not very fat but is big boned and quite tall so that he weighed over 7 ½ lbs. anyway.

I hope you got our cable all right. I sent it yesterday at 2 o'clock and as our time is 14 hours ahead of yours Dad ought to have found it waiting for him when he arrived at his office. I sent it to Mason City as that is a registered international cable office and Clear Lake is not.

Letter written by Rob to his sister Nan

Peitaiho / Sept 8, 1913

Well, the summer is over and we have to begin to think about getting home. We will leave Thursday morning for Tientsin, stay there over Sunday and then go home Monday. We will stay with the Cunninghams three or four days until we can get our stuff moved over.

I am sending you an account of a trip Mr. Van Norden (formerly Editor of Van Norden's Magazine), who was out here a couple of years ago wrote about a trip he took with Mr. Thwing, the man with whom Karl [Edith's brother] is associated. It is very well written and gives you a good idea of the country North of Peking and West of here. I thought you would find it interesting.

Bishop Lewis preached here yesterday. He is the founder of Morningside College, you know. He is now Bishop of Foochow. He just got back from a money raising trip home.

We have traded our organ for a Victrola and we are just going to gorge ourselves with music this fall. That is the one thing a person misses out here more than anything else, the lack of good concerts. When we come home on our vacation we'll try to make up for lost time. I'll send you a list of what records we have when we see what we've got.

Letter written by Rob to his sister Celia

Paotingfu / Sept. 22, 1913

We left Peitaiho a week ago Thursday. We stayed over in Tientsin till Monday to give Edith and Gordon a chance to rest up good. Miss Harris stayed with us till Sunday, which was a great help. Monday morning we went on to Peking, had a four hour rest there and then came on to Paotingfu, getting here at dark, just in time for the beginning of the eclipse of the moon.

Anyone would have thought there was a great celebration going on from the noise when we arrived. You know the Chinese always pound drums and gongs during an eclipse in order to scare away the dog which is eating the moon.

We are beginning to get our Association work going again. I went out to the Veterinary College Saturday night and organized a Bible class there. There were thirty-one joined out of seventy-five students in the school. Of course, it's an easy school to work in for the Director and several of the students are Christians. Mr. Cunningham also has a class of forty in the Normal School, and we have had calls to start classes in three or four other schools already. We'll probably start some English classes next week at the Y.M.C.A. building.

I have to go out with Mr. Hu, our treasurer, this afternoon to call on the city officials and see how much money we can get out of them. The International Committee in New York pays the salaries of the foreigners, but the other expenses of the Association have to be raised here, and we have about $600 gold to raise this year. For the next year or two I have to give half my time to language study, so you see I'll be kept pretty busy. I'm also working now on some Bible study courses which will help to fill in the time when I'm resting.

Letter written by Edith to Rob's mother

Paotingfu, N. China / Oct. 6, 1913

Rob is so very busy these days that I am afraid he isn't going to get time to write his home letter this week, so I will have to do it for him. Rob has to go into the city and teach a class in English from 6 to 8 o'clock every evening but Sunday. He is there now, and Gordon and I are all alone. We have dinner after Rob gets back. It just occurred to me that it would be nice for you to have a list of the foreigners here and where they live.

Presbyterian (or West Suburb)
    Dr. Maud Mackey
    Miss Gumbrell
    Miss Newton
    Mr. and Mrs. Mather and little son Brewster
    Mrs. Burroughs (is Mrs. Mather's mother)
    Mr. and Mrs. Whallon
    Dr. and Mrs. Lewis and their children John and Anne.
    Mr. and Mrs. Cunningham
    Mr. and Mrs. Clack and Gordon
American Board (South Suburb)
    Mr. and Mrs. Galt
    Mr. and Mrs. Price
    Mr. and Mrs. Hubbard
    Mrs. King
    Miss Phelps
    Mr. and Mrs. McCann and their four children are expected back about Xmas.

Mr. Long lives in Normal School in the North Suburb.

Letter written by Rob to his sister Ida

Paotingfu / Oct. 14, 1913

I didn't get any time to write you Sunday or yesterday, but cut out my Chinese lesson this morning and got time that way. I'm even busier than ever these days as Mr. Cunningham has gone to Shanghai for a month, which throws his two Bible classes and the management of the religious services of the Y.M.C.A. over on to me. However, we are expecting Hubbard to arrive the first of next week, which will lighten things up a trifle.

Gordon continues to thrive. Did I tell you that the servants call him "Hsiao Yeh" (the little grandfather)? That's the regular Chinese expression for the son of one of the upper class. Our sewing woman calls him "the white baby."

Letter written by Edith to Rob's sister Nan

Paotingfu, N. China / Oct. 20, 1913

Mr. and Mrs. Hubbard came last Sat. We are going to have them over to tiffin tomorrow. He came home from meeting with Rob yesterday afternoon. He looks the same as ever. They were leading spirits in our crowd that first summer at Peitaiho when Rob and I met. They were only engaged then. Were married last Xmas. We are very fond of them and are so glad to have them here at Paofu. Mr. Hubbard is an expert at telling yarns, too. I wish you could meet all our friends out here.

Letter written by Rob to his sister Celia

Paofu / Oct. 26, 1913

We've been quite dissipated this week. Had guests to tiffin twice. Tuesday the Hubbards were over and Friday we had Mr. and Mrs. Mather, Mrs. Burroughs (Mrs. Mather's mother) and Mrs. Cunningham over. Mr. Cunningham has gone to Shanghai to attend the China Council of Presbyterian Churches. Has been gone about a month, but will be back this week. I'll certainly be glad to have him back, as I depend on him so much to help me in my work. He is the man who a year ago thought that Y.M.C.A. work was not worthwhile. However, when the students from the Y.M.C.A. classes began to come to him in large numbers applying for admission to the church, he changed his mind and now gives more time to the Y.M.C.A. than any two of the other missionaries.

My work certainly keeps me busy. My regular daily schedule is about as follows: 8-12 study Chinese, 1-4 write letters, pay calls, work on Bible lessons, and any other administration work that comes up, 4-6 tea and recreation (except that I don't get much time for the recreation), 6-8 English classes, after which I can go home and get my supper just in time to get to bed. After this though Hubbard will take the English classes twice a week so I'll have two days off. I also have three Bible classes of my own each week besides substituting on and off for the other teachers. I don't lack for something to keep me busy.

The Y.M.C.A. is going to give a big reception for Hubbard and me on Tuesday. All members are invited, and besides all the officials are coming. It's really to be quite a swell affair.

Letter written by Edith to her mother (in China)
Paotingfu, N. China / Nov. 3, 1913

    We had General and Mrs. Chang with us over Sat. night. He is the President of the National Anti-Opium Society. He came down to lecture for the Y.M.C.A. so of course they stopped here. He has just returned from a trip to England in the interests of the Anti-Opium Society. I guess his mission was not so very successful. He is a southerner but his wife is Pekingese. They were very pleasant people. This was the first time Mrs. Chang had ever been away from Peking. She is just my age. We enjoyed having them here so much.

Letter written by Rob to his father
Paotingfu / Nov. 3, 1913

    The Y.M.C.A. had a reception Tuesday for Hubbard and me. All the big city officials were there. They seemed to be very much interested. I wonder if they will be so interested when we send our subscription blank around to them.
    General Chang, of the Board of War, was here Saturday and Sunday. He came down here to give a lecture and brought is wife with him and they stopped with us. He is President of the National Anti-Opium Society and has just returned from England where he spent several months trying to get the British government to give the Chinese some show to get rid of the opium traffic. He speaks English very well, but his wife who has never been out of Peking before doesn't speak any. However, as she is pure Pekingese we could get along all right. We never have much trouble understanding anybody from this province, but from some of the other provinces it's an entirely different language. The other day an official from Kweichow (one of the southern provinces) called at the Y.M.C.A. to see about his son studying English. I had to call in one of the other Chinese to translate, and he finally had to call in the official's little son, who speaks both Kweichou and Pekingese, before he could understand.
    Mr. Hu, the Postal Inspector, who has done most of the work in organizing the Y.M.C.A., has been transferred to Shuntêfu, the next Fu city on the railroad south. He doesn't leave till the end of the month, but his wife and little girls left today. They were both very popular both among the Chinese and foreigners and there was a huge crowd at the station to see them off.

Letter written by Rob to his mother
Paofu / Nov. 10, 1913

    I sent off those little presents for Dad to give away this week. There were two parcels, one, a wooden box containing five little gilded mud images of the Goddess of Mercy; one little Buddha in a wooden case; two glass scent bottles painted on the inside, one string of Mandarin beads in a blue cloth box, 5 little embroidered silk scent bags; 3 little brass boxes, one imitation jade ring; two little stone lions on pedestals; one porcelain shoe just the size the Chinese ladies wear, one little China box with a cover; one red porcelain ink well; two little Chinese vases. That parcel is worth about $3 gold. The other parcel contains 12 pairs Mandarin squares, six pairs of embroidered cuffs; and two embroidered handkerchief cases, value about $4 gold.

I am enclosing a copy of the new Chinese Constitution which has just been established. It gives the President a great deal more power than he had under the Provisional Constitution and is a great victory for Yüan all around. He has struck while the iron is hot, too. Last week he issued an order expelling all members of the Kuo Min Tang (the political party which engineered last summer's revolt in Central China) from the National Assembly and they were immediately visited by the police and their election certificates taken away. Also any who stirs up any trouble will be immediately arrested and dealt with as traitors. It was quite a drastic step, but was fully justified by the situation and most of the people are behind Yüan, so it greatly strengthens his hand.

This leaves Parliament without a quorum until new members can be elected (which will not be till January or February) and meanwhile Yüan, under the Constitution has almost the powers of a dictator. It is just what the country needs, as now he can restore order without being continually hampered by Parliament. They have been absolutely worthless so far; the only business they have done in their six month's session is to vote themselves excessive salaries. This delaying the game has been almost entirely caused by the Kuo Min Tang, too; so they ought to get along better now.

Letter written by Rob to sister Ida

Nov. 17, 1913 (Monday)

Last Tuesday was quite an exciting day on this compound. In the morning Dr. and Mrs. Wampler arrived from America. They are Virginians and he just graduated from Rush [Rush Medical College, Chicago] last spring, and has been appointed doctor for the Dunkard Mission at Pingtingchou over in Shansi. They decided that instead of having him take his internship in Chicago, where he could sit back thirty or forty feet and watch the surgeons operate several times a week, they would send him out here and let him help Dr. Lewis for a year, where he can begin doing many of the minor operations himself immediately and can help in anywhere from three to eight major operations a day, besides picking up considerably more Chinese than he would in Chicago. They both seem to be very nice people.

Then we had Mrs. King and Miss Phelps over from the American Board for tiffin, and in the afternoon had another arrival at the compound, an English lady, who has written several books and is now writing another. She is a typical English old maid, pug dog and all.

Then later in the afternoon we had still another arrival, Mr. Richard Brewster Mather, weight nine pounds, so Gordon's nose is out of joint, he's no longer the youngest member of the Paotingfu foreign community. Both Mrs. Mather and the baby are getting along fine. This compound has certainly improved since I came to Paotingfu. Then there were no children here, now there are two little Lewises, two little Mathers and a little Clack, four boys and a little girl.

Chang P'ei Chih, Chinese secretary of the Peking Y.M.C.A. was here over Sunday to give a lecture and stayed with us. He's great fun. He doesn't talk English, but speaks the purest kind of Pekingese and is very easy to understand, so we enjoyed very much having him here.

I'm going up to Peking Saturday [November 22] to attend the annual dinner of the American College Club. Mr. Reinsch, the new minister who has just arrived, is to be the guest of honor.

Letter written by Edith to Rob's mother

Paotingfu, N. China / Nov. 26, 1913

I just received a card from our friends Mr. and Mrs. Nowack. They came out to China on the same boat Mother and I came on the first time. I will repeat word for word what she wrote:

Nov. 23
"Dear Edith,
Our consul has ordered us to leave at once. Robbers are rampant everywhere. It is terrible the damage they do. Could you tell us if we could rent rooms there furnished or unfurnished? At what price? Have written several parties. Our lives are indeed in great danger. A speedy reply will be welcomed. Would bring 3 servants and our family of seven.
Sincerely yours, Katherine Nowack, Pi Yang Hsien, Honan."

So we must rush around tomorrow and see if we can possibly find them a place. I am so anxious about them. The robbers are something awful off there in that district. They are two days and a half (west) from the railroad. I hope and trust nothing serious happens to them.

Letter written by Rob to his sister, Nan

Paofu / Dec. 1, 1913

We had a busy time the past two weeks. A week ago Thursday we had a big Chinese Feast in honor of Mr. Hu of the Post Office who has been transferred to Peking. I don't know how we are going to get along without him in the Y.M.C.A. as he has been the backbone of it from the Chinese side right along. Perhaps, though, it will be good for the other fellows as it will give them a better chance to develop.

Then Saturday I went to Peking to attend the annual dinner of the American College Club. There were over 200 present – about half Chinese graduates of American schools and the other half Americans. The dinner was in honor of Mr. Reinsch, the new minister. There was only one other Grinnell man there, Dr. Adams, advisor to the Board of Communications. He was considerably before my time though, having graduated in '74. Mr. Reinsch has made a great hit already. He called together a meeting of the leading missionaries and the Y.M.C.A. secretaries in Peking last Monday and told them he would do anything in his power to help them. He also announced that the American government, in its dealings with the Chinese government, was to be governed by the same code of ethics as obtained between gentlemen in their dealings with each other. This is certainly quite a contrast to the stand the European powers have taken, and it has already greatly increased the already strong friendship the Chinese have developed for the Americans.

Wednesday noon Mr. Brockman, Senior Secretary of the National Committee of the Y.M.C.A., who has just returned from a six month's campaign in America, came and stayed until Thursday afternoon. We put in a mighty busy twenty-four hours making plans and stirring up the Chinese a little. Mr. Brockman's secretary, Mr. Wilson, a young fellow just out, was with him.

We got off our Christmas parcels this week. The pair of brass candlesticks are for Dad and mamma. The vase is for Melville and the small ink jar is for Ray and Gladys. It is small, but is very old. The Peacock feathers are for you girls, one each. They are what were originally worn by high officials on their hats and were worth $50 or $60 dollars apiece, but now since the country is a Republic they have depreciated amazingly. Edith has a hat trimmed with them and thought you would like some. [see photo on back cover]

Letter written by Rob to his sister Celia Paotingfu / Dec. 15, 1913

We have decided not to go to Tientsin after all. The trip would be so hard on Gordon [4 months old], and we didn't like to spend the money, besides. Then Edith is helping to bring a little eight weeks old baby who pretty nearly starved to death back to life, and doesn't like to leave him. His father is a Y.M.C.A. secretary now in Peking studying the language, and his mother almost died when he was born and is still pretty sick though entirely out of danger. Of course she couldn't feed him, so finally they sent him down here to see if Doctor Mackey could do anything. She got a Chinese woman, who washes for the hospital and has a baby eight months old, to give him five feedings a day, and Edith gives him one, and then during the night they feed him from a bottle. Though he hadn't gained a bit in the eight weeks before they brought him down [from Peking to Paotingfu], now he has gained ten ounces in four days and has perked up wonderfully. He is still mostly bones, however. Gordon doesn't seem to miss the extra feeding a bit.

Letter written by Edith to her mother Paotingfu, N. China / Dec. 22, 1913

No, it is not Charley Stanley's baby I am helping, but Rubert Stanley of the Y.M.C.A. They have only been out a year, and since the baby came she [Mrs. Stanley] has been desperately ill, and for a while they feared for both their lives. Now they are both out of danger and we are so grateful. The baby gained a pound last week and Sat. evening he smiled up at me so sweetly. He looks and acts so much better.

Letter written by Rob to his father Paotingfu / Christmas Day 1913

We were awakened this morning by the boys from the Boy's school singing a Chinese Christmas carol under our window. The tune however was quite English, and it made us think of the old English stories we used to read when we were little. The Chinese have so little that is really good in the holiday line, that the Christians make a great deal of Christmas, and it is surprising how many of our good old Anglo-Saxon customs they have adopted. For example just imagine a Chinese Santa Claus. We made the acquaintance of one yesterday, only he was a woman. Dr. Mackey had a Christmas tree yesterday afternoon for the babies of the compound, that is, the babies of the servants and mission helpers, and all the little foreign babies were invited, too. We took Gordon over and left him upstairs with one of the nurses, while we attended the ceremonies for him. The nurses had charge of the affair and they had a fine tree fixed up, candles and all. There were about twenty of the Chinese babies present and I wish you could have seen them stare at the tree.

(breaking here while we go over to the church to see a wedding)

Just returned from the wedding. The church was crowded. They followed the foreign service very closely; had a best man and a bridesmaid, and the bride wore a veil and a gorgeous green skirt. I also got a picture of the church decorations which I'll send next week. I'll bet that you never knew that there were Chinese angels, but as soon as you see this picture, you will know that there are, slant eyes and all.

Did Mr. Marzoff see Mr. Ewing in Kansas City? We know him very well indeed. His daughter used to live with Edith in Tientsin, so that she could go to the English school as their home was out at Hsiku, 7 miles out. I stayed with Mr. Ewing the last day or two before we were married, and he was at the wedding.

**Dr. and Mrs. Chauncey Goodrich – Missionary with
the American Board of Commissioners for Foreign Missions**

Members of the Paotingfu Presbyterian Church
(Dr. Goodrich standing on far right)

An 'angel' in the Presbyterian Church (photo Christmas Day 1913)

14   End of First Full Year with the Y.M.C.A.

Highlights: January-June 1914

⌘ The letters from January through June 1914 cover the second half of Rob's first year as General Secretary of the newly-formed Y.M.C.A. in Paotingfu. He continued to teach Bible classes and also an English class in order to meet students to bring them into the church and the Y.M.C.A.

⌘ A few of the letters in January mention that Edith's brother, Moore Gordon, visited Rob's family in Iowa during Christmas 1913.

⌘ At the end of June, Rob attended the Y.M.C.A. Wo Fo Ssŭ Conference in Peking while Edith and baby Gordon were summering in Peitaiho.

⌘ Edith's brother, Karl Gordon, was living in Peking during this time. One of his letters is included toward the end of this chapter. Also included are a few paragraphs written later by Edith's mother, Elma Butler Gordon, in her "Memoir" about her life in China.

THE LETTERS

Letter written by Rob to his mother

Paotingfu / Jan 4, 1914

    Tuesday night we had a Victrola Concert for all the people on the compound and their guests. There were three people from Peking. We gave them *Poet and Peasant Overture* from "William Tell"; *The Bedouin Love Song*; *Amaryllis*; Schubert's *Ave Maria* played by Maud Powell; *The Rosary* by Schuman-Heink; *The Pilgrim Chorus*; *Hymn to the Evening Star*; *Sing Me to Sleep*; Chopin's *Funeral March*; *Kennst du das Land* from Mignon; *Träumerei* by Maud Powell; *Absent*; and the *Hallelujah Chorus*.

    Thursday was New Year's Day, and I had quite a lot of callers. The Chinese make much more of New Year's calls than even the English, but except for those who are in official positions or who have been in contact with foreigners they do their calling at the Chinese New Year time, (from three to six weeks after ours). The cutest callers we had were Elder Li's two children (a boy of eight and a girl of six) and three of their playmates. It was awfully funny to see them; none of their elders could have been more punctilious about observing all the "li" (a very good Chinese word which can't be exactly expressed in English but means practically every formal thing which ought to be done). Then there were a bunch of children from the hospital, who were not so punctilious as to their "li" but whose avowed purpose was the getting of the cakes which were served to all callers.

    The schools all reopen again this week and all of our Bible classes will be resumed. Also I am going to teach English two hours a week at the Agricultural College. It will give me a good chance to get a hold on the students over there. There will remain then only three of the twelve colleges and High schools of the place where we haven't some foothold, and I think we can get into them all right before Mr. Eddy comes next fall. We certainly have been wonderfully fortunate in our work, as we have brought about thirty government school students into the church since we started our work a year ago, which is several times more than all the previous years together. And we have as many more who are enrolled as probationers and will probably be received before summer.

Letter written by Rob to his sister Ida

Paotingfu / Jan. 15, 1914

The books from you and Nan came last week. Thank you both ever so much. We read "The Spoilers" Sunday. It certainly keeps you keyed up, so that you can't put it down till you finish. Then Edith read the "Blue Flower" to me while I was laid up. It is quite the opposite to "The Spoilers", so soothing and sweet. I never get tired of "The Other Wise Man." I guess I've read it twenty times and each time I like it better. I don't think there is anything in English literature that surpasses it, either in subtlety of thought, or beauty of style.

Roy sent word the other day that Bill Zeigler could have his place at Pei Yang next year if he wanted it. Bill wrote me several weeks ago that he'd like to come out here, so I sent his letter on to Roy, and President Wang, of the University, seemed to be much pleased with the chance to get him. I wonder if he'll bring Isabel Rutledge with him if he comes out. He told me in his letter that he'd just been to see her.

Letter written by Rob to his sister Nan

Paotingfu / Jan. 19, 1914

We got our books last week. Have read the "Tinder Box" and thought it was fine. We have just started the "Judgment House", but it certainly starts off promising. Thank you ever and ever so much. I don't know how we would ever keep up with what is doing in the book line if it wasn't for you girls, as they don't have American books out here much. The foreign business houses are mostly British. I have a firm in Shanghai from whom I can get standard American books, but they are not up much on the new ones.

Yesterday was quite a holiday for the Chinese. It was the day of the ascent of the Kitchen god. In all the non-Christian homes they have a big paper idol which is kept on the wall above the stove. He is supposed to keep track of the deeds of all the members of the family and to report them to the Emperor of Heaven once a year. He goes up eight days before the New Year (Chinese, of course), and does not come back till New Year's day, so that for that period the people may do as they please without fearing any but earthly punishment. They have a way, however, of getting ahead of the kitchen god, for the day before his trip they feed him a lot of very sticky candy, so that he can't get his mouth open to tell on them. Of course, the candy costs money, but the thrifty Chinaman can easily overcome that, so he doesn't feed the idol real candy, but makes paper candy which looks just like the real article and eats the real himself. This is just as good, for the Chinese gods are much inferior to human beings in intelligence and so are easily fooled. The god is sent to Heaven by taking him out and burning him, and he comes back when the families go out and buy a new one. I asked Li Chang if the people really thought that was true. "Well," he said, "If you believe it, it's true," which philosophy I was unable to gainsay.

Officially, of course, the old calendar is no longer recognized, but I notice that the people in general are making just as big preparations as ever for the celebration, which comes a week from today. They have one very fine custom. Everybody is supposed to pay his debts before the

New Year, and if a creditor can't find his debtor then, the debtor can let the account run for another year and not lose any face over it. However, you frequently see creditors running around ten or eleven o'clock New Year's morning carrying a lantern looking for their debtors. The theory is that if the man carries a lantern he doesn't know that it is daylight yet, so it is still the Old Year, and if he finds the debtor, he has to pay.

Letter written by Rob to his father

Paotingfu / Feb. 2, 1914

I was telling my Chinese teacher about the groundhog today and he said that he could remember his grandmother telling him a similar story about some kind of bird when he was a little boy. I'd like to be able to trace down the connection between the two. I've heard that the American story came originally from the Indians, and they certainly were originally Chinese. You see typical American Indians here all the time.

The Chinese are gradually getting settled down again after their New Year's. The country people celebrate it just exactly the same as before; I don't suppose most of them even know that there is a foreign calendar. But things have changed here in the city. Formerly they kept all the shops closed for two weeks, but they have most of them been reopened now, and it is only a week since New Year's Day.

Did I tell you that Bill Zeigler had been offered Roy's place in Tientsin? I don't know whether he'll accept or not, but I think he will, as he wrote me some time ago that he wanted to come to China. I have written him that if he does come he must come early and spend the summer with us at Peitaiho.

I want you to be sure to send us a good supply of seeds this year. You better send them right away, as it will be about time to get them in when they get here. We would like sugar corn, field corn, radishes, onions, cauliflower, tomatoes, celery, lettuce, cabbage, etc. We have some land here we can use, and also the servants have some land they'll be glad to raise foreign vegetables on and sell to us at the regular market rate, which is about one tenth what they cost at home.

Letter written by Rob to his mother

February 15, 1914

We have company for over Sunday. Drusie Malott, who belongs to a mission in southern Honan, has been in Tientsin all fall and winter, but is just returning to her station, and being an old friend of Edith's, stopped off over Sunday with us. She is a little bit of a woman, only a trifle over four feet tall, but is an expert stenographer and has been helping out at the Business Agency in Tientsin.

Yüan Shih K'ai is beginning to show who is boss. He has abolished the Provincial Assemblies, which really is a fine thing for the country as the Assemblies didn't do much except borrow money for their members to squeeze and plan uprisings which would give them a little more power so they could borrow more money. This makes Yüan practically Dictator, though he has gathered together a number of the strongest men of the country into a sort of Administrative Council. We are all hoping and praying that he'll keep his power as he will be able to bring some order out of the chaos if he has time enough. The Chinese, except a few foreign educated students who have lost their chances for graft, are very well satisfied with the stand Yüan is taking. The great mass of the people never were in sympathy with the sweeping reforms the Young China Party tried to introduce, anyway. All they ask is to be let alone, and Yüan is very wise to change the old order as slowly as possible. He is certainly a wonderful man. Though he hasn't made nearly the splurge that Sun Yat Sen made, there is no comparison between the abilities of the two. Sun is a little too much on the Dickie Kabrick order, great on theories but small on practice.

The White Wolf [*Bai Lang*] still continues his rampage south of the Yellow River. He has made a bad mistake now, however. He has become so bold that he has left his mountains in western Honan and gone across the plain into Anhui, where it will be easy to cut off his retreat and surround him. They are preparing a big army to send against him now. It is to be commanded by General Chang Hsün who captured Nanking and looted it after the rebellion last summer. While Chang isn't much of a man otherwise, he is a good fighter, and I think the White Wolf's days are numbered.

I had a nice letter from the man who pays my salary yesterday. His name is John B. Lord, of the Ayer & Lord Tie Company, Railroad Exchange Building, Chicago. If any of you are in Chicago he would probably like to have you call on him.

Letter written by Rob to his sister Ida

Paotingfu / March 1, 1914

I didn't get a letter written last week. It seems as if the only possible way I can get a letter written Sunday is to stay home from church, which I am doing today. Last Sunday was a specially busy day. It was the Day of Prayer for students, so we had a little extra in our services. Then besides, I had to lead the foreign service after having three others in a row, two of which I had to lead, one of them in Chinese, which is a lot harder work. I just gave them an address of John R. Mott's on "Intercession". I've had a little more to do than usual the past two weeks because our Chinese secretary was called to Chefoo by sickness in the family.

Letter written by Rob to his father

Paotingfu / Mar. 30, 1914

I didn't get a letter off last week as I was in Peking from Saturday to Wednesday and was too busy there. I received word the first of the week that Mr. Messer, general secretary of the Chicago Y.M.C.A. was to be there on his trip around the world so a conference was called for North China. Hubbard and [H.L.] Sun and I all went up; the two secretaries from Chinanfu came; four American and nine Chinese secretaries from Tientsin and the fourteen foreign and fourteen Chinese secretaries from Peking most of whom, however, are only in Peking for language study and training, so they represented Kaifêngfu, Taiyüanfu, Kirin and Mukden besides. Then Brockman, Pettys, Crocker and Wilson of the National Committee of Shanghai were there, and Birks of Montreal so we had quite a formidable gathering. Mr. Messer gave seven addresses on the methods they use in Chicago where he has been for over twenty-five years, and each was followed by half an hour or so of general questions and discussions.

I also got a chance for a long personal talk with him which was very helpful; as I am supported by the Chicago Association, or rather by one of the members, Mr. J.B. Lord. When I go home on furlough I will spend some time there in Chicago helping them to work up interest in foreign work, and incidentally getting some pointers on the latest methods.

Letter written by Rob to his mother

Paotingfu / Apl 6, 1914

This last week has been a rather strenuous one. Mr. and Mrs. Burgess came down from Peking Thursday for a short visit. Mr. Burgess went back this morning, but she is going over to stay with Mrs. Whallon till Thursday. Mr. Burgess has charge of the student work in Peking and the Summer Conference and was getting pretty well tired out, so wanted to get a few day's rest. They have a lot harder time of it in Peking than we do here, as there is always a string of globe trotters butting in on them, and besides there are so many other foreigners there that the social burden is rather heavy as the Association has to keep in touch with all the different interests.

Mr. and Mrs. Guttery, who just came out to the language school last fall, were down over Sunday visiting the Lewises, too, and we had them in to tiffin today. They are very nice people.

Edith and I went over to the hospital and were vaccinated last week. We don't have smallpox scares out here as the Chinese always have it. They regard it as just as necessary as chicken pox used to be regarded in America. I think that at least fifty out of every hundred Chinese is pockmarked, and the rest have all had it.

I guess we wrote you about the English authoress who has been staying at the Lewis's this winter, Mrs. Mary Gaunt. She set off today on a trip overland to Kashgar, the farthest western city of China. She will be the first white woman who has made the trip. One of my former students is going as interpreter, and our best mason is to act as guide. It's rather risky starting out now as they have to pass just north of Sianfu where the White Wolf [*Bai Lang*] is now operating, but I think they'll get through all right. If you see any of her books advertised you might find them interesting.

Letter written by Rob to his sister Ida

Paotingfu / April 19, 1914

I didn't get my letter off last week again. Seems as if, if I can't get it in Sunday morning at church time I don't get it written at all, as my Sunday afternoons are full up. I have a Bible Class from the Agricultural College from 1:30 to 2:30; Y.M.C.A. prayer meeting 2:30 to 3:30, Bible Class from Yü Tê Middle School 3:30 to 4:30 and another from the Industrial College from 4:30 to 5:30, and by that time I'm too tired to do any writing. It would be a hard afternoon's work in English, but in Chinese it's lots worse.

We are going to take Gordon to Tientsin Wednesday to see his Grandma Gordon. I expect we'll stay a week, and Karl will be down from Peking over Sunday with us.

The All British Sports come off Saturday, and this year the Americans have organized a track team and are going to try to win them, so I am going to "put the shot" for them. We have a number of mighty good men. Walker, of the Anglo-Chinese College, did 6 ft 3 in. in the high jump last year; Porter, of the American Board Mission at Tungchou, used to run the hurdles at

Yale and I guess Roy will help him out. Hunter, of the Peking Y.M.C.A., was a member of the Illinois mile relay team who broke the world's record last year; and Howell, of the Peking Y.M.C.A., used to run the mile at Princeton. Besides that I suppose there will be a number of American soldiers enter, though they have never done anything much before.

We are expecting to spend one day with Roy and Lynne, as they will be leaving in less than two months so I expect we won't see them again. Monday evening we are going to a band concert by the German Military Band from Tsingtao, so you see we'll have quite a gay time of it. We are expecting to stop in Peking a day on the way back.

Letter written by Edith to Rob's father
Paotingfu, N. China / May 17, 1914 [Sunday]

We have just had Mr. Jenkins, the business manager of the International Y.M.C.A. office in N.Y. City, with us for a day. He was accompanied by Mr. Wilbur of the Shanghai Y.M.C.A.. They were both such nice men. Mr. Jenkins is looking over all the stations out here and seeing in what way things can be improved. He has one plan that we sincerely hope may be put thru. It is having each secretary stay out only three years and then spend six full months in the homeland. Won't that be fine? Of course, that won't affect us this time, but it will afterwards. I will have been out in China eight years and a half when we start home. I certainly will be behind the times, won't I?

Letter written by Edith to her mother
Paotingfu, N. China / June 2, 1914

Miss Paxton was here over Sunday, to see if we couldn't get a Y.W.C.A. started here. We organized our Executive Committee while she was here. Mrs. Hubbard, Mrs. Mather and myself are the foreigners on it. I don't know who are the Chinese. We wanted to have Mr. Eddy speak to the women as he does to the men, and after his meetings we want to get them into Bible classes.

Rob was just telling me tho' that it is doubtful if Mr. Eddy will come here this trip as the Missions feel they couldn't take care of the results of the meetings, but that isn't decided yet.

Letter from Karl Gordon (Edith's brother) to Rob's sister in Iowa
Peking, China / June 24, 1914

My dear Miss Clack:

Rob sent me your note of May 11th a few days ago. I am glad that you disposed of so much of the goods you had on hand & I want you to feel that you are entitled to the few things you have left. I feel that I did very well on the small amount I invested & I trust your share of the profits made it worthwhile for the time you spent selling the goods.

I have been thinking that I would send you a small parcel of Chinese *cloisonné*, but as it is expensive stuff & easily damaged I have hesitated to do so. I fear the American people would not appreciate it. Altho' I think it is far superior to the Japanese product. They make all sorts of articles such as napkin rings, salt cups, pepper shakers, paper knives, card cases & trays, pen holders, ink stands, vases all sizes and shapes, etc. They are very beautifully designed & coloured. No doubt Rob has sent you some pieces, so you know what it is. When in San Francisco & Los Angeles I looked for it, but could find only the Japanese. Napkin rings can be delivered to at 30¢ & 80¢ each (two kinds). This does not include duty. Let me know what you think about sending a trial parcel.

You ask how soon I expect to go to America again. Well, if I keep well, not before 1920. I hope I may meet you & the rest of the family next time. I am glad Moore was able to meet you & I know you all liked him, but you must not judge the rest of us by him, for you will go a long way before you will find another man like my brothers Moore & Rob. I hope you & all the family are keeping well.

Yours faithfully, Karl M. Gordon

TRANSITIONAL SUMMARY

Written on August 23, 1914 by Edith's mother, Elma Butler Gordon, in her Memoir while at Peitaiho, China

Many things have happened to hinder me from writing more since July 20th last year. At that time Karl [Elma's son] had just returned to China, to help Rev. E.W. Thwing in his anti-opium work. Karl, Robert, Edith and I were pleasantly located at East Cliff for the summer. Little Karl David Gordon Clack joined us Aug. 21st. [1913 - Edith and Rob Clack's first child]

Early in July this year [1914], I came to this same spot again, and have my dear Mary Wood with me. She came from Nanking to work with me last November, and expected to go on to America at least by this October. She was a great help to me in my work in Tientsin, where I have a night Mission for the U.S. soldiers. I teach English to Chinese young men and boys during the afternoon, music afternoons to soldiers and Chinese, and hold services evenings – speak to the soldiers three evenings each week, and attend their Wednesday evening Prayer Meeting. All this in my school room which is open every evening to soldiers. A Dr. Whitmore, from the Y.M.C.A., gives them an hour every Monday night for Bible study.

First of July he [Dr. Whitmore] had to leave for America, and since then, Karl has that, and every other evening. Karl's year ended with Dr. Thwing, and he came to be in Tientsin with me, until such time as God should open other doors for him. Last November I opened my house as a stopping place for missionaries – some few came. Karl took charge of the home July 1st, as I was coming to Peitaiho. Shortly afterward the ladies of the American M.E. Mission asked him to help them. They are erecting a Hospital, a Girls School, and a Ladies' Home, and Karl superintends the work under the instructions of a fine architect. This gives him a few hours every a.m., and p.m., in the open air, besides giving him a reasonable salary, and gives him some valuable training in building. Some day he hopes to use that knowledge if God permits him to open an "Industrial Work" for Chinese.

Women's Hospital, Presbyterian Mission (photo 1914)

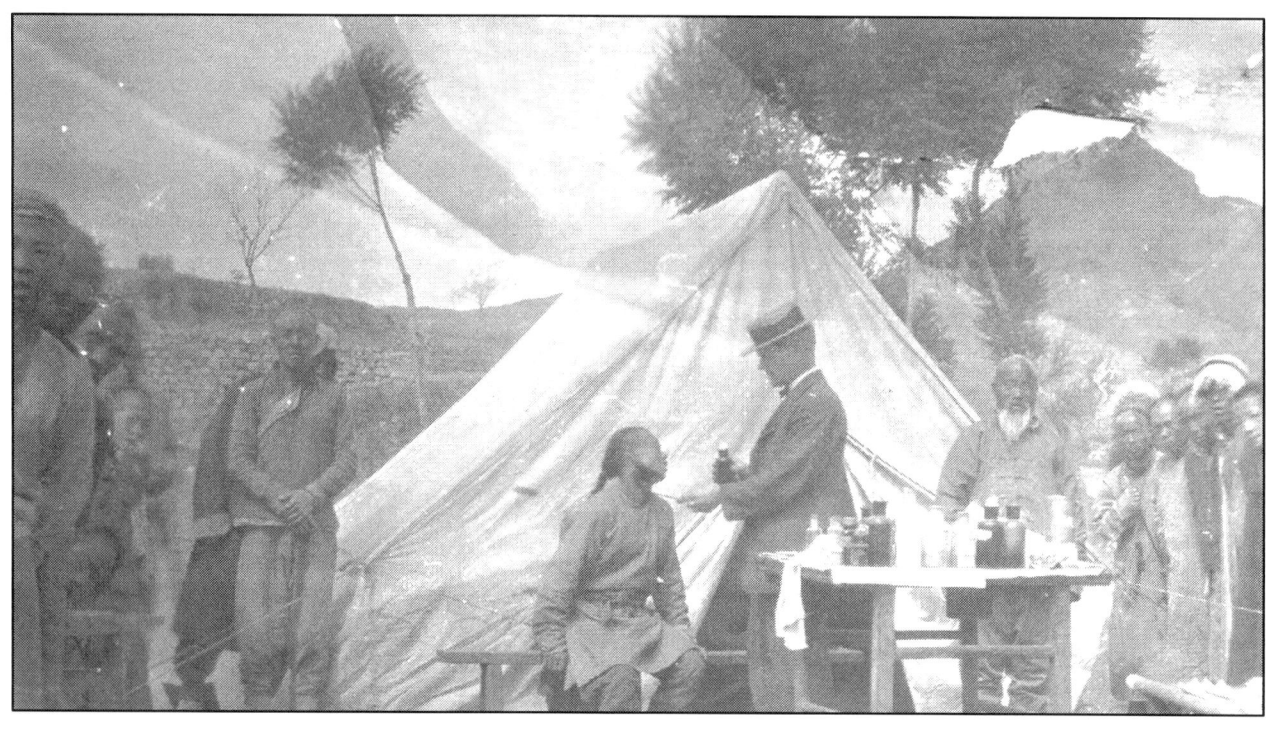

Paotingfu, Dr. Lewis, country clinic (photo 1914)

15 Beginning of Second Fiscal Year with the Y.M.C.A.

Highlights: July-December 1914

⌘ In June Rob took Edith and baby Gordon to Peitaiho, their usual summer vacation site. Edith and Gordon remained there while Rob attended Y.M.C.A. activities, including the Wo Fo Ssŭ Conference near Peking. This year Rob was the conference Treasurer and also taught a Bible class.

⌘ Edith's letter of September 14 to Rob's parents contained the first reference to what was to develop into the "Great War" (World War I) – "trouble in Shantung between the Germans and the Japs" and on October 5: "We are hoping that China will keep out of the fuss."
[Editor's note – China was neutral during the first three years of this worldwide military conflict and it was not until August 1917, that China declared war on Germany.]

⌘ By October Rob was occupied with starting Y.M.C.A. classes and training Chinese teachers for this work. In one school alone there were more than 100 students. He was also teaching English rugby, "Basket Ball", and "Volley Ball". Because Rob was so busy, Edith was doing most of the correspondence with family members.

Y.M.C.A. ANNUAL REPORT, PAOTINGFU
Year ended September 30, 1914
Written by Robert W. Clack, General Secretary (following are excerpts from the Report)

"Our Association has been in existence barely more than a year, so that the year has been in many ways only a trying out and training of the workers, and we could not expect a great amount of growth. A number of those who joined at the beginning allowed their memberships to lapse, and for several months during the winter we were not able to keep up with current expenses even, to say nothing of paying off the debt on our equipment. We have also had a number of extra expenses which we have been able to meet. Prof. Robertson was here for a lecture campaign in May; we sent a good delegation to the North China Student Conference in July, and the past week we have had another series of lectures by Prof. Robertson, followed by an evangelistic campaign led by Mr. Eddy.

- Staff – Several Chinese are being trained for this work. Mr. Hubbard will be free from his language study after this year, which will give me a chance to finish up my own study, and get some needed training along other lines. I also hope to be able to go to Peking or Tientsin for several months' training in Association methods.
- Student Conference – A number of the missionaries are helping us more and more with our work. One very encouraging feature of the past year's work was the increase in our delegation to the student conference at Wo Fo Ssŭ in July.
- Athletics – We were able to make a little start in athletics during the year. Mr. Hubbard and I went frequently to the Normal School for football and track. We had the satisfaction

of running off the "home meet" of eight events during the last week of school and had the first track meet ever held in Paotingfu.
- Religious Work – It is our religious work which has been the most encouraging. And again this fall the Bible classes were reopened at the request of the students themselves.

Hindrances – At present, our greatest problem is that of finance. I was finally able to convince the Board of Directors to borrow money on a joint personal note to pay up the debts of the Association. Mr. Eddy has raised the money for a building, and it seems very probable that we will have a site within a few weeks, but I recommend that no start be made toward building operations until all debts are paid, and a large enough income is pledged to keep the building running for a year or more after its completion." 3

THE LETTERS

Letter written by Rob to his sister Ida Peitaiho / July 14, 1914

We had a fine conference at Wo Fo Ssŭ. Had over two hundred present, of whom over two thirds were students. I was treasurer and had a Bible class besides so I was kept pretty busy. We came out in great shape on our finances. It cost us about $300 less than last year, with a larger number of delegates, too. We had twelve delegates from Paotingfu, as against one last year and the year before. I had the whole management of the conference the last two days as Burgess was called away and that left me senior secretary.

Well, I must stop as it is time for the milkman to come. He drives his cows around and I have to stand right over him to see that he washes off the cow and his hands properly and that everything is as clean as it can be made. That is the only way we dare to use the milk for Gordon without boiling it. He seems to be thriving on it so far.

Letter written by Rob to his sister Nan Peitaiho / Aug. 2, 1914

If you want to get operating experience you better come and live with us a while. Dr. Lewis never speaks of *operation*; it's always plural. He arranges about forty a week, and once this spring he did thirty-three in two days. He has only lost two patients since I have been in China, too. Both appendicitis, which had gone so far that the appendix had burst.

Mr. Stelle, who lives next to us had quite an experience week before last. He was going with a party of fellows on a trip to Jehol (pronounced about like this "rŭ her) north of Peking, where the Manchu emperors have their large family estate. They were going over a small mountain pass in a heavy rain when donkey got his foot caught in a crevice, and in endeavoring to extricate himself plunged over the cliff and they dropped fifty feet to the rocks below. It killed the donkey instantly but Mr. Stelle got off with a number of cuts and bruises and a broken rib, which wasn't discovered till yesterday after it was about well. He fell almost into a village and the people all thought he must be a special favorite of the gods, or he would have been killed.

Letter written by Rob to his sister Celia

Peitaiho / Aug. 10, 1914

I'm afraid you folks lost our last letter home, as the Siberian mail service stopped just after it was mailed, and I suppose our friends the Russians just dumped the mail bags in the nearest creek. We'll send all our letters via the Pacific now until this European war is over. The war comes pretty close to home to us here, as we had a large number of Germans here at Peitaiho who were called to Tsingtao to help defend it. It isn't certain yet that it will be attacked, but there is quite a large English and French force out here and they may decide to take it. The Germans think so at any rate, as they have ordered all foreigners to leave.

We had a mighty full week last week, and have another this week. Last Wednesday the Fitches of the Shanghai Y.M.C.A. had a big party and Thursday morning Fred Pyke, of the Tientsin Methodist Mission, and Frances Taft, of the Y.M.C.A. were married, and practically all of Peitaiho was invited to the reception. Then Friday we started the children's sports but had to stop in the middle for a big storm which lasted almost all night. The Garniers from East Cliff with their two babies stayed overnight with us, as it was too stormy for them to go home. Saturday we finished up the children sports and had a small field meet of our own beforehand.

Eddy came yesterday and is holding a series of meetings this week on Evangelism in preparation for the fall campaign. If today's meeting is any criterion we are to have a great series. If I am any judge the results of the campaign this fall will surprise the world, for humanly speaking, at any rate, there never was a campaign better planned and organized, or where the field was as ready.

The first meetings start in Tientsin in about five weeks, and then Peking and Paotingfu follow in order. Then Eddy goes to central China to Hankow, Wuch'ang, Changsha, Hangchow and Soochow. Then he goes to Fuchow, and from there conducts a campaign all over Fukien province (Ed Munson is the one in charge of it) then south to Amoy, Hong Kong and Canton, and then back to Shanghai and Nanking, ending up the first week in December. Robertson will precede him all around the circuit preparing the way.

Karl [Edith's brother] came up from Tientsin Saturday and will stay till tomorrow so he and Mother Gordon are spending the day over here. He is feeling much better since he left the Anti-Opium work. He is now spending most of his time supervising a lot of building for the Methodist Mission in Tientsin.

Letter written by Rob to his mother

Paotingfu / Aug. 31, 1914

Well, here we are home again, and mighty glad to be here. That's one of the great advantages of a vacation; you're always so glad to get back home. We left Peitaiho Wednesday morning and spent Thursday in Tientsin, and came on home Friday.

I'm sending the last pictures we had taken at Peitaiho. I hope they get to you all right, but the Post Offices in Tientsin have put out a notice that all parcels and registered letters will be accepted only at the sender's risk, so I suppose it's all a gamble whether any mail gets through or not. It ought not to take long, however, to drive all the Germans out of the Pacific and get all the boats running as usual again.

I found everything at the Y.M.C.A. in pretty good shape, though it will take me some days to get the odds and ends straightened out. I don't expect to take over the English classes or start Bible classes until next week, so that will give me a little breathing space. Then we'll plunge into preparations for the fall campaign, and I expect I'll be almost swamped from then on till almost Christmas time.

Letter written by Edith to Rob's sister Ida

Paotingfu, N. China / Sept. 14, 1914

It never occurred to me until just this minute that you people might be worrying about us because of the trouble in Shantung between the Germans and the Japs. That is a long way from here and we can't see that it will affect us personally in the least. We are awfully sorry that the Germans didn't turn Tsingtao over to the Chinese in the first place. Then they could have saved not only their "face" but their lives too. We very much fear that they will all be killed. They have sent all the women and children to Tientsin. Poor women, some of them haven't any means of support at all with their husbands taken from them.

One thing that will help the Germans out for the present at least is that the Yellow River has overflowed its banks and is miles wide, so the Japs who have landed troops north of the river are helpless to get at the Germans. And the Japs are rather afraid to attack from the sea as the Germans have mined everywhere. Oh! I think this war is horrible, but I try to think of it as little as possible.

Letter written by Edith to Rob's sister Nan

Paotingfu, N. China / Sept. 23, 1914

Ida asked in her letter if we could send some squares etc. and a brass tea-pot to her, but I think we will have to wait until this awful war is over, as things do get lost coming thru' Japan. After this war is over (if it ever is) she can write again and tell us just exactly what she wants and we will get them if we can. We can't get old brass tea-pots, but it is very easy to get old vases & incense burners etc. The old brass is certainly much finer than the new.

Letter written by Rob to his father

Paotingfu, N. China / Oct. 11th, 1914

Since writing last week we heard that Pres. Yüan's advisors had urged him to declare war on Japan because of their encroachments on China. But nothing has come of it as Yüan realizes, as all thinking people do, that nothing could possibly be gained, while very much indeed could be lost. Japan has taken lots of undue liberties with China under pretext of attacking the Germans, and we are all very provoked with them, nevertheless China will just have to endure the indignities, because if she did declare war the Japs would just take Manchuria right away and possibly Shantung too. My, I wonder if this horrible war will ever cease.

Letter written by Rob to his sister Nan

Paotingfu / Nov. 17, 1914

    We had a party Saturday for the Yü Tê (Nurture Virtue) Middle School Bible classes. There are three classes with about 110 students altogether. They came over led by their director, and we first showed them all over the compound, especially the hospital, and then they split up into classes, going to their teachers houses for tea (Lewis, Whallon and I each have a class). They seemed to enjoy themselves immensely, and were all eyes, for it was the first time most of them had ever been in a foreign house. We hope to have the other Bible classes over soon.

    Sunday evening we had Mr. Palmer, formerly in the Normal College, over for supper. He is now one of the Salt Commissioners. Salt is a government monopoly, you know, and pays a big tax of about $1.00 on the same amount, so you see the temptation to evade the tax is pretty strong. It is a little over a year since foreign commissioners (about 35 of them) were appointed to supervise the collection of the tax, but they are collecting over four times what was collected under the old regime. Most of the difference went into the pockets of the Chinese Officials. Yüan is certainly doing a lot to root out squeezing. He had one high official beheaded a few weeks ago for taking a bribe of $1,000. That method might free us of such episodes as the Lorimer affair in America.

    The Wamplers leave for their station (Pingtingchou, Shansi) next week, so we are having them in tonight. We will miss them a lot. They are Virginians, though he took his medical course at Rush [Medical College, Chicago].

    The package you sent Gordon has not yet arrived. I'm afraid the Japs took it. They have a habit of doing such things, you know. The amount they have stolen from the poor Chinese in Shantung under the pretense of acting against Ch'ingtao is something enormous. And the worst of it is, the Chinese can only protest, as they know that the Japs are just looking for a good excuse to take Manchuria and Shantung away from them.

Letter written by Rob to his father

Paotingfu / Dec. 7, 1914

    I didn't get time for a letter last week but have a few minutes now before I have to go over to the Normal College to help them with their English rugby. I haven't been over for three weeks, so I feel as if I had to go today. We have basketball started in three schools now. Whallon is teaching the boys in the Presbyterian school and I am helping those in the two Middle (High) schools. They had their first interscholastic game last week. The "Nurture Virtue" School (semi-private) beat the regular Government School 4 to 0. It was really a much better game than the score would indicate, for though they were perfectly rotten at throwing baskets, they did pretty well with their passing and teamwork.

    We had a great time Thanksgiving. All went to the Whallon's for dinner and then had service and supper at the South Suburb. Edith and Gordon rode over in a chair and also enjoyed the affair. The Burgesses and the two Misses Beard (teachers in the new American Children's School) came down for a few days. The Lewises, however, all went to Shuntêfu where Dr. Elizabeth is stationed. It's about 100 miles south of here on the road to Hankow.

Coal Hill, Peking, from the East (photo Summer 1914)

Peking street scene (photo Summer 1914)

Peking / view across the bridge (Robert Clack on bridge) (photo Summer 1914)

White Marble Bridge in Pei Hai (North Lake) the Forbidden City Park, Peking
(photo Summer 1914) (Robert Clack on left)

The Executive Committee of the Y.M.C.A. Conference (Robert in middle in white)

The Western Hills out from Peking / Paotingfu delegation (Robert far right)

WoFoSsŭ Conference, R.R. Gailey and Hsü Pao Ch'in (photo July 1914)

Peitaiho / West from Rocky Point (photo 1914)

Peitaiho Assembly Hall (photo 1914)

Peitaiho / FishHook Point Lighthouse in distance (photo 1914)

16 Third Year with the Y.M.C.A.

Highlights: 1915

- Rob and Edith's second child, Constance Elizabeth Clack, was born January 20 in Paotingfu.
- During March, the Y.M.C.A. staff in Paotingfu moved from temporary quarters to a rented building adjoining the lot they bought for constructing their permanent headquarters when funds become available.
- Rob took Chinese language exams to assess his next course of study.
- Rob escorted students to a field meet in Peking in late March. In mid-June he served as executive secretary for the entire Wo Fo Ssŭ Conference.
- In early September, the Clack family returned to Paotingfu from their summer retreat in Peitaiho. They purchased a lot at East Cliff, Peitaiho, for future development.
- October 11 letter written by Edith – "Rob is planning to go to Shanghai the end of the month, to be gone three weeks." This is where the Far Eastern Olympics games were played, and Rob also attended a Y.M.C.A. National Secretaries Conference while there.

Y.M.C.A. ANNUAL REPORT, PAOTINGFU
Year ended September 30, 1915

Written by Robert W. Clack, General Secretary (following are excerpts from the Report)

Number of Members – 58
Number of Active Members – 37
Number in Bible Study Classes –100-plus

Of greatest importance for the future of our work in Paotingfu is that we have at last a trained Chinese secretary on our staff – Mr. Shih Ch'ing who was at the Tientsin Training School for Secretaries. …

- Building Site – We have obtained a large building site in the city and Mr. Eddy has raised the funds necessary for a building. We have transferred our temporary quarters to a rented building adjoining the land, where we are preparing a number of athletic courts.
- Religious Work – Because of Mr. Eddy's meetings last fall, we had 500 people who enquired. Of those, 300 were enrolled in Bible classes and 29 of these men were led to decisions for Christ, and seventeen were baptized and entered the Church. Our change of quarters in the spring necessitated the dropping temporarily of our Sunday service, as our new building had no room large enough. Our night school is developing very satisfactorily and we have almost fifty students who fill four English classes, one arithmetic class, and one Bible class.
- Athletics – We have as yet no regular classes in physical training, but have basketball and tennis courts in use. Mr. Hubbard and I were able to take teams from three government schools to the North China Meet at Tientsin. We also held a city basketball tournament on our court from seven schools. It is a very significant fact that we have had at least two Bible classes in each of the schools where we have been helping with the athletics.

- <u>Hindrances</u> – Our greatest difficulty now is to get teachers for our Bible classes. Also, financially we are handicapped by the fact that at present our constituency consists mostly of students. Paotingfu has never been much of a commercial center, and now that most of the officials have gone to Tientsin, we have few wealthy men on whom we can call for contributions. Our lack of building and suitable equipment makes it impossible to get many members.

Mrs. Clack has also been very ill this fall, which has kept me rather closely confined at home. She has been in China over six years now, during which time she married and has borne and nursed two big children, besides taking care of her mother through a year of illness, so that she is rather worn out. This will make it necessary for me to relieve her from as much responsibility as possible for a while, until she gets rested.

Personally, I feel very much the lack of special training before beginning my work here. I hope very much to get a large amount of practical experience when on my furlough [in America], and, if possible, to get a few months' work in Peking or Tientsin within the next few years. Of course, this is absolutely impossible at present, as there is no one available to relieve me here.

I served as executive secretary for the Wo Fo Ssŭ Conference which took all my time during June-July. [4] *[Editor's note – Summer Conference for Government students at a temple in the Western Hills north of Peking; focus was "Present Day Problems and Christianity".]*

THE LETTERS

Letter written by Rob to his sister Ida

Paotingfu / Jan. 3, 1915

Here it is 1915. "How tempus does fugit." It won't be long till 1917 at this rate. In lots of ways it doesn't seem almost five years that I've been out here, but in other ways I seem to have been here always. We were all at the Lewis' for dinner Christmas evening. Had turkey. The Hamiltons at Shuntêfu (south of here) have a lot of turkeys and send them up on the train when anyone here wants one. The Chinese think they are awfully funny as they have nothing like them. They call them "American chickens".

Letter written by Rob to his parents

Paotingfu / Sunday eve, Jan. 24, 1915

Well, your granddaughter, Constance Elizabeth, arrived safely Wednesday evening [January 20] and is beginning to get a little acquainted with this big world. She is not very big, 6-3/4 lbs, but has a good framework to build upon and is absolutely sound.

Letter written by Rob to his sister Nan

Paotingfu / Mar. 14, 1915

Here it is two weeks again since I wrote home. I just never seem to get time to write. That, however, seems to be the chronic state in the Y.M.C.A., so I might as well get used to it. They are notorious out here for each having at least two ordinary missionaries' work to do.

Mother Gordon sprung a surprise on us last week. We got a telegram from her Monday noon that she was coming on the afternoon train. She had been intending to come the last of the month, but got a chance to come with the Ellises (Mrs. Hubbard's brother) and so decided to come now. She stayed until Friday. She is planning to leave for America April first. She will probably make you folks a visit in May sometime, as a Chinese gentleman [Mr. Kwong] who was himself educated in America is sending his children to go to school at Springfield, Mass., and he has asked her to see them through to their destination, and she is planning to make several visits on the way back to California.

I have an all day job on tomorrow. The "Nurture Virtue" Middle School has their tenth anniversary and are going to celebrate with an athletic carnival which I am to take charge of. They start at ten in the morning with a tennis tournament. Then a basketball tournament, then a feast, and after that a field meet, ending up with several association football games. Then in the evening they have theatricals, which I will dodge for reasons which you could not appreciate unless you had heard Chinese theatricals. They always make one think that he has been living a wicked life and has died.

I'm expecting to get into a couple of good field meets this spring. They have always had a meet for the various Legation Guards in Peking every spring, but this year since only the Americans have more than a dozen men left, they have decided to turn it into an International Meet, Chinese, Japs and all. I'm expecting to go up and take any of the local students who show any kind of form. Then May 15–22 they have the Far Eastern Olympics (China, Japan, Siam, Philippines) in Shanghai, and we are going to have a National Secretaries Conference at the same time, so I'll be able to get in on the International Meet on the Tientsin Treaty Port team. We will divide up by treaty ports, which gives Tientsin a good chance, as Peking and all Chihli Province belong to the Tientsin district.

Dr. Lewis got back from his Siberian trip last week. He visited a number of the German prisoners camps and says the tales about their being mistreated and starved are all fairy stories. The Russians treat them as well as they do their own soldiers, which is all they really have a right to expect, even though it is less than they are used to. The complaints seem to originate with the German officers, who are treated just the same as the common soldiers, and so are dreadfully abused. If they could only make the Kaiser stand some of it, it might help the International Peace Propaganda.

Elma Gordon (middle, back row) ready to sail with the Kwong children on the "Empress of Asia" (photo March 17, 1915)

Letter written by Rob (including a note from Edith) to his family

Paotingfu / March 28, 1915

    Tell Dad the seed came through O.K. We start our garden in a few days now as the frost is all out of the ground. We will have it over at Lewises' this year as we shall move over there July first. We are hoping to have a house of our own in another year. When the Association building is built here, they will build us a house, too. The American Board Mission has offered us a place for it in their compound. We shall like it better over there as the people there are Westerners and are more neighborly. On this compound they are mostly Easterners, and are more wrapped up in themselves and their own particular work. We have made out our house plans already, but they have to be approved by the International Committee architects before we can use them. We get $3500 to build with.

    We are very busy now moving our Association quarters. We have rented another building adjoining the lot we have bought and will make that our headquarters till the big building is finished. We are working now on the plans for it. We have to work out about what we want and then go over the plans in New York and put them into proper shape architecturally. We don't want too large a building or we can't raise enough to run it, but on the other hand we don't want to build such a small one that we'll outgrow it in a few years, so it takes a lot of figuring.

    I went to Peking Tuesday and came back Thursday. Took the language school exams. I've never taken any language exams before, so had to see where I was at. Edwards of the Peking

Y.M.C.A. has charge of the language work of all the other North China secretaries, and he will look over my papers and tell me what to study next. I wish I could give more time to language study as it is fascinating, especially studying the characters. They are not all mixed up as they seem at first, but are really a very highly developed system. There are some mighty good sermons in some of them.

Letter written by Rob to Edith's brother, Karl, in China

Paotingfu / June 14, 1915

We are expecting Charlie Harvey [Y.M.C.A. National Secretary for North China] this afternoon for twenty-four hours. He is now in Peking and is coming down to look over our building sites and talk things over. I've been trying all year to get one of the National Secretaries here to look things over, but haven't succeeded before. We have all the old buildings torn down and have a basketball court made already on the ruins. We will make a number of courts for other sports in the fall. We have a basketball tournament on now, with seven schools in. The Presbyterians have a team but we couldn't get them to enter.

The Bible classes were officially closed yesterday, though one or two will be started especially for those who remain here this summer. Altogether 17 joined the church from our classes this year, and 12 others were enrolled as catechumens.

We are planning to leave for Peitaiho Friday, taking the night train from Peking and arriving at Peitaiho 8:00 Saturday morning. Then I shall return Tuesday for a couple of days, then going to Peking to take charge of the Wo Fo Ssŭ Conference. The Burgesses are going to Japan because of her health so I have to take Stew's place as executive secretary of the conference. I expect I'll get back to Peitaiho about the 11th or 12th of July.

Letter written by Edith Clack to her mother in California

Paotingfu, N. China / Sept. 7th, 1915

We have moved and gotten settled in Dr. Lewis' house, and it looks fine. Our furniture fits into the rooms much better than their's did. But I hope the next time we move we can move into our own house.

We have bought a lot [parcel of land] up at Peitaiho. It's at East Cliff just back of the Fenn's. Mr. Ellis and we bought the two lots just back of the Taylors and Fenns. It is a very good location, and a week later we were offered by Mr. Richard Evans $75.00 more than what we paid for it. But we told him it was not for sale.

914. Front gate of Yamen purchased by Y.M.C.A., Paotingfu

915. Dr. Chêng, President of Y.M.C.A. & Sun Hê Lu, Chinese secretary on newly purchased land.

Apr. 1

931. Front gate of new Y.M.C.A. property

Y.M.C.A. property looking north (photo April 1, 1915)
"We have transferred our temporary quarters to a rented building adjoining the land, where we are preparing a number of athletic courts."

Door of Paotingfu Y.M.C.A. and Chinese secretaries (photo April 1915)

Robert Clack in center. Y.M.C.A. banners translate as "Enthusiastic in Service" and "Help Young People" (photo ca. 1915)

West Lake Bridge (Hangzhou, Zhejiang Province, East China) (photo 1915)

Left – Needle Pagoda, West Lake - Hangchow, China (collapsed in 1924)

Right – Monuments to Infamy / Yueh Fei's Betrayers

Left – Entrance to cave in Spirits Retreat

Right – Bridge in Spirits Retreat Monastery

Y.M.C.A. of China, employed officers (Shanghai conference) (photo Nov. 1915)
R.W. Clack (in white) seated to right

Y.M.C.A. officials: Gailey (Peking), Tung (Shanghai), and Lyon (National Committee) at Hangchou (photo May 1915)

Willow-Ware Teahouse, Shanghai (China's Central Coast)

Family portrait (December 1915)

Robert W. and Edith Clack with their two children

K.D. Gordon Clack (2 years, 4 mos.) and Constance Elizabeth Clack (11 months).

17 Fourth Year with the Y.M.C.A. and Beginning of Homeland Sabbatical

Highlights: 1916

⌘ In April 1916 there was a scarlet fever epidemic in China. Rob contracted this disease in May and spent a month in quarantine.

⌘ For 15 months – from June 1916 to September 1917 – Rob went on a Y.M.C.A. furlough to the U.S. with Edith and their two children, Gordon (3) and Constance (1-1/2). They arrived in Seattle, Washington, then visited with Edith's family members in California before going to Rob's hometown of Clear Lake, Iowa, in mid-August.

⌘ The family stayed with Rob's parents in Clear Lake for about two and one-half months.

⌘ At the end of October, they relocated to Cleveland, Ohio, to be near the Y.M.C.A. regional office. They stayed there for about seven months – early November 1916 through May 1917. Edith and Constance left Cleveland earlier than Rob did so she could visit family members in California prior to their return to China.

THE LETTERS

Letter written by Edith to her mother (visiting family in California)
Paotingfu, N. China / Jan. 18, 1916

There is one thing that pleases us very much. A year ago last fall when Mr. and Mrs. Eddy were here the Director of the Girls Schools wouldn't dismiss the schools to go to his meetings. He allowed Mrs. Eddy to speak in the school but was very unfriendly otherwise. Last Sunday morning at nine o'clock Mr. Yung Tao preached a regular Gospel sermon to them, and 49 girls gave in their names for Bibles! Also, in the afternoon at the big meeting the Director of the Schools came to Mr. Clack and begged to be allowed to be one of the ushers!! My! we are so thankful for an opening at last into that school.

Letter written by Edith to her mother in California
Paotingfu, N. China / Feb. 14, 1916

Four months from today we leave here for Shanghai, where we sail for San Francisco on the "China". It leaves Shanghai June 24th and arrives in S.F. July 13th. Hurrah! Aren't you surprised? We have been hoping and planning for our vacation for several months now, but we didn't want to tell you all until we were certain. Rob just returned from Peking yesterday after a conference with Mr. Chas. Harvey and everything is all settled. Oh! we are all so delighted that we don't have to wait another year.

We will be in the homeland just a little over 13 months, but Rob has to spend from Oct. to May at Y.M.C.A. training school. He will have about a month to spend in California both coming and going. I wish it might be longer, but we can do lots of visiting in that time, can't we?

Letter written by Edith to her brother Moore (in California)
Paotingfu, N. China / April 9, 1916

Mrs. Mather just came in a little while ago to tell us that Mr. M. has just received a letter from their Board saying that you had been appointed to Tungchow College, to take Mr. Corbett's place, as he goes on furlough this spring. My! it is such a surprise we can hardly believe it, but we are so happy for you that such a very nice place has been opened for you. I only wish you could bring a wife out with you. But then, if you don't maybe you will find her out here. Such things have happened, you know. And we also are so pleased for Karl's sake. He was so dreading being left out here alone without any of his own people here, and I was dreading leaving him. But if he knows you are coming he won't mind our going nearly so much.

Don't plan to come out on any of the Japanese boats. I heard from several different people that they were running their boats as cheaply as possible now. They have reduced the table fare from $1.45 a person to 90¢; they have a very poor ice supply, and of course you can imagine the state into which their meats, vegetables, etc. get, and that vermin is rampant. The Dilly's almost lost their baby from the impure water. They take enough water on in Japan to last them till they get back. Of course you won't sail till after we get back home, but since you do have to sail we would like to have you do it before we have to go east.

Our boat has been changed to leave Shanghai two days later (June 26th) and also we go by Yokohama, so we won't get into S.F. till July 17th instead of the 13th. The boat Dr. Mackey and Miss Gumbrell and Miss Judson were planning to go on (the "Chiyo Maru") was broken in two by a storm off Hong Kong [March 31; no casualties] and they have been transferred to our boat. We have cabin #2, Mrs. Burroughs has lower berth in #3 and they have #4. Six grownups and two children from Paofu. Mr. and Mrs. Hicks and son go on the same boat too, and no telling who else. Maybe you could return on the "China". I'm sure Karl would be glad if you could.

There has been a dreadful epidemic of scarlet fever and measles around. So many poor little kiddies are dying every day. Mrs. Elmer Galt and her baby boy are sick, also Dorothy Galt, Mr. H. Galt's little girl who was visiting here. We are praying that we may be spared.

Letter written by Edith to her mother (in California)
Paotingfu, N. China / Mon. 24th, Apr. 1916

Two months from today we will be in Shanghai. I guess I told you that our boat doesn't leave there till the 26th. We will be in Yokohama June 30th and Honolulu July 12th and S.F. July 17th.

We received yours and Moore's letter telling about Moore being appointed to the "Peking University". There is something twisted somewhere. Mrs. Mather says the letter from the Board say he is appointed to the Tungchow College. I only know of two Peking Universities, one is Government and the other is Methodist. All of our Presbyterian friends are so rejoiced to have him as one of them.

Mrs. Galt's little boy is very sick with diphtheria. We are all very anxious for him. You remember they lost their other boy when he was a year old, so this child is especially precious. There is an awful lot of diphtheria, measles & scarlet fever around. The Chinese children have been dying like flies, almost. We keep our children entirely away from all the Chinese we can.

Letter written by Edith to her mother and brother (in California)
                                                            Paotingfu / Sun. May 14th, 1916

    The last word from Karl says everything was quiet there now [Peking], but simply because the city was deserted. We do hope nothing serious will happen. If we can't go to see him maybe he can come to Tientsin for a day or so and see us off. We will be sorry to not get our visit with him, but we feel we hardly dare run the risk. No telling what we would run into around Nanking. It is always such a hot bed.

    We are all well now. Of course Rob is still in quarantine [from scarlet fever], but Gordon is feeling so fine and Sister and I are too.

Y.M.C.A. ANNUAL REPORT, PAOTINGFU
Year Ending September 30, 1916
Written by Robert W. Clack, General Secretary (following are excerpts from the Report)

Note – The Clack family went to the USA for a Y.M.C.A. training furlough from June 1916 through September 1917.

At present I can give only a partial report of the activities of the Paotingfu Association for the past year, for it has been almost four months since we left for our year's furlough in America. As our work in the summer is almost at a standstill, there is little more than the summer conference to report, but that is the crown of our year's work, and so is very important.

Three Years Old – It is now a little more than three years since the launching of the Paotingfu Association. The first year was marked by the excitement and popularity of a new venture, followed the second year by reaction and little progress as the first enthusiasm died away, but this last year we have gotten our bearings and there was a steady and encouraging progress throughout the year.

Mr. Hubbard was able to give more of his time and energy to the Association, and he finally took over complete charge when I was taken with the scarlet fever in May. Mr. Shih, our Chinese secretary has developed remarkably as more responsibility has been placed upon him. We all attended the Employed Officers' Conference in Hangchow in November, and it was a great inspiration and education to us. Mr. Shih has given special attention to our finances and just added a printing press to our equipment. Since there is no paper published in the city and no other good printing press, this should add considerably to our revenue.

We spent a considerable sum during the year on our rented quarters making them better suited to our purposes. Nine rooms are now fitted up as dormitories, and are packed with students throughout the year. We had thirty-five from the Military College and ten from other schools. Almost all of them were in Bible classes, and several made decisions for Christ during the year. We also rented an adjoining building, tearing out the partitions and using it for an auditorium and gymnasium. Our [new] building site was leveled off, and is being made into a fine athletic field, which can probably be retained even after we build.

Bible Study

In January we had the opportunity to help Mr. Yung T'ao, the famous merchant and philanthropist of Peking, in one of his Bible distribution campaigns. Mr. Yung had long been an ardent Confucianist, but desiring to do something to stem the tide of moral and political degradation in his country, he took up a systematic study of the great religions of the world in order to find out what useful elements were in them. He immediately recognized the superiority of Christian ethics over the other systems, and set to work to present these ethics to his people by distributing Bibles. … In Paotingfu 1500 people attended Mr. Yung's meetings of whom about 1100 finally received Bibles.

China's West Point Opened

Owing to their strict rules only a few students of the Military School were able to attend Mr. Yung's meetings. A few days later we received a petition signed by 700 out of the 2000 students in the institution asking for Bibles. Mr. Yung could make no provision for these men, but luckily Mr. Hubbard had a small fund given by a friend for just such a purpose, and we were able to supply pocket Testaments to the whole seven hundred. The opportunity for expanding our Y.M.C.A. work in this school now seems possible.

Directing the Athletics of the City

Our greatest opening has been along athletic lines. Our new athletic field has been of great help to us and has naturally become the athletic centre of the city. We also trained all the track men for the North China Meet at Peking. During the winter we had our first gymnasium classes for our own members and night school students.

Hindrances

We are still very badly handicapped in our Bible study work by the lack of suitable teachers. The unsettled state of the government has been a serious financial handicap. Our building situation brings our worst problem. We cannot go much beyond the student work till we get a proper building; but we have not yet had time to develop a financial constituency that can support a building. A site was obtained last year, but there was no suitable outlet to the street, and nothing further can be done till that is bought.

Recommendations

The matter of a residence [for the General Secretary] in Paotingfu should be acted upon very soon. The Presbyterian Mission is getting three new families, so will no longer be able to let us have a house. Next year we shall be able to get Mr. Galt's house in the American Board compound while he is on furlough, but after he returns there will be nothing available. The committee purchased a very fine site adjoining the American Board compound this spring, and the residence should be completed before the summer of 1918. The appropriation made by the American Board for a residence in North China is, I believe, $3,500. [5]

Secretaries of Paotingfu Y.M.C.A., February 1916 (R.W. Clack on right)

Photo of Y.M.C.A. group, 1916 (R.W. Clack in center)
[Translations in the photo are from Yiding Gao, 2018]

Editor's note – Rob, Edith, Gordon, and Constance departed from Hong Kong on June 29, 1916 aboard a ship owned by the China Mail Steamship Company, Ltd. They arrived in Honolulu, Hawaii, July 21 and subsequently arrived in the Port of San Francisco on July 24, 1916. After spending some time visiting Edith's relatives in California, they arrived in Clear Lake, Iowa, on August 12, to stay with Rob's parents.

The Gordon family in San Francisco, August 1916 (photo from Clack family album)

Standing (L-R):
Clark Gordon (Edith's brother, resident of San Francisco), Robert Clack, Moore Gordon (Edith's brother)

Seated (L-R):
Gladys Gordon, Ethel Gordon, "Grandma" Elma Gordon (with Constance Clack on her lap), Edith (Gordon) Clack (with Gordon Clack on her lap), Weston Gordon
[Gladys and Weston are the children of Clark and Ethel Gordon]

18 Fifth Year with the Y.M.C.A. and End of Homeland Sabbatical

Highlights: 1917

⌘ In June 1916, the Clack family started on a 15-month furlough to the U.S. for Robert's Y.M.C.A. training. At first they stayed with Robert's parents in Clear Lake, Iowa. Then they rented a house in Cleveland in December 1916 with a lease that expired May 1, 1917. Robert stayed in Cleveland for additional training, so during June, Edith took Connie and went to visit some of her relatives on her way to California. Gordon stayed with his father during this time.

⌘ Following Edith's visits with Gordon family members in California, including her mother (who was staying in the U.S. at this time), on August 30 the Clack family set sail from Vancouver, Canada, to return to China. When they arrived they found that much of North China was overwhelmed with major floods.

Y.M.C.A. ANNUAL REPORT, PAOTINGFU
Year Ended September 30, 1917

Written by Robert Wood Clack, General Secretary (following are excerpts from the Report)

Number of members – 57; Number of active members – 27; Number in Bible classes – 100

We left China in July last year [1916] and have been spending the year on furlough in America. We are returning to Paotingfu the latter part of September. During our absence Mr. Hugh W. Hubbard, of the American Board of Mission, who has been my associate for several years, had had entire charge. Messrs. Sun and Shih remained with the Association, and one full time man, Mr. Huang, a graduate of Union College, has been added as educational director.

Education – Under Mr. Huang's leadership the educational department has enlarged its field to include a day school and a free school for the poor. We are also to open a commercial school this fall. The post office and the Commercial Press (largest native firm in China) have guaranteed us enough students to pay expenses, and we have an honor graduate of the commercial school of Peking Association as chief instructor. The Bible class enrollment was about the same as last year, the number of classes being limited only by the number of capable teachers. The Sunday evangelistic services filled the auditorium every Sunday, and a large number were from the Military College. The most encouraging event was the organizing of a Military College Y.M.C.A. Student Branch.

Physical Education – continues to give us our largest point of contact with the students. In all, we have given direct help to eleven different schools, and have thus been thrown into personal contact with over 1,000 students. The First Annual Field Meet with twelve middle schools entered was held in October and the Association was asked to take charge.

City Prospers – The sudden recovery of the city from depression which has held it since it was looted and burned during the Revolution [1911] has put us in a position for more rapid expansion than we thought possible a year ago. The city has again been made the military capital, and the Military Governor of the Province has been brought back after an absence of over a decade. With him came some hundred lesser officials ... adding some 10,000 to the population. This made it necessary for the Association to move into larger quarters, and we succeeded in getting the largest building in the city at half the usual rent. The building was dedicated by the American Ambassador to China, Doctor Reinsch, at our fourth anniversary.

Interpretation of Political Events – Because of their effect on our work, it might not be out of place in conclusion to give a short statement of recent political events. Ever since the Manchus were driven out in 1911, there has been a struggle between the two elements of the Republicans, the military and civil, as to which should dominate the government. While Yuan Shih K'ai lived, his strong personality forced all others to the background, but with his death [1916] the contest became more pronounced and finally reached a crisis this spring.

Chang Hsün was one of the Manchu generals, and he had never really given his allegiance to the Republic. He made his headquarters at Hauchoufu, on the Tientsin-Pukow Railway, and has for a number of years been Military Governor of Anhui Province. He has obeyed the laws of the Republic only when it pleased him, and his rowdy troops have terrorized the Province for five years. He has practically monopolized that part of the railway in Anhui, and his men have made things so disagreeable that travelers have gone through only in cases of necessity. The Peking government has longed to get rid of him, but his position was so strong, and his troops so devoted to him personally that they did not feel able. However, this spring when the tension in the Republican ranks became so strong, the Military party invited him to bring his army to Peking to overawe the Civil party. When he arrive he took control of the capital, soon compelled President Li [Yüan Hung] to resign, and then proclaimed the recall of the Manchu Emperor, believing that he would be supported either from desire or fear by all military leaders.

But he had been mistaken in his estimate of the shallowness of their conversion to republicanism. Party lines were forgotten and all rallied to the defense of the Republic. Chang Hsün's undisciplined rowdies were no match for the trained troops of Young China, and in a few days they were defeated and dispersed, and Chang had to flee for his life. Thus one of the greatest internal menaces of the Republic has been removed, and all parties are united as never before since the Revolution. The Military party is still in control, but prospects are bright for the peaceful return of civil government. But more than ever before the Chinese are realizing that only the development of trained, unselfish leaders will save them from national death. And it will be the opportunity of the Association [Y.M.C.A.] to meet this need.

Hindrances – Before we left China it was understood that on our return Mr. Hubbard was to devote the coming year to the work of the American Board, to take the place of Mr. Galt, who is on furlough; but then to return to the Association next year. His last letter, however, seems to indicate that he has been withdrawn permanently. If this is true, it will leave Paotingfu very short-handed, and postpone a large expansion of our work to the indefinite future. Mr. Hubbard and Mr. Rugh have both pointed out the very great use that could be made of a stereopticon [slide projector] and some playground equipment.

I spent the major portion of my furlough in the office of the Cleveland Central Association. While I learned a great deal from this experience, I feel that there should be a better understanding between the International Committee and the heads of the Cleveland Association as to what training should be given, and that there should be a proper guarantee that that agreement will be lived up to, before any more prospective foreign secretaries or secretaries on furlough are sent there.

Distribution of Time – I spent seven months of the past year in the Cleveland Central general office. In June I attended the foreign work conference in Chicago and the Student Conference at Lake Geneva [Wisconsin]. July was spent at my father's home in Iowa, where I was able to give some help in raising the Iowa portion of the War Work fund. Most of August was spent with Mrs. Clack's relatives in California. We expect to be back and settled in Paotingfu by October first. [6]

THE LETTERS

Letter written by Rob to his mother

PUBLIC CORRESPONDENCE TABLES

CENTRAL BRANCH

YOUNG MEN'S CHRISTIAN ASSOCIATION

CLEVELAND, OHIO

May 6, 1917

Today I am going out to the railroad Y.M.C.A. and investigate it thoroughly; especially the way they run their restaurant.

No, the war won't make any difference about our going back. You see, I am registered as a resident of Tientsin so that if I am conscripted it must be through Tientsin and I can't be held in this country on that account. Of course I could go into the Army Y.M.C.A. work during the duration of the war, but the foreign work is so much more important for world peace, even from a selfish American point of view. We have got to see to it that when China does get awake she won't be dominated by any Prussian ideals. Japan has got them, but luckily she hasn't enough power to dare to make the attempt as the Kaiser had. I tell you we've got such a big work and influence now in China that when one thinks of the possibilities and the responsibility it is simply staggering. Why, our little group of a hundred men absolutely have the whole future of the world in our hands. It's pretty hard for anyone who has not been on the inside to realize, but it's true. China is either to be materialistic or altruistic, and the matter will be decided in the next generation, and the whole question depends upon whether her leaders become Christian (in the true sense of the word) or not. Why, in Paotingfu we have our Military College. All the future military leaders of China will be educated there. We have a student Association organized in the school now. Are those students going to be men like Von Tirpitz and Hindenberg or are they going to be men like Cromwell and Stonewall Jackson, who prayed before they went into battle? The whole matter rests on two or three men, of whom I am one. Do you wonder that I get scared sometimes at my own selfishness and inefficiency and that I am willing to put up with a good deal if it will make me any more efficient?

We have a Conference of the foreign secretaries in Caldwell, New Jersey, May 25 to 29, and Edith and I are both supposed to attend. ... I am hoping, then, to come back with Edith to Clear Lake for a day or two, then take them all to Grinnell for Commencement, take them from there to see Edith's Uncle Major [Gordon] in Braymer, Mo., from where I can go direct to Chicago and the Student Conference at Lake Geneva, and then back here in time for the Boys Summer Camps.

Letter written by Edith to her mother and brother Karl (in California)
Paotingfu / Sept. 26, 1917

A month ago today we were in Eugene, now here we are almost settled in our home. We arrived here last Thursday, Sept. 20th, but we have just been so very busy that I couldn't get time to write before.

We are to live in the McCann house (the west house) this year instead of the Galt house. Mr. Price [a widower] is to have three of the rooms and he is either going to eat at the Hubbard's or keep house himself. The new people are going to have the Galt's house partly furnished. Mr. and Mrs. Robinson is their name. They just got here Monday.

We are having most awful rains and floods. The paper says there is six ft. of water running thru the streets of Tientsin native city and some in the Japanese Concession, but not so much. There is also a foot in the other Concessions. The stores have moved all their goods to the second floors. It is rumored that the people of Honan have gotten desperate and have cut the dykes of the Yellow River and it has returned to its old bed which is the Pei He.

We are very thankful to have gotten here so easily. So many from Shansi & Shantung are having such a time to get to their homes after the summer. Some of our baggage is still on the river and our Montgomery Ward stuff is still in Japan, I guess. It makes it easier to straighten things up a few at a time.

Letter written by Edith to her mother and brother Karl (in California)
Paotingfu / Oct. 8th, 1917

I suppose you have read about the awful floods we have been having in N. China since August. It was quite bad here in August, but now the roads around here are about normal, but in Tientsin they have had anywhere from 3 to six ft. of water all over the place. In front of the Business Agency it was three ft. It was about that deep all over the Concessions except the German. The Y.M.C.A. families (at least some of them) have gone back to Peitaiho. They say the smell of the water is awful. They have boats in the streets now instead of rickshas. In the new compound at Têchow there is over seven ft. of water and the water has come two feet into the houses. The families have started for Tientsin. I suppose they are there by now. It's rather like jumping out of the frying pan into the fire to go to Tientsin.

If we can't live here next year and if we can't have our house built we are going to rent the house that the Lattimores lived in over at the old College Compound. It will make a lovely place to live, much nicer than anything in the city.

Formal photograph taken at Y.M.C.A.-Central Branch, Cleveland, Ohio (1916 or 1917)

(Robert Clack seated at table on right, third from front) (photo from Clack family album)

The William R. Clack family in Clear Lake, Iowa, 1916

Standing (L-R):
"Grandpa" William R. Clack, Celia (Clack) Hughes, Melville Prince Hughes, (unidentified woman), Robert Clack

Seated (L-R):
"Grandma" Adda Clack (holding Mary Ann Hughes), Ida Clack (holding Gordon Clack), Nan Clack (holding Melville "Bud" Hughes), Edith Clack (holding Constance Clack)

Notes about children (all grandchildren of William R. and Adda Clack) (L-R)
- Mary Ann "Molly" Hughes, daughter of Melville and Celia (Clack) Hughes
- Gordon Clack, son of Robert and Edith (Gordon) Clack
- Melville "Bud" Hughes, son of Melville and Celia (Clack) Hughes
- Constance Elizabeth Clack, daughter of Robert and Edith (Gordon) Clack

Y.M.C.A. Association Building, Paotingfu; West Street from top of building, Nov. 1917

Our house in the American Board Compound, 1917-1918 [formerly the McCann house] (sharing house with American Board Member Mr. Price who has three rooms to himself)

Editor's note – Mrs. Price died August 1916 (according to Edith's letter of Sept. 21, 1916)

19 Sixth Year with the Y.M.C.A.

Highlights: 1918

- 1918 was Rob's sixth year with the Y.M.C.A. and his first full year following his year-long training sabbatical in the United States. According to one of Edith's letters, "Rob is having quite a time to keep the Y.M.C.A. financed. He has to make calls every day soliciting money for it." Edith is now writing most of the family correspondence.
- There may be some letters missing from this year because of the World War. It is evident that some of the letters are not getting through the mails to the United States.
- During this time Edith is pregnant and, in addition, is being monitored by the doctor for persistent heart concerns. Edith's mother has been living in California for more than a year with Edith's brother, Karl, who is on sabbatical from China because of health issues.
- During the spring, flooding in North China created major problems which, in turn, caused famines. Rob was a part of the Flood Relief Committee headquartered in Peking.
- Edith and their two children went to Peitaiho for the hot summer months and Rob also spent a short time there. Upon returning to Paotingfu, their third child, Robert William Douglas Clack, was born in the hospital on September 6.
- The World War officially ended on November 11, 1918.
 (see letters of November 13 and 22, and December 27)

Y.M.C.A. ANNUAL REPORT, PAOTINGFU
Year Ended September 30, 1918
Written by Robert W. Clack, General Secretary (following are excerpts from the Report)

The government schools continue to give us our greatest opportunity for student participants. Our membership campaign has, however, given us a new field among the teachers, minor officials, and gentry, which must be developed. As yet we have very little contact with the merchant class. They belong properly to the regular mission work, and both missions have chapels in the City established especially for them. There are also always a large number of soldiers stationed here, for whom we must begin some kind of work as soon as we can.

Hindrances – Our Bible class enrollment has remained practically stationary for several years, and I feel that we are not doing the religious work that we should be doing with the opportunity we have. This is largely due to the lack of well-qualified teachers.

Mr. Hubbard has been withdrawn by the American Mission Board until next summer. During the past year he has had to give all of his time to flood relief, so has not even had time to teach a Bible class. We have tried repeatedly during the past year to get another man temporarily from the National Committee to help out, but have not even been able to get one of the traveling secretaries to stop off and look things over when passing through. The Chinese board members feel that they are not being treated exactly square.

Policy for Next Year – We expect this year to push athletics harder than ever. We will try to resume our Sunday preaching services and start a course of Saturday evening lectures. We are also attempting to get in more students in our day and night schools. We are badly handicapped here by having no dormitories.

We should like again from the International Committee an exact statement of the conditions on which the building fund raised by Mr. Eddy will be granted to us. We feel that we are at last in a position where we can really plan for the building in the not distant future.

My time this year has been given almost entirely to regular Association work. I attended no conferences. I had most of August at the seacoast, but that part of July usually spent on vacation and at the summer conference I gave to flood relief work.

Housing – Our housing problem is settled for the present, and I think we shall be very comfortable in our Chinese house. Mrs. Clack's inability to go up or down stairs makes the Chinese style of house especially acceptable. [7]

THE LETTERS

Letter written by Edith to her mother and brother Karl (in California)
Paotingfu / Feb. 6th, 1918

Rob went to Tientsin on a short business trip. The Governor was here a few days. Rob called on him and he gave us $1000.00 for the Y.M.C.A. in Tientsin notes which means 100 cents on the dollar. The Peking notes are only 60 cents on the dollar. Most of the contributions Rob has gotten have been in Peking notes and when he told Rob he would give $1000.00 Rob still supposed it would be in Peking notes. The Governor sent a servant out for the money and he brought the Peking notes. "No No!" the Governor said, "Take these back and get Tientsin notes. I know that some people give those other notes, but it's pu hao, pu hao kuei chê." So Rob has gone up to deposit the money. He returns tomorrow. The Governor was the man that Rob stayed in Tientsin for a week to see at Thanksgiving time.

The plague is bad again. It started away up in Mongolia about two or three months ago. The Government asked Dr. Lewis to go up and see what could be done to keep it from spreading, but the officials up there were very hostile and wouldn't do a thing to help. Several Drs. went up with Dr. Lewis. They were nearly mobbed at one place, so they came back. Then Dr. Lewis was called to Taiyuanfu to help the Drs. there but now it is spreading everywhere. The last we heard was that it was about 100 miles south of here. The Drs. are all nearly worked to death trying to keep it from spreading. Of course Chinese New Year will help, and as soon as spring comes it will stop. Wouldn't it be awful if it would get among our flooded people? Mr. Hubbard has a proposition on hand that if it goes thru' will give 2000 men work. Pray that it will go thru!

Miss Gumbrell and Mrs. Mather have opened up a "jo" kitchen for the poor country people who have come into the city to beg. They have enough money on hands to give a big bowl of porridge to 40 women and children for two months. $1.50 Mex will feed one person a month. Mrs. Mather says this forty is only about 1/10 of the number they could feed if they only had the money.

This is part of Rob's letter from Peking that I thought would interest you –

    Mr. & Mrs. Hicks came up on the train with me so it was not as unpleasant as it might have been. I spent part of my time waiting at Paofu talking to Dr. Lewis who was awaiting the special [train] of C.C. Wang and his corps of doctors who are putting quarantine into effect all along the line. Dr. Lewis just got back last night from Tingchow. There were three deaths from plague in a village a mile from Tingchow yesterday, some people who had just come across country from Shansi. He thinks though that the quarantine starting today will keep it from spreading in Chihli to any great extent. No trains will stop at stations near where there is plague, and at all other stations everyone must present a certificate from the local police that he is resident or else will have to undergo five days quarantine before he can get on the train. That is to prevent people from the infected districts traveling across country to get the train somewhere else.

Letter written by Edith to her mother and brother Karl (in California)
                                                                           Paotingfu / Feb. 25th, 1918

    The plague is still at it. At Ting Hsien where they thought they had it so well under control they found that the people and police had been hiding cases from them. One suspect whom they left in quarantine with the police, Dr. Ingram found out he had been allowed to go to a "Miao" and so infected the whole crowd. Dr. Ingram wrote asking Dr. Lewis if he couldn't get him the authority to have the soldiers who are acting as police killed (shot) when they so flatly disobey orders. Of course they can't get such an order, but it seems like they ought to have some severe punishment to hold over them. It's awful for them to allow so many people to be exposed. We still haven't heard of any cases around here.

    The famine relief work is going on all right, but sometimes it seems awfully slow. That money you sent and the Wilcoxes' and some that Moore had and we added a bit which brought it up to $20.65 Mex., I gave to Miss Chapin for her "jo" kitchen. I saw one poor woman with a family of 4, husband sick, and all they have is what she and the children can get begging. They are giving her help and Oh! they are so grateful.

Letter written by Edith to her mother and brother Karl (in California)
                                                                           Paotingfu / Mar. 19th, 1918

    I don't know whether we will build [the Y.M.C.A.] this coming year or not. Mr. C.W. Harvey has just passed thru' here on his way to Peking. Rob has gone to Peking with him and will come back tomorrow. He will know then whether there is any hopes or not. Personally, we can't see any use of waiting for exchange to improve because it will be years before it will ever get back to where it was, that is, if it ever does. But of course, now all the time and most of the money is being spent on War Work. Mr. Edwards of the Peking Y.M.C.A. who went home on furlough this year has been asked to assume the responsibility for all the Y.M.C.A. work for American soldiers in France.

    We are expecting Mr. Eddy and Mrs. Eddy and party the first part of next month. We do hope and pray that their coming may prove the blessing we are praying for. I must close and take a walk. I don't get out as much as I should. There are so many beggars that I don't walk outside the compound very often.

Letter written by Rob to his father

Spring 1918

I don't think we better try to send any more parcels by mail unless it's absolutely necessary while service is so poor. It's not worth the risk of losing them. It looks now as if by another Christmas there might be the beginning of a return to the old safe and sane days. It certainly is great to get the papers these days. I have a big map of France & Belgium where I keep track of the line from day to day with pins. That is about the only recreation I get.

We are extra busy now getting ready for the Central Chihli Meet next Monday and Tuesday; track, basketball and tennis. We are coaching three schools, the Government Middle; Yü Tê Middle, and Industrial. I expect the Govt. Middle to win the basketball and the Yü Tê to win the tennis and get second in both other sports.

Letter written by Edith to her brother Karl (in California)

Paotingfu / Wed. April 3rd, 1918

Your letter of Feb. 24th just arrived last evening. My! you don't know how happy your check for $33.20 made us. Dad sent us $50.00 both together they equal about $110.00 Mex. We are getting about $1.30 now for $1.00. The first money out of these sums is to go to dressing three newborn babies and giving their mothers clean clothes in exchange for the dirty, lousy things they're using now. Also to give the mothers extra food, so they will have enough for the babies. Most of the money will be spent feeding mothers and children. I am so glad it has come just now as this next month or two are going to be the very worst. Please don't think we spend most of our time just thinking of these poor hungry people, because we don't; we simply don't dare. We have to keep fit so as to have more to give them. We are having beautiful warm weather now which relieves their suffering from the cold.

Letter written by Edith to her mother (in California)

Paotingfu / Apr. 22nd, 1918

We have found a Chinese house right next to this compound that we can rent and which will be very nice indeed after putting in new floors, windows, etc. and papering and calcimining and fumigating etc. I think we will get the house about the first of June so it will be all finished so Rob can "pan chia" before he comes to Peitaiho the last of July. He only plans to spend Aug. at Peitaiho this year. He wants to start a special summer school this spring and summer.

They started a membership campaign last Sunday. They have various teams, but there is one boy out on his own hook. He has gotten 22 paid up members; 8 old ones but the rest are new.

Rob is enclosing a map that he thought you and Karl would especially be interested in. Your money has been very gratefully received by both Mrs. Mathers and Miss Chapin. And some of it we gave to Drusie along with some Miss Chapin gave her to open up a soup kitchen for the next two months in Chentingfu.

Rob has to go up to Peking every week now to take Hugh's [Hugh Hubbard] place on the Flood Relief Com. He saw Moore [Edith's brother] yesterday. Moore expects to go into Honan this week to buy millet for his men. If he has time he is going to stop off a day on his way back.

Letter written by Rob to his father in Iowa

Paotingfu, June 16, 1918

We are having our Chinese house fixed up now and I'll have to keep a pretty close tab on that. I may also have to take charge of a gang of flood refugees and build a road in the West Suburb, too. We are trying to get a couple of American Board Missionaries who have just been driven out of Turkey and come across this way to take charge, but if they can't I guess it's up to Hugh and me. He will get things started and then I'll finish them up. One of the men we want to get is Dr. George White, of Grinnell [College].

Letter written by Rob to his mother

Paotingfu, June 30, 1918

This is Sunday afternoon, and I just got back from Peking where I went yesterday to attend the meeting of the Flood Relief Committee. I found your letter of May 26 waiting for me when I got here.

Tell Dad he better invest the children's money in the next Liberty Loan. We can at least do that much toward knocking the Kaiser. It will please Gordon very much to know he is helping. He takes great interest in the war, and always wants all the cartoons about it in the Literary Digest explained, tho' I am afraid his ideas on the matter are rather vague. He does recognize all pictures of the Kaiser, though.

I took Edith and the children up to Peitaiho a week ago Friday and Saturday. Edith stood the trip exceedingly well and I do not think was as tired Saturday evening as she has usually been down here in spite of the trip. They have run a branch line of the railway over to the beach so we don't have that long trip on donkeys and chairs that we used to have, being now only about as far from the station as we are at Clear Lake [Iowa].

I came back Monday. I have two hundred men in from the flooded districts building a road, whom I am looking after for a month. We got $1500 from the B.A.T. for them. Also both our Chinese secretaries at the Y.M.C.A. are away, so I have to keep my eye on things there. Of course, our work in the schools is closed for the summer, but we have several classes of our own running in night school. Also I have to spend a little time overseeing the workmen who are fixing up our Chinese house. I expect to move things over the middle of July.

It has not been excessively hot yet. Over ninety most every day, but not yet up to a hundred. We have been having quite a little rain, but today there is a dry hot wind. We are just finishing the dykes on the Sha Hê (our nearest river to the south) so that unless there are again excessive rains as last year, we have it in control. On the P'u T'ao Hê, still farther south, where they have not yet gotten the dykes repaired, however, these last rains have again caused floods. The trouble is that there was so much silt last year that the old bed all filled up, so there is no way for any extra water to flow off.

We are trying to put thru a million dollar dyke project down there, but it is still up in the air. A number of villages have built small dykes surrounding their fields and village, so that they, as least, are safe for the present, but that can be only a temporary measure. All around here where the water had gone down and where the land was not spoiled by gravel, they have just harvested the best wheat crop in years. That, of course, will bring the price of grain down a lot and make our money go farther in relieving those who are still destitute, besides taking a lot of the refugees off our hands. If only the rains will stay to normal this summer we ought to have things back in pretty good shape by next spring.

Letter written by Rob to his sister Ida

Paotingfu, July 9, 1918

Our new house is all finished but part of the painting, so I guess I can get things moved over the first of next week. It is really going to be quite a cozy little place. We have a nice big front court with a little side yard where the children can play, and then a large back yard for our goats and our garden. Hugh is leaving tomorrow and then I will be the only foreigner left in the South Suburb. In the West Suburb there will still be Mr. Herman, the business manager of the hospital, and his family. He is a Hungarian citizen, so has been interned here by the Gov't and can't leave. Then McCoy, of the Standard Oil [Company], and Cotton, of the B.A.T. are here off and on. I expect to get away in about three more weeks for three weeks.

Letter written by Rob to his sister Celia

Peitaiho, Aug. 2, 1918

Well, I have finally gotten up here for my vacation at last. We got our road all finished up and the men paid off last week Thursday, and then I moved Friday and settled Saturday, left Paofu Sunday afternoon and got here early Monday morning. I have my summer's work all done up now except balancing up the books on the dyke work, which will only be a matter of an hour or two when all the accounts are in. We have had only light rains so far at Peitaiho, so it looks as if we would have no new floods this fall in our immediate field.

Our new house is going to be very comfortable, though we will have to build on a new room or two as soon as the children begin to get big enough to want rooms of their own. I am sending a picture of the main part of the house taken from the street.

We are planning to have a Grinnell [College, Iowa] picnic next week. We will have quite a number of Grinnell people: Paul and Helen MacEachion '09, Lyman Cady '10, Miss Anderson '16, Alice Reed '13, William Gleysteen (he is Cynthia Meyer's uncle), Mrs. LaForce, who was one of the oldest Bonsquet girls, and Susan Arvis '02. I think you knew her brother John '09. Ida does, I know. She was a missionary in Turkey, but a large party of them were driven across into Russia last year and so came out thru Siberia. A lot of them are staying here to help the American Board, several permanently probably.

Letter written by Rob to his mother

Peitaiho, August 15, 1918

I took Gordon to the Y.M.C.A. picnic at East Cliff day before yesterday. There were about thirty there. Next to the Burgesses who came out six months before I did, I was the veteran of the bunch. That gives a good idea of how the Association has grown in China the last few years. They are trying now to get 20 foreigners (who speak Chinese) and 100 Chinese secretaries to go to France to work among the Chinese Coolies there.

Dr. Lewis was here over Sunday on his way to Vladivostok. A lot of American and English doctors and nurses are going up into Siberia to take charge of the hospitals of the Czecho-Slav army that is starting to clean up the Bolsheviki and their German and Austrian auxiliaries that they have recruited from among the prisoners-of-war who were interned there. The Japanese and Chinese are also sending armies, while the Americans, French and British will send a regiment or two.

Letter written by Rob to his sister Ida

Paotingfu, Oct 10, 1918

I will take advantage of a holiday to get off another letter to you folks. Today is the seventh anniversary of the beginning of the Revolution, so is being appropriately celebrated by the inauguration of the new president, Hsü Shih Ch'ang, who it is hoped will be able to reunite the North and South and bring peace. He is the former tutor of the little Emperor, but really is not as conservative as one would think from that. At any rate, he is very anxious for peace with the South, so that the country can do something to aid against the Germans, which is the main thing.

The election for Vice President is to be held today, and it is almost certain that our local Governor, Ts'ao K'un, will be elected. I fear the Chinese have yet a long way to go before they have a real republican form of government, as I understand the delegates have been selling their votes openly to the highest bidder. However, even with all the corruption, they are infinitely better off than they would be under Japanese control.

Letter written by Rob to his sister Nan

Paotingfu, Nov. 13, 1918

We just ran off our Central Chihli Middle School Athletic meet last week, for which we have been preparing all fall. Teams Hubbard and I were coaching won both first and second in the track and field meet, first and second in basketball, and first in tennis, so we were quite pleased over it. The Yü Tê Middle School won all three events last year. It was quite a surprise in the track and field, as both Hubbard and I (who were coaching both teams and knew the men as well as anyone could) picked the Government Middle School to win.

We just got word of the surrender of Germany and the armistice. Isn't it great? I am wondering what effect it will have on your [nursing] work. I suppose the Americans in Europe at present will stay a long time yet, but don't see the reason for sending any more or keeping up the training camps much longer. We'll need all the men we can get to produce food for Europe this winter and get it to them. Well, I must close and go to class.

Letter written by Edith to Rob's family Paotingfu, N. China / Nov. 22, 1918

A Merry Christmas and a Happy New Year to you all from us five. This ought to be about the happiest holiday season of our lives. When we think of the fact that that awful war is over it seems like we can't be grateful and thankful and happy enough. I find it hard to realize that it is really over. I have to pinch myself several times a day. I feel like going around and saying like we do on Easter morning, "Christ is Risen", "He is risen indeed." "The war is over", "It is over, indeed." Or rather, better yet to say "The war is <u>won</u>." "It is won, indeed."

What a Thanksgiving it will be this year! When Bulgaria broke we began to say to each other half hoping, half doubting, "We may have a real Thanksgiving yet," but sure enough we are going to have. Of course we realize that the reconstruction is going to be difficult but still that is quite different from knowing that people are being hurt and killed all the time. We hung up our flags and stood at attention while they were being put up and saluted and sang "Three Cheers for the Red, White and Blue," and shouted "Hip-hip-hurrah!"

We are going to have a big compound dinner at the Robinson's this year. We didn't have any last Thanksgiving because of the flood and famine, so we are going to make up for it now. There will be nineteen of us at the table. The Robinson's are planning to have four guests from Peking and the single ladies are to have two guests and we are to have one. And we are planning to have a grand time.

I want to tell you about the guest we are to have. Her name is Miss [Drusie] Malott. She is a dwarf about four feet high. She came to China in the same party that Karl came with in 1904. She came as a stenographer to Mr. Houlding and stayed there a few years, then went up into Honan with some other independent missionaries, but three or four years ago she got the "Gift of Tongues". As these other missionaries didn't believe in that she had to leave. So she came to some other missionaries of that belief who live in a city about 90 miles south of here. But the head of that mission went off on "Seventh Day worship" which was too much for her so she started out to have a mission by herself. She is about forty. She believes so sincerely in what she does believe that none of us can find it in our hearts to discourage her. She is "trusting the Lord" as she puts it, not only for her own support, but she has two street chapels running which requires the services of an Evangelist and a small day school which has to have a teacher.

And, as if that wasn't enough, she has two little famine girls that she supports. She has been living in six wee Chinese rooms, dirt floors and everything, just like the Chinese. She said in her last letter tho' that she was moving into some rooms off the street chapel so they could open the other chapel as the $2.00–$2.50 rent that they had to pay took an awful big slice out of the $25 to $35 that came in every month "because" she added, "not only myself but the two girls and Mr. Lee and his family and Mr. Ma and his family all have to live off it." So if you folks have any stray $5.00 that you don't know where to put just send them along and I'll place them for you. She could earn a good living any time if she was willing to go to Tientsin to Mr. Grimes, but she is determined to do her mission work so we, as her friends, have to see that she doesn't starve to death. I had her down for a week's visit last spring which seemed to do her lots of good, and as she was sick in the summer and had the influenza this fall I thought a change and feed would do her good. She has to live on the poorest kind of Chinese food most of the time.

Dad's letter of Oct.10th–19th came today. We are going to return part of it to show what clever censors we had.

I am enclosing a picture of the four Chinese women who saw me thru' when Douglas was born [September 6, 1918]. The one highest on the stairs will graduate from Peking Medical School this year and will then be Dr. Sun. Her father died just before the Boxer trouble and her mother was killed by the Boxers which left her alone. Dr. Mackey adopted her and sent her thru' school. When she finished she said she wanted to be a doctor, but she seemed like such a frail little thing that Dr. Mackey didn't think she could stand the training and so she didn't encourage her in it. But Miss Sun was as determined as some other people we might mention so she got Dr. Elizabeth Lewis to loan her the money to take her training, and judging from the efficient way she cared for me I think she will be a great success.

Standing next to her is Miss Lee who is a perfect dear. She took care of me when Constance was born too. She too has a very interesting history. She never knew her parents. She – with a boy about the same age – were both adopted by a small official and engaged to each other. The official died; his wife was a very flighty sort of a creature, but she put the two children in the Mission schools and paid for their schooling for two or three years when she suddenly disappeared, leaving the children dependent on the missionaries here. The boy didn't seem to care and after a year he ran away, but Miss Lee felt dreadfully humiliated but as she was helpless she had to accept charity. Miss Newton paid her expenses until she finished school. When she finished school they asked her what she wanted to do. She said, I want to learn to be a nurse so I can earn my own living. She is an excellent maternity nurse. She was married two weeks to the day after Douglas was born, and I was able to attend the wedding. She was engaged to a widower and planned to have been married shortly after Constance was born, but the man died suddenly. She was dreadfully cut up at the time, so much so that Dr. Mackey was afraid she would take a vow not to marry, so Dr. Mackey made her promise not to do that as she might feel differently later. Just fancy being so upset over a man you had never laid eyes on! The man she just married was a very close friend of the former and was not a widower. They are both educated and according to the Chinese ought to have a happy home altho' they had to do all their getting acquainted after the marriage. She was the prettiest bride. Her clothes were the very palest green, silk with silk stockings and satin shoes to match. The latter were covered with the tiniest embroidered butterflies. I forgot to say her husband is pastor of one of the Presbyterian Mission Churches. She was so afraid that she wouldn't get to care for me and baby Douglas.

Miss Lin who is standing just below Miss Lee was the very first patient they had in the Hospital in Peking when it opened after the Boxer trouble. She had tubercular bones and glands. She has one wooden leg and has had to have parts of bones and glands taken out in various places. She has been operated on a number of times. There are just she and her mother. When her mother found out that Miss Lin would have to have her foot off she said "Well we might as well go and commit suicide, as no man would want to marry a cripple." Dr. Mackey told her that wasn't at all necessary. That if she would work and educate the girl they would make her self-supporting so she wouldn't have to be married. She is now Dr. Mackey's right hand man. She is very efficient and Dr. Mackey couldn't possibly get along without her. Rob calls her "the boss."

Miss Chang who is standing next to her was my regular nurse. Her mother is dead. She wants to earn her own living so she won't have to be married off against her will or wishes. She was awfully sick for over a year. Dr. Lewis as well as Dr. Mackey treated her for everything that they could imagine that ailed her without having any effect, so they at last decided on an operation. And what do you think ailed her? Just tapeworms! It isn't every small boy who has so many interesting people to care for him, is it?

Dec. 1st, 1918

Thanksgiving is over and we had a perfectly lovely time. Miss Malott came Tuesday. Thurs. morning at ten o'clock we all went over to Mrs. Lewis' house to Thanksgiving service then came home and we all had a big Thanksgiving dinner at Mrs. Robinson's. We had several outside guests and had a very interesting time altogether. Miss Phelps gave a very clever reproduction of village life in China while Miss Chapin told us of many interesting things that happened in the siege of Peking during 1900. Miss Chapin is the only American woman to have the Victoria Cross for women. She had charge of the kitchen in the hospital and was very clever at making tasty dishes out of the limited supplies, horse and mule meat soup, etc.

We had a high tea at the Ladies house yesterday afternoon and had a big crowd, a number of people were down from Peking and it surely was fine to see so many nice people altogether. We had between thirty and forty present. Dr. Lewis is still in Russia. Mrs. L. hasn't heard from him since peace, so she don't know but what he may be home soon. She is always so cheerful and brave when he runs these great risks taking care of the plague and war etc.

Letter written by Edith to her mother and brother (in California)
Paotingfu / Dec. 4th, 1918

Isn't it wonderful to know that the war is won and over? They have been having great celebrations in Peking and Tientsin. We had a very happy time here on Thanksgiving Day. We had our Service at Mrs. Lewis' house and then we came home and had a big Compound dinner at Mrs. Robinson's home. There were eighteen of us at the two tables. We had Drusie down and Mrs. R. had three guests and, of course, the bigger children were at the table too.

Poor Drusie seemed to enjoy the change so much. She has been living mostly on millet and "dough-strings." She brought her littlest girl with her, Lilly Pearl. She was a pretty child. We found some of Constance's old clothes and fitted her up in them and she looked so cute. She was a very well behaved child and if Drusie doesn't spoil her she ought to be a great comfort to her. I have offered Drusie the privilege of coming and living here in our house next summer. It will be so much nicer for her than her place in Chengting. She was so very pleased with the idea. I think I will ask Mrs. Faulke and her two girls to come too. Rose Mary, the youngest one, wasn't very well last summer and I think a change would do them all good. I only wish we could afford to have them all up at Peitaiho with us.

Letter written by Rob to his family Paotingfu / Dec. 27, 1918

It is rather hard to adjust oneself to the fact that the war is really over and the world is again at peace, isn't it? And if it is hard for us who were engaged in work which was so very little directly affected by the war, what must it be for those who were actually on the firing line?

The greatest effect noticeable out here is that America's stock among the Chinese has gone even higher than ever, and the bad effect of the American-Japanese agreement last winter in regard to China has been wiped out completely. The people are putting all their hopes on America taking a stand for them against Japanese aggression in the Peace Conference. [President] Wilson is especially popular. The old "Wilhelm Strasse" in the former German Concession in Tientsin has been named "Woodrow Wilson Street".

It begins to look as though we might have internal peace in China soon, too, in spite of efforts of "a certain nation" to keep things stirred up. The new president, Hsü, is showing himself much more of a statesman than people thought possible when he was elected and seems ready to make almost any kind of reasonable sacrifice to bring back internal peace. His attitude has been much more conciliatory than that of the Southern party, though he really has much less reason to be so than they.

Yü Tê Track Team (middle school in Paotingfu)**, Champions of North China**
(Hugh Hubbard and R.W. Clack in center of second row) (photo 1918)

Men from flooded districts working on roads (photo 1918)

Flood refugees - stone crushers, rebuilding roads in 1918

Our Chinese House in the South Suburb (photo 1918)
(see letter of April 22, 1918)

20 Seventh Year with the Y.M.C.A.

Highlights of 1919

- The goal of the Y.M.C.A. was to "put Christian principles into practice by developing a healthy body, mind, and spirit". As executive secretary of the Paotingfu Y.M.C.A., Rob was very active in encouraging physical fitness participation and – as an extension – organizing athletic activities.
- In addition to coordinating local school athletic activities and events, he helped prepare for the North China Athletic Federation meet in Taiyuanfu, Shansi. He also served as president of the China Amateur Athletic Union beginning in 1919 (through 1921). In that capacity he oversaw the Chinese team of about 200 athletes who competed against Japanese and Philippine athletes in the Far Eastern Olympian Championship Games in Manila in May 1919.
- Another outreach project was to start publishing a monthly magazine, "Paotingfu Young Men". There were no regular newspapers of any kind published in Paotingfu because of its proximity to Peking and Tientsin, so the paper was well received and had a circulation of more than 800.

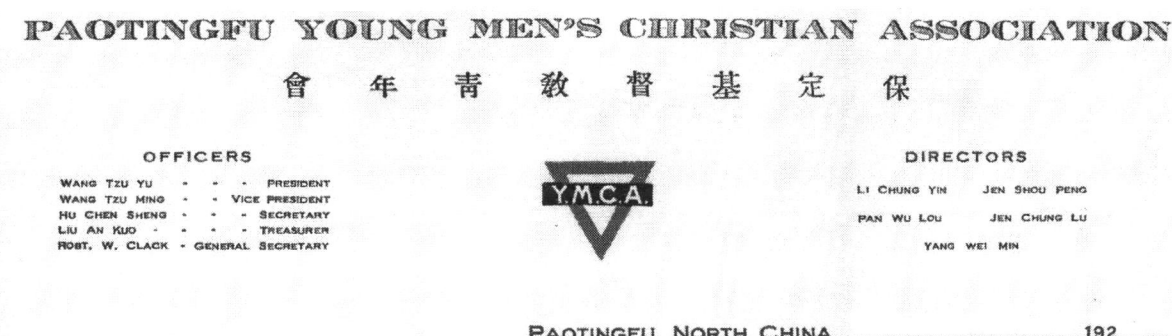

Y.M.C.A. ANNUAL REPORT, PAOTINGFU
Year Ended September 30, 1919
Written by Robert W. Clack, General Secretary (following are excerpts from the Report)

1919 - YEAR ENDED SEPTEMBER 30 (Vol. I)

Men Won for the Church – I have just returned from a very impressive service at the Presbyterian Church at which, among others received into membership was Ts'ou Hsi, the inter-scholastic mile champion of the Far East. He has been a member of the Association Bible classes throughout his four years of High School. Aside from Ts'ou Hsi, a dozen others of the student class have entered the local Churches during the past year either directly or indirectly through Association influence.

Among the older men won, the most influential is Major Li, one of the teachers in the Military College. This summer he was elected to the Board of Directors of the Association, where, because of his aggressive spirit for service, he is a very valuable asset.

None but Chinese Directors Now – Several changes have taken place in the Board of Directors. It is now composed entirely of Chinese. We started six years ago with a majority of foreigners on the Board, but as their terms have expired these have one by one been replaced by Chinese.

The president, Mr. Wang Tzu Yu, has had a very interesting career and is a living example of the power of God to change lives. He was formerly an official with all the official sins – embezzlement of public funds, gambling, and opium smoking. Finally, however, he became a Christian, gave up his position, broke off his bad habits, and has become a fine reliable man. He now earns his living by superintending the language study of the American Board missionaries. The vice-president, Dr. Wangsun, is a second generation Christian. He was educated in the mission schools, graduating from the North China Union College, and then from the Union Medical College. He is now the head of the Chinese staff in the Presbyterian Hospital. The secretary, Dr. Hu Chen Sheng, is a doctor of the old school, and proprietor of one of the leading drug stores of the city. Dr. Liu, the treasurer, having gone to Shansi, that position is now vacant. The other members are Mr. Jen Shou Peng, principal of the American Board boys' school; Mr. Yang Wei Min, one of the teachers in that school; and Dr. Pan Wu Liu, a prominent physician.

We have been exceedingly fortunate in obtaining Mr. Liu Kuo Chu from the American Board Mission to organize and take charge of the new Boys' Department. Mr. Liu was city evangelist for the American Board and was so successful in organizing boys' clubs that the Mission were very willing to let us have him that he might give all his time to working with boys. In the last six months he has built up a flourishing Boys' Department of almost a hundred members. He has also been very valuable in organizing our religious work. The Sunday services have been placed in his charge with a marked gain both in their character and their attendance.

Owing to the shortage of workers in the American Board Mission last fall and the recurrence of floods with the spring freshets, we were deprived of Mr. Hubbard's services during the past year. Even though there was no responsible head for that work, the student Bible classes showed a substantial gain with a membership of almost 150.

Local and Regional Athletics – A large portion of my own time has been taken up with government school athletics. We had complete charge of athletics in the Government Middle School, the Yu Te Middle School, and the Industrial School during the fall term. After the New Year, as the only member of the Games Committee of the North China Athletic Federation who had had previous experience in running off a big meet, I was obliged to spend a good deal of time in preparations for the North China meet, which was held in Taiyuanfu, Shansi, in April. I was also secretary of the committee which had charge of rewriting the constitution of the Federation.

The Far Eastern Games – When Mr. Swan, head of the Physical Department of the National Committee, left for America on furlough in April, I went to Shanghai to take his place as executive secretary of the Committee for China of the Far Eastern Athletic Association. We took a team of over a hundred athletes to Manila. We finished second in the Games. We took advantage of having representatives from all parts of the country together at Manila to initiate a National Athletic Union, something which has never before been attempted. I was appointed head of a committee to draw up a constitution and rules.

Editor's note – The First [Modern] Olympic Games were held in 1894, but China was not represented at the first nine Olympic Games. In 1920 the International Olympics Committee (IOC) recognized the Far Eastern Championship Games and the Far Eastern Amateur Athletic Federation, the first regional international sports organization to enter relations with the IOC. As an active member of the Federation, China participated in the ten Far Eastern Championship Games held during the period of 1913-34. [8]

United Evangelism in the City – Our relations with the Churches have continued to be very satisfactory. We have welcomed a new organization to the city, the Salvation Army, and were able to be of service to them in finding suitable quarters and otherwise getting started. We also arranged for weekly evangelistic meetings in the three prisons of the city. The impression on the prison authorities was so good that they also consented to let us do direct personal work with the prisoners.

Expanded Activities – We now have twenty-three students in day school, and a still large number studying English in the night school.

We started a monthly magazine in January, "Paotingfu Young Men". There are no regular newspapers of any kind published here, because of our nearness to Peking and Tientsin, so our paper has been well received and has a circulation of over 800.

The second annual membership campaign was carried to a very successful conclusion entirely by the Chinese. Eight teams of five men each went to work with the goal set at three hundred new members. They got 550, which brought the total membership up to 651. Our financial campaign also did well, with Governor-General Ts'ao K'un generously repeating his last year's gift of Mexican $1000 for current expenses.

Our increase in membership a year ago made it necessary for us to move to a larger building last fall, and we got the largest building we could find in the city, but with our further increase this year, even this building is very inadequate. We are trying to obtain a suitable site to build on.

Seed of the Martyrs – A Preaching General
In conclusion I wish to tell of a letter which has just come to Rev. A. M. Cunningham, of the Presbyterian Mission, from Hunan Province where the Sixteenth Division of Chihli troops (mostly recruited from the Paotingfu district) are stationed. These troops are under the command of Major General Wu P'ei Fu and Brigadier General Feng Yü Hsiang, both of whom are former members of, and liberal contributors, to the Paotingfu Association.

Since the armistice between the two parties, General Feng has been stationed in Hunan, with nothing special to do; so, assisted by several of his Christian officers, he started an evangelistic campaign among his men. This was carried on without missionary instigation or assistance until a couple of weeks ago, when Rev. Jonathan Goforth, of the Canadian Presbyterians, was called in to baptize those who were ready to join the Church. He baptized 507 men, of whom about two-thirds were officers.

These officers decided that they also wished to have Christian homes, so they asked Dr. T. K. Fu, formerly a very active member of our Association, to write for his wife to come down to Hunan to work with the officers' wives. General Feng has just written Mr. and Mrs. Cunningham to come for a month to give them further Bible training and help them to organize better to extend their evangelistic campaign into other divisions of the army.

This truly seems to be the beginning of the movement we have all been praying for, whereby the whole Chinese nation will be evangelized not by the inadequate efforts of a few scattered foreigners, but by leaders who God will raise up from among the Chinese themselves. It will be our work to help find these leaders and pass on to them the blessings and training and experience which generations of Christianity have given us. [9]

1919 - YEAR ENDED SEPTEMBER 30 (Vol. II)

Survey of the Field – To the classes mentioned in last year's report, which remain practically unchanged, we must add the large number of merchants of the better class, who have come into the Association in the membership campaign this year and whom we formerly considered to belong especially to the field of the missions.

Problems and Handicaps – In spite of our greatly increased membership, the number from the Association uniting with the churches remains practically the same. While we are reaching, superficially a great many more, we are getting into intimate relationships with only about the same number as before. This is largely due to the fact that our building cannot accommodate a very large number, and we have about reached the limit of those we can get into intimate relationships with by going outside of the building for personal calls.

Another reason why it is hard to get men to the churches is because of their locations. Our work must, of necessity, centre inside the walled city, while the two churches are in connection with the mission compounds, one outside the west suburb, and the other outside the south suburb. If a member wishes to be introduced to the church leaders, it is necessary for the secretary to take him the long trip outside the city and back. We should have room in our building for church offices, where the pastors or other church representatives could meet those interested and sit down for quiet uninterrupted talks to get acquainted. In our present overcrowded quarters, not only is it impossible to set aside such office room but we even have no place where one of the secretaries can take a member for a private conference.

Policy – We shall continue to work on the same lines as last year, but in addition shall attempt:
(a) to reorganize our committees and membership department so that the responsibilities are carried by a larger proportion of the membership;

(b) to organize Bible classes among the merchants and gentry in the membership;
(c) to get as many people as possible interested in teaching the new phonetic alphabet to illiterates;
(d) to get a suitable building site, and if possible, to get work started on our new building;
(e) to work out, in cooperation with the churches, a program of voluntary service, so that there is a task for every man who is willing to help.

Distribution of Time – September to March was spent on regular Association work; April and May were given to the North China and Far Eastern Athletic Meets; I was taken sick the first of June and spent most of the month recuperating; July was spent in regular work; August at the seashore; September, back at work again.

Health – Mrs. Clack's heart is gradually getting stronger, though she will need to be careful of strains and shocks for a long time yet. I had a severe attack of dengue fever [mosquito-borne tropical disease] on my return from Manila which left me rather shaky for several weeks, and I notice that I still get tired more easily than usual. Last year was a very heavy year, but with Hubbard back this year to help share the responsibility it will not be so wearing. [10]

THE LETTERS

Letter written by Rob to his sister Nan

Paotingfu / Jan. 10, 1919

I got an interview with the Governor General last week and he gave me $1000 to start the Y.M.C.A.'s new year budget with. That means we will have at least this year free from financial worries, as when he gives so substantially, all the other officials have to give proportionate subscriptions as a matter of face. In fact we don't intend to use the governor's gift at all if we can help it, but keep it for a rainy day. I took it to Tientsin and bought gold with it, for it is certain that when trade begins to pick up gold will gradually work back towards its old value. I had to pay $1.00 Mex for $1.00 gold, and also get 4% interest on the money.

Letter written by Rob to his sister Ida

Paotingfu / Jan. 17, 1919

Wasn't Teddy's death a shock, though, of course, during the epidemic it was liable to get anyone. *[Editor's note – former President Theodore Roosevelt died January 6, 1919, Oyster Bay, NY]* Mother asked in her letter if there was any ground to the theory that the "flu" was the same as the pneumonic plague. I fear that was advanced by a man who knew very little of the plague. Of course the "flu" was really worse in the total number of deaths because practically everybody had it, but I don't believe that anywhere the death rate was more than 30% or 40%, while as for the plague in the two epidemics of 1911 and 1918, there is only one absolute authenticated case of recovery, and even if the supposed cases of plague which recovered are allowed, the death rate was between 98% and 99%.

Letter written by Rob to his mother

Paotingfu / Jan. 29, 1919

    Saturday, Feb. 1, will be the Chinese New Year so everybody is having vacations or getting ready for it. All the schools closed last week for a three weeks' vacation including ours, and the secretaries are all gone home for ten days or a fortnight, so I am running things alone. I am keeping one class of older men who live here in the city going, but that is all. The schools are being out, our game room is crowded all day long with small boys, so I have to be on the job at least part of the day to settle quarrels, and keep one crowd from monopolizing the games all the time.

    We have just engaged one of the American Board workers who has shown a special aptitude for dealing with small boys as Boy's Secretary so we will start a regular boy's department after the New Year, which will ultimately undoubtedly grow to be our biggest piece of work. Even now we are going to have to use, not only our own building, but all the mission chapels in the city as centres for the boy's clubs.

Letter written by Edith to her mother in California

Paotingfu / Feb. 17th, 1919

    Saturday was the 15th of the first moon, and Oh! it was lively around here. They had firecrackers etc. in the city and they also had two huge drums, but the Governor wouldn't allow them in the city so they spent the evening circulating thru' this suburb. One drum was fully ten feet in diameter and about three feet thick, while the smaller one was about seven feet. They were mounted on low push carts. They were about ten men to beat each drum, besides a number of cymbals and strings of metal and a fife or two. They stopped right out here in front of our house about ten o'clock at night and I never in my life heard such a noise. The big drum shook the house so it felt like an earthquake. There were about two hundred in the crowd and about a dozen odd shaped lanterns in the crowd. It was the most weird unearthly scene I ever saw in my life and the noisiest.

Letter written by Rob to his father

Paotingfu / Feb. 18, 1919

    Everything here is in a rush now getting ready for Chinese New Year day after tomorrow. I suppose you have been reading of the student agitation in the larger cities. It is not so bad here as outside the Military College, where the students are under martial law, the students are almost all of only high school grade. Furthermore we have no Japs. The real issue is between the students and the military party who are now in control of the government. The militarists have hardly passed a chance to bungle affairs and to alienate the merchants and gentry, who are the real backbone of the country. At first the merchants and gentry opposed the student agitation, but have gradually been driven to line up with them, until in some places, for example Tientsin, the Commercial Club and Student's Union have amalgamated into a People's Union. And the Japs don't miss a chance to play into their hands by their tactless aggression. The militarists are pro-Japanese, you know, just as they were pro-German before.

Letter written by Rob to his father

Paotingfu / Feb. 22, 1919

I suppose you have been keeping up on the Peace Conference and have seen how the Japs got shown up trying to gag the Chinese delegates. Of course we all have been deeply grieved to see how our illustrious ally has overreached herself. I am afraid the Japs didn't know the Chinese delegates as well as some of the rest of us did. Wellington Koo, I have just met, but C.T. Wang is a close personal friend. He was in the Y.M.C.A. for a long time, you know. He is one of the spitfire type, and only just a little harder to put a gag on than Teddy Roosevelt was. I only hope the Powers have finally got wise enough to the Japs so that they will try to give Korea some freedom. There was probably no one of the Austrian subject races which has been oppressed half as bad as the Koreans.

Letter written by Rob to his father

March 1919

I'm keeping pretty busy now getting ready for the North China & Far Eastern Meets. North China Meet is to be held in Taiyüanfu, Shansi, Apl. 14 & 15. I am the only out-of-town man on the Committee. I have already been up once and have to go again about a week before the meet and stay till it's over.

It's quite a hard trip. Leave here at 2 A.M. and go to Shihchiachuang. Get there at 6:00 and then leave at 8:00 on the narrow gauge French railway. We entered the mountains about 20 miles away and climb up to about 4000 feet by noon. It's beautiful scenery. We follow up the gorge of the Sha River, one of the ones which give us so much trouble during the rainy season, but the railway is high enough above it and the roadbed is mostly cut right out of the rock so the floods never bother it. There is hardly a straight track all the way and 18 tunnels, but none over a quarter mile. From noon on we go down again but more gradually, getting down to Taiyüanfu about 5 P.M. It is about 3000 feet up. It is a little larger city than Paotingfu but, except for the fact that they have electric lights, much less well kept.

They are building an athletic field especially for the meet in the southeast corner of the city, and are terracing the city wall to make grandstands. It makes a great amphitheatre; will seat 15,000 I should estimate. The Governor, Yen, the youngest and most progressive governor in China is financing it. Pays all my expenses when I go up. In fact, I made money. I went second class and they insisted on my taking expense money for first class.

The Far Eastern Games are in Manila. I am on the committee to select the track and field men. I may go to Manila with the team if I can manage things here to get away.

Letter written by Rob to his father

Chengchow, Honan / Apl. 12, 1919

I have a short time here before train time so I will make good use of it in getting off a note to you folks. I certainly have been on the go the last week or so. A week ago Thursday I received a special delivery letter from Swan, our National Physical Director, who has been the head of the Committee for China in the Far Eastern Athletic Association, saying that he had suddenly been called home to America, and that the Committee (which consists chiefly of Tang Shao I, the southern delegate to the Peace Conference in Shanghai; Chu, the northern delegate; Dr. Tsui, former president of Tsing Hua College, and secretary of the Peace Conference, and C.C. Heih, head of the Shanghai Chamber of Commerce) had me to take his place and wanted me to come to Shanghai at once to take things over.

So I left the next afternoon for Tientsin where I unloaded most of my responsibility for the North China Meet on P.C. Chang, the president of the N.C. Federation, (brother of Chang Po Ling, of Nankai School) and then went on to Shanghai getting there Sunday night. I spent Monday, Tuesday and Wednesday going over correspondence files and conferring with Swan and the Committee to find out what had been done and what still remains to be done, and then got started back north again day before yesterday.

I am trying to get to Taiyüanfu in time for the North China Meet which starts Monday, and unless I miss connections at Shihchiachuang, I'll get there Sunday afternoon. Altogether I will have traveled almost 2500 miles on nine different trains in nine days. After the meet at Taiyüanfu I will get back to Paotingfu for three or four days, and then back to Shanghai again to make the final preparations. We leave Shanghai May 3, and get to Manila May 7, the meet lasting the week from May 12 to 17. We come back by way of Hong Kong and will probably get back home again the first week in June.

This appointment is really quite an honor as it makes me the executive head of all athletics in China. The reason they passed over the heads of the regular physical directors and took me is because they had to have a man who is not only thoroughly familiar with all kinds of athletics, but a trained executive as well, and of course very few physical directors have that training. Swan has done a fine job of setting things up so that now the main things left for me to do are to pick the athletes and coaches who are to go, and take charge of getting them there and back. We have the arrangements all finished for getting them from Shanghai to Manila, and negotiations in progress in regard to getting the Northern men to Shanghai and getting the whole bunch back.

We have to raise $20,000 to finance the trip, but as practically every one of the Chinese on the Committee could give the whole sum personally without even missing it, I am not planning to spend much time on that.

We have already decided to send the South China volleyball, football, tennis and swimming teams, and the North China basketball team, so that the chief thing now is to pick the track men. About three-fourths of them will have to come from North China. I will pick the North China men at Taiyüanfu, and then we have another big meet in Shanghai April 26 to pick the rest from Central and South China.

Editor's note – Rob was in transit during the time of the "May Fourth Incident" when more than 3,000 college students in Peking protested against the decision of the Paris Peace Conference to transfer to Japan all of the land, railways, mines, forests, etc. previously occupied by Germany. [11]

Letter written by Rob to his mother

Approaching Island of Luzon, P.I. / May 7, 1919

Well, here we are approaching the Philippines. Expect to be in Manila by this time tomorrow afternoon. We have had a very smooth trip, hardly any whitecaps even most of the time, but in spite of that quite a number of our boys have been seasick. Chinese are very poor sailors. However they have four days in Manila before the games begin so ought to get back in good shape. We have a party of forty-eight athletes, three Chinese coaches and eight Americans (counting the reporter).

The Americans are Dr. McCracken, of Shanghai (All-American guard and one-time holder of World's record in the hammer throw) and Dr. Jee, of Tientsin, (an American born and trained Chinese) who are the physicians of the party, Dr. Shoemaker, physical director of Peking Higher Normal College, Bradshaw, Amoy Y.M.C.A.; Leake, Foochow Y.M.C.A.; Kulp, physical director of Shanghai Baptist College (another All-American football man); Doyle, reporter of the Chinese Press; and myself, manager of the bunch. We have the whole track team and the basketball team with us. The soccer team, volleyball team, tennis team and swimmers are from South China and have gone directly across from Hong Kong. We stop over at Hong Kong and Canton on the way back. We get back to Shanghai about May 24th.

We are beginning to realize we are in the tropics. We are about 18° now. (Manila is about 14°). The sun is directly overhead here at noon this time of year and, believe me, it does burn through. The field meet will be held in the morning and late afternoon, as everybody takes a siesta in the middle of the day. The water is such a deep blue, and there are flying fish in sight all of the time.

I certainly have been on the move lately. In the three weeks from April 4 to April 25, I was on the train 15 days (shortest trip one day 90 miles). We will be 8 days in Manila which will be our longest stop, and I'll get back home about May 29th.

Apparently I'll not be through then either. Just as I got on the boat at Shanghai I got a telegram appointing me to take charge of the Chinese Army Y.M.C.A. for Siberia for the summer. Headquarters are at Nicolevsk (I think that is spelled properly) about fifty miles out from Vladivostok. I replied that I would accept if I didn't have to go before July first. If I go I won't get any vacation, but this trip, and the change of work up there ought to be all the rest I need. Edith will have some people with her at Peitaiho, so I will feel quite easy about her. It will be good for our Chinese secretaries at Paotingfu to have the responsibility of the Y.M.C.A. for a while.

Letter written by Rob to his sister Ida

Between Hong Kong & Shanghai / May 24, 1919

Well, our Manila visit is over and we are on the way back. We were there twelve days, May 8 to 20th. We went across to Hong Kong on the "Empress of Asia" stopped there overnight and left yesterday, May 23. We get to Shanghai May 26. I have to stop there a day or two to settle up and then on to home. Will probably get there about a week from today. I am afraid I'll miss the big wedding, Miss Savige and Dr. Honnestadt, the first foreign wedding in Paotingfu, but will get back in time for Moore's [Edith's brother] and Jessie's wedding which will be about the middle of June, I guess.

We did not win the games as we hoped, but made the best showing yet made by a team away from home in the Far Eastern games, and beat time out of the Japs, which was the main thing. We also stole the limelight from the Filipinos by winning two of the feature events, the pentathlon and decathlon.

Chu En Tê [Ente] of the Peking Normal College, Far Eastern Championship Games

What made it even more of a headliner was the fact that both were won by one man, Chu En Tê, of the Peking Normal College, a stunt which has never been pulled off before in the Far East, and only Jim Thorpe has done it in the European Olympics. To cap the climax he raised the pentathlon record from 341 to 360 and the decathlon 711 to 755. They were both whirlwind finishes, too.

In the pentathlon he came up to the mile just at noon in that awful heat after going through the first five decathlon events and the other four pentathlon, and was told he had to run the mile in 5'07" to win, when his best previous record in the mile was 5'25" and that was made when he was fresh and not under a tropical sun. Most men would have quit then and there, and no one would have criticized them for it, but he made the attempt. He set an awfully hard pace and when he got to the three quarters I thought he was done, but he went on, literally staggering all over the track for the last quarter and finished with two seconds to spare in 5'05". Of course we all thought that finished him for the decathlon next day, as it didn't seem possible that a man could run himself to exhaustion like that and still be able to go on with only one night's rest. But he showed up the next morning as determined as ever for the last five decathlon events, even though he had big dark circles under the eyes and lacked his usual springiness.

When they came to the mile again, which is also the last decathlon event, he again needed to make up a big margin. Taduran, a Filipino half miler, was leading in points and Chu had to beat him 17 seconds to win. Even had it been a case of just barely beating him it would have seemed desperate for Taduran was fairly fresh and was a trained distance runner, while Chu ought to have been exhausted from the day before and is supposed to be a weight thrower rather than a distance man. However he said to me, "I'll do it" and gritted his teeth and set in. He set the same pace he had the day before. Taduran, of course, didn't dare to let him get too much of a lead so had to follow the pace. Chu ran him off his feet in the first three quarters, and then finished on his nerve as he had the day before, pulling away from Taduran at the finish and beating him 19 seconds in 5'07", only two seconds slower than the day before.

Results

Altogether the Filipinos won first in baseball (by default), swimming, basketball, volleyball and track and field, and got second in the marathon and football, and the decathlon. We won football, the decathlon and pentathlon, and second in pentathlon, track and field, swimming, basketball and volleyball. The Japs won the marathon and broke even with the Filipinos on tennis but got no other first or second in swimming which is supposed to be their long suit. Baseball had no second as neither China or Japan sent a team. The next games are to be in Shanghai about October 1, 1921. We ought then to have a good chance to win everything but the track and field, where the Filipinos are too strong for us. We had a team this year who could do as well or better than the Far Eastern records in more than half the events, but even that was far from good enough. The Filipinos broke fourteen and tied one record in eighteen events. In several cases we had two or three men better than the old record, and didn't even get third place.

Letter written by Rob to his father in Iowa

Peitaiho / August 18, 1919

Mother's letter from Mabel of July 13 just came and a few days before that a number of letters written way back in June. The mail has been very irregular again for the last month or so, because the cholera has been so bad in Shanghai that a lot of the Trans Pacific boats don't stop there anymore. They either put Shanghai mail and passengers off in Japan or else carry them on to Hong Kong, and from there they go to Shanghai on local boats which are not bothered so much by the quarantine regulations.

Our new house over at East Cliff is getting along in good shape. They are just beginning to put the roof on. It ought to be all done but the inside finishing by the last of next week when we go back home. I believe I sent a plan of it in the last letter. It will cost about $2500 when it is all finished. We will have to pay about $150 a year interest on the money we borrowed to build it, but we would have to pay $350 rent, so we will have a margin of about $200 to pay on the principal.

Letter written by Edith to Rob's sister Ida

Paotingfu, N. China / Sept. 24, 1919

Gordon wants me to tell you about the robber. One came this morning in broad day-light and took the [servant] boy's bedding, watch, etc. out of the gate-house which is right by the big gate that opens on the street. The children are very much excited about it all. It is really the servants' own fault as they ought to keep that gate closed and locked, but they all hate to run and open the gate when the bell rings so that they just leave it open.

Our Peitaiho house was almost finished when we left. It is so very nice and we have such beautiful views from our porch. I told Rob it was hard to realize that it was really ours. He said we would realize it was ours all right before we got it paid for. It surely is a joy to think of going to our own place next summer, and not have to hunt around for a house to rent. They are going to make a good rickshaw road from Rocky-Point to East Cliff which will be a great improvement for us all. I hate to ride the donkeys so, so have had to walk it most of the time, as chairs cost too much money. It is about two miles one way. Gordon and Constance both walked both ways two or three times this summer.

Rob is going to have to go to Hangchow, Central China, to a Y.M.C.A. Conference about the middle of Nov. I do wish I could afford to go with him. He says it is so lovely down there. Quite different than around here.

Letter written by Rob to his mother

Hangchow, Sunday afternoon / Nov. 23, 1919

We are having our [Y.M.C.A.] National Secretaries' Conference here for eight days and don't get much time to loaf. Regular sessions are from 8 to 11:30; 1 to 4:30 and 7 to 8:30; and we have committee meetings outside that so it keeps us pretty busy. Today they are having a number of special religious services which are not connected with the work of the conference proper, but I fear that the attendance is not very big. We have in all 60 American secretaries and

110 Chinese in attendance, which is about half our total force in China, in fact a little more than half of the foreigners. Ed Munson is here, and there are three other Iowa men in the crowd; Oliver, of Hangchow is a Cornell man; and Smith, of Kaifengfu, and Verink, who is still in the language school, are from Coe. We are trying to get up a basketball game with some other state, but have not yet succeeded in finding any other state with enough men.

We left home a week ago Wednesday, Hubbard and I and Verink came down from Peking on the same train. We stopped off at Shuntefu overnight, as we were traveling third class and did not want to spend two nights on the train. Then we went on the next morning, getting to Hankow Friday morning. We spent the day there and in Wuchang, which is across the river. I had tiffin and a good visit with S.B. Harvey, who used to teach with me in the college at Paotingfu. We left that evening on the boat for Shanghai, getting there Monday noon. It is a delightfully restful 600 mile trip down the river, though the scenery is nothing special. There are one or two picturesque spots though. The last half day's trip the river is so wide that one cannot see across from one side to the other, so it gives the impression of being on the sea except that there is no swell, and one can't get seasick. We came down here Wednesday evening.

This place is about 100 miles south of Shanghai. It is the most picturesque spot in China, and a great resort. We are living in a hotel overlooking the famous West Lake, with its islands and causeways, hills and temples. The Chinese proverb says, "Above is Heaven, below are Soo (chow) and Hang (chow)."

We are taking advantage of having delegates from all over the country to organize a National Athletic Union. We had a meeting in Shanghai before we came down, and have a final meeting the day we get back, next Friday. I think, however, I will find it necessary to go back a day early, Thursday, as that is Thanksgiving Day, and they are having the first game of American football in China for several years between the men from the fleet and the civilians. I am rooting for the Navy this time, as I helped coach them the two days I stopped in Shanghai on the way down. The civilians are a bunch of old college stars, but while they are more experienced, I think the Navy have it on them in condition.

Letter written by Rob to his sister Ida

Paotingfu / Dec. 10, 1919

Well, here I am back home again after three weeks in the south. I got back a week ago. Went up from Hangchow to Shanghai Thanksgiving morning and got there just in time for the football game. I refereed. It was between the Shanghai civilians and the men from the American gunboats in port. The civilians won 6 to 0. The civilian team was made up of old college stars from the American firms in Shanghai. Most of them have come out in the last year. They say over 80 new American firms have opened offices in Shanghai in the last three months. They took a lot of moving pictures of the game, so you may see it in the movies yet.

There was a bunch of Universal Film people coming up on the train from Shanghai to Peking with me. They are out here getting pictures for "The Lotus Petals of Laocius". They took a number of shots of the train and stations on the way up. The film will be released next summer, so if you get a chance to see it you want to go. You can be sure that all the views of Chinese trains are real because I saw them made. A lot were taken at the Têchow station, where the Grinnell people are. I also told them where to get the Gobi desert stuff, camels, sand storms and so forth, without having to go more than ten miles out of Peking.

Waterfall just above Niangtzukuan – Shansi Railroad
(photo taken from aboard a moving train, 1919)

Cave dwellings at south end of Yellow River Bridge, Peking-Hankow Railroad (photo 1919)

Niangtzukuan, location of the Niangzi Pass (photo 1919)
(famous pass in the Great Wall known as the ninth pass under the heaven)

North China Meet, Taiyuanfu, Governor's Stand (photo April 1919)

Paotingfu Representatives on the Chinese National Team (photo May 1919)

Robert Wood Clack at the Manila Far Eastern Games (photo May 1919)

21 Warlords, Famine, and More

Highlights: January-July 1920

- In April Rob was negotiating with the local officials for a two-acre piece of land just inside the south gate for a Y.M.C.A. building site and athletic field. "If we do get it, we can probably start our new building plans right away, and may even be able to start building in the fall."
- In addition to his Y.M.C.A. work, Rob also served as Chinese representative to the International Olympic Federation from 1920 to 1923.
- The Wo Fo Ssŭ (Sleeping Buddha Temple) Y.M.C.A. Conference was held near Peking in early July.
- There was no Y.M.C.A. Annual Report written for September 30, 1920, because the international requirements changed to a two-year reporting standard.

THE LETTERS

Letter written by Rob to his family in Iowa

Paotingfu / Jan. 2, 1920

Hugh has gone to Shansi on a hunting trip, Wang is in the South until the Chinese New Year studying Association methods, and our two day-school teachers are in Peking over Christmas and New Year's, so Liu, the Boys secretary and I are running things alone for a while, and with our yearly statistical and financial reports to the National Committee and all, I manage to keep out of mischief.

I will probably have to go to Peking or Tientsin for a meeting of the Executive Committee of the North China Athletic Association in the next week or ten days, and will get a good chance to read then. I like to read on the train, you remember.

There has been quite a bit of influenza again this winter, though the last few weeks there has been a let up. Charles Ogilvey, of the Presbyterian mission, probably the best all round young fellow in North China died of it yesterday in Peking.

Letter written by Rob to his sister Nan

Paotingfu / Jan. 15, 1920

Moore [Edith's brother] left for America Monday morning for a six month's trip to get men and stock for the large agricultural experiment station which is to be launched under the auspices of the University. A large Chinese hotel owner by the name of Ch'in is responsible for the idea and offered to put up the money, but now President Hsü Shih Ch'ang and several other wealthy men have gone in so it is assured of success. They have bought or leased a large tract of land just south of Peking. Moore will be director of it.

Letter written by Edith to Rob's mother

Paotingfu, N. China / March 24, 1920

A week ago Friday we had a reception at Mrs. Mather's for both the Fosters and the Longs. The Fosters left the next Monday. They are the loveliest people. We tried to get them to promise to visit you, but traveling is so very hard on Mrs. Foster that she felt it would be too much to promise. They return to China in the fall. He is to teach in the same University where Moore is. He is going home just now as a delegate to the big China-American Chamber of Commerce Convention that is to be held in San Francisco either the last of April or the first of May. Their daughter, Constance Hubbard and husband and two children are coming out to Hong Kong soon after Mrs. Foster gets home. Mr. Hubbard is being sent out by his firm.

Day after tomorrow we are expecting four Y.M.C.A. people for a day's trip, Mr. and Mrs. Brockman, his private secretary and another man. Mr. Brockman is Mr. Mott's right-hand man. And Oh! he is the nicest man. We are in hopes that this visit of theirs will mean that we may have our house enlarged. We are awfully crowded now. There is hardly two feet of wall space that is vacant thru'out the house. I hate to be so crowded. By spending about $500.00 we could fix us eleven rooms to use instead of six as we have now. The children need bedrooms by themselves now and Mother will need two rooms. I certainly hope we can make some changes, because I will go crazy if we are so crowded for a whole winter as we are now.

Letter written by Rob to his sister Nan

Paotingfu, North China / April 14, 1920

I had a chance to go back into school work again just last week. They offered me a position in Pei Yang University. But some way just teaching doesn't appeal to me as a man-sized job anymore. When one has been an executive at the head of things for a while, he is rather spoiled for settling down into a prescribed routine without much chance for individual initiative, as a teacher does. Of course, a teacher does have a great chance for leaving his impress on students who will afterwards do great things, but in Association work we have the same chance, and in addition can pull wires and initiate some big institutions ourselves. Especially working in a heathen country like this there is always a delightful uncertainty as to how popular opinion is going to jump on big moral and religious issues that appeals to my sporting instincts.

I am at present negotiating with the local officials for a two-acre piece of land just inside the south gate for a building site and athletic field. I don't know how we are going to come out yet, though the local county magistrate says he thinks there is no question but that we will get it. However, in China, nothing in the land line is certain till you get your deed and get it registered and have it approved by the National Committee.

If we do get it, we can probably start our new building plans right away, and may even be able to start building in the fall. Then I will have a man-sized job, as at no other place in China have they attempted to run a modern building without four or five foreign secretaries. Well, I must close and write President Main [John H. T. Main, president of Grinnell College] a letter on the Grinnell-in-China work in Shantung.

Letter written by Rob to his family

Paotingfu / July 7, 1920

    I just got back here last night after ten days at Wo Fo Ssŭ after taking the family to Peitaiho the week before. We had a fine conference at Wo Fo Ssŭ. There were about 300 students there. Over twenty from Paotingfu, the largest delegation we have yet had at a conference. Three of them applied for church membership, and eight of the Christians volunteered for the ministry, which is especially encouraging, as the native ministry is very much in need of a lot of new blood from the student class.

    They have been having some diphtheria at Peitaiho near us, and the children were all exposed, so have been under a partial quarantine. Constance had a little fever the other day so the Doctor came over and gave her a shot of anti-toxin, but evidently it did the business, as she had had no unfavorable symptoms since. Edith is still keeping her in bed though. Douglas and Gordon seem to keep as lively as ever. I hope to get back there the first of next week.

    The Chinese political situation is in a state of flux again. The pro-Japanese section of the military party has been in power for the last couple of years, but they seem to have been outmaneuvered the last few weeks by the Chihli militarists (anti-Japanese) and some of the most powerful and corrupt have been forced out of office. Gen. Ts'ao K'un, our Governor here, is the leader of the Chihli party. The man who holds the whip hand, however, seems to be Gen. Wu P'ei-fu, who has been in the south for a couple of years holding the southerners back, but who has just come back and is here at present. He is a military man, but is anti-militaristic in his politics, and he has the best disciplined and most loyal troops in China, whose only politics are to do as he says. So he is in a position to dictate to all parties as he holds the balance of power. He is a really fine fellow. I know him quite well personally, and he was very instrumental in putting our local Y.M.C.A. on their feet financially by starting off our first financial campaign two years ago last winter. I am going around to see him tomorrow and discuss the relation between Jesus' and Confucians' ethics, which is his favorite topic. I think without question he will come out for Christianity before long.

Letter written by Edith to Rob's father

East Cliff, Peitaiho / July 28, 1920

    In my last letter to Nan I promised to write again in a few days but things have been happening so thick and fast that I haven't gotten around to it. I meant as much as could be to write you a birthday letter and tell you how much I loved you and how glad I am to have such a nice Dad and how proud I am of you, but I was just so worried about your son that I couldn't think of anyone else. And if I had known where that son of yours was all those days I think I would have surely died of fright. But Oh! dear, I'm as proud as punch of him, now that I have him safe at home again. I will let him tell you in his own way of his adventures. He is writing them up now for his report and will write you all about them in a few days.

    I received a telegram from him from Peking which had been sent Thursday afternoon and arrived here Friday morning saying that he probably would arrive here Saturday, and sure enough Saturday morning he got here (today is Wednesday). Yesterday afternoon we all went over to Rocky Point as Rob was going to play ball, East Cliff against Rocky Point. I held what you might call a small reception because I was the wife of "the great man" of the moment.

Our Peitaiho summer home under construction (photo 1920)
(on right – Gordon, Edith, and Constance)

See Edith's letter of September 7, 1915 – "… bought lot in East Cliff just back of the Fenn's …".

Note: East Cliff is on the Gulf of Chihli near Lighthouse Point.

22 Tuchuns' War – July 1920: Robert W. Clack Serves as Interpreter

The Warlord Era (1916–1928) was a period in the history of the Republic of China when control of the country was divided among former military cliques of the Beiyang Army and other regional factions which were spread across the mainland. This era was characterized by constant military conflicts between different factions, and the largest conflict was the Central Plains War which involved more than one million soldiers.

The following letter explains how Robert W. Clack became involved as an interpreter for General Wu P'ei-fu for one week and what he experienced during that eventful week.

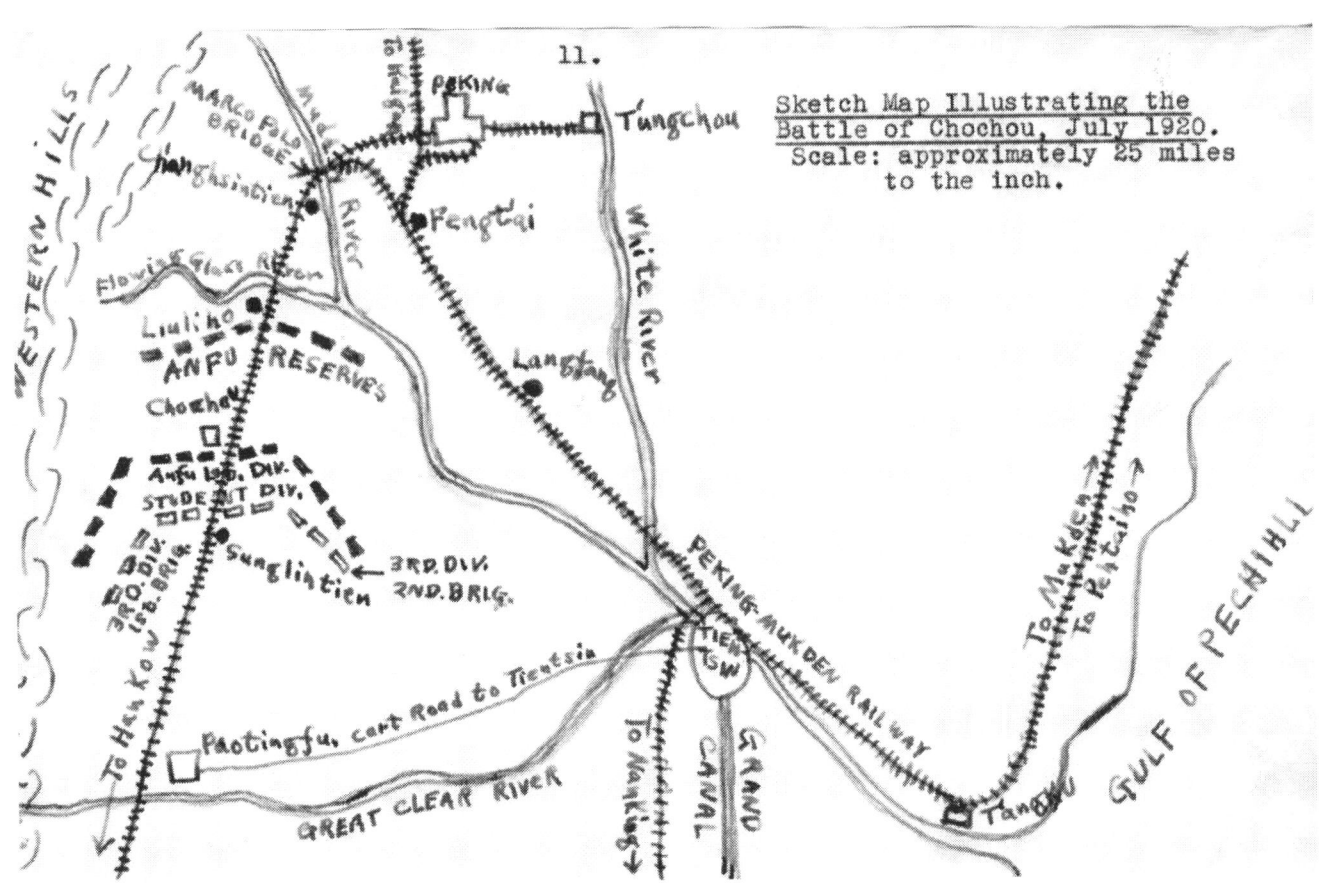

Map drawn by Robert Clack

CHINESE LEADERS
MENTIONED IN THE LETTER DATED AUGUST 1, 1920ŭ

Descriptions are from the letter written by R.W. Clack

Chang Hsŭn
– Leader of the abortive attempt to restore the Manchus in 1917.

Tuan Ch'i Jui
– Leader of Anfu Club; largely responsible for Chang Hsŭn's defeat in 1917; now almost seventy years of age.

Hsü Shih Ch'ang
– President of China; supporter of the Chihli party, but not a military man himself.

Hsü Shu Cheng (Little Hsü)
– Commander in Chief of Anfu troops; able but corrupt.

Chang Chin Yao
– Anfu governor of Hunan; an opium smoker; noted for his cruelty and corruption; his personal troops were all (un)reformed brigands.

Ts'ao K'un
– Governor General of Chihli; head of the Chihli Party.

Chang Tso Lin
– Governor General of Manchuria; allied with the Chihli Party.

Ch'ü T'ung Feng
– Commander of the first line of Anfu troops.
        (Previously the head of the National Military Academy at Paotingfu.)

Tuan Chih Kuei
– Commander of Anfu reserves; nephew of Tuan Ch'i Jui.

Wu P'ei-fu
– Commander in Chief of Chihli troops; his personal character is probably best shown by the fact that though his opportunities for graft have been limitless he is still a poor man.

Letter written by Rob to his family in Iowa

Peitaiho / August 1, 1920

I have just returned from one of the most interesting experiences through which it has ever been my privilege to pass, and like most of the exciting experiences we have here in China I dropped into it without the slightest warning. That is I was one of the only two foreigners to witness the actual fighting in this summer's "Tuchuns' War" and was for six days the guest of Wu P'ei Fu, the Liberal generalissimo, on his private car, on the fighting line.

The political situation here in China, as you probably know, is exceedingly complex, so much so that even those of us who live in the midst of it do not pretend to understand all of its ins and outs. To attempt anything like an exhaustive exposition of the subject would take a good sized volume, so I shall not attempt to do more than outline the general situation here in the North.

Since Chang Hsŭn's abortive attempt to restore the Manchus three years ago the Peking Government has been in control of the Peiyang Military Party under the leadership of Tuan Ch'i Jui (see last page for list of names of Chinese leaders). There has been a gradual split in this party into two sections, the pro-Japanese Anhui Party (or Anfu Club) and the Chihli Party. The President, Hsü Shih Ch'ang, has been a sympathizer with the Chihli group, but the Cabinet and the Parliament have been under the control of the Anfu Club. The military governorships have been about equally divided between the two sections, but the Anfu Club with its control of Peking and the national finances has been considered much the stronger. Their chief military strength has been in the so-called "Frontier Defense Army", equipped and trained by the Japanese, ostensibly for the protection of the Mongolian frontier against the Bolsheviks, but actually to give themselves the balance of power in China. These troops were under the command of Gen. Hsü Shu-Cheng ("Little Hsü"), the ablest, but the most corrupt and unscrupulous of the Anfu leaders. The Anfu Club have borrowed freely from Japan, mortgaging much of the most valuable national resources, the money being used, not for public improvements as is stated in the loan agreements, but for personal ends and to strengthen the hold of the Anfu Club on the government. It has also been freely charged, with no attempt at denial, that most of the Anfu Club leaders were in the direct pay of the Japanese Military Party.

The agitation among the student and merchant classes during the past year has been directed chiefly against the Anfu Club, but as these classes lacked military support, they have succeeded in forcing only minor concessions from the Government. The Chihli Party apparently did not feel itself strong enough to come to an open break, and so has kept quiet. To make themselves more secure the Government has kept Gen. Wu P'ei Fu, by far the ablest and most highly principled of the Chihli Party, in the south bolstering up the corrupt Anfu military governor of Hunan, Chang Chin Yao. Gen. Wu has frequently been accused by the Anfuites of being in sympathy with the Southerners, but nothing could be proved against him, especially as he held the complete confidence of his direct superior, Gen. Ts'ao K'un, Governor General of Chihli and leader of the Chihli Party. The Anfu Club have further tried to weaken the Chihli Party by withholding all military supplies from their troops and by keeping the Chihli soldiers months in arrears on their pay.

Gen. Chang Tso Lin, the Governor General of Manchuria, has apparently been neutral until the last few weeks, when he has thrown his support to the Chihli faction. Encouraged by this, Wu P'ei Fu, apparently with the complete approval of Ts'ao K'un, sent word to the Government that he was withdrawing his troops from Hunan and returning North with them. This caused the complete collapse of the Anfu governor, Chang Chin Yao, and he and his army of brigands were driven in complete rout from the province by the native Hunanese troops, who have been allied with the Southerners.

The Anfu Club took fright at this and did their best to hinder Gen. Wu's return north by keeping all transportation away from him, but only succeeded in delaying him slightly. Just at this point the Manchurian Governor General, with only a small bodyguard, took a hurried trip to Peking, and by his very audacity in thus entering the stronghold of the Anfuites practically unprotected, forced the dismissal of "Little Hsü" from the command of the Frontier Defense Forces on the ground that he had been disobedient in bringing his army when it was needed to defend Mongolia.

The Anfu Club immediately rallied to the support of Little Hsü, and refused to accept his dismissal unless Wu also be dismissed for his retirement from Hunan. An attempt was made to seize Chang Tso Lin, but the Manchurian Governor was too wary and made his escape back to Mukden. The Anfuites immediately called in their real leader, Tuan Ch'i Jui, to take charge of affairs as Dictator, while the President was made a prisoner in his palace.

It was just at this juncture that our student summer conference at Wo Fo Ssŭ closed and I went back to Paotingfu, intending to stay a couple of days to see that everything was in ship-shape, and then leave to join my family at the seacoast for my summer vacation. The day after I returned Ts'ao K'un sent a delegate to Peking to demand the release of the President and the retirement of Tuan, but Tuan refused even to see the delegate. Railway communication was immediately cut off and both sides rushed troops out along the railroad. No actual fighting took place for a week, however, as each side hoped that the other would back down without a fight.

There was great excitement among the civil population at Paotingfu when communications were cut. We had open only the military road to Tientsin, and that was closed to all travel except military automobiles. All our newspapers and other mail come down from Peking, and when this service was cut off, the people, naturally panicky and given to spreading rumors because of the high percentage of illiteracy, began to imagine all sorts of disasters. One day robber bands would be coming up from the south to attack the city while the troops were away at the front, while the next day it would be rumored that our troops at the front had been defeated and Little Hsü and his troops would arrive exactly at midnight to loot the city. The American Consul at Tientsin telegraphed for all Americans to leave immediately, but after discussing the situation thoroughly, the few of us who had not yet gone on vacation decided to stay in order to help quiet the fears of the populace, to whom the flight of the American community would mean the verification of all the rumors.

The Commercial Club of the city (which is the nearest approach to a Board of Aldermen a Chinese city has) appointed a special committee of six to act in an emergency, and three others, two of whom were Wang Tzu Yu, our President, and myself, were appointed to represent the non-commercial interests. We prepared for disorder by raising a home guard of 500 men to supplement the police force, and by equipping a number of buildings, one of which was the Y.M.C.A., with supplies of grain and with temporary defenses, so that they could be used as refuges for the women and children in case of looting. As one of the old merchants said, "The mutiny of the soldiers in 1912 caught us absolutely unprepared to protect ourselves. We do not propose to be so caught again."

We had just gotten things nicely set up, and I was out of a job again, when Major Philoon, military attaché of the American Legation in Peking, arrived in one of the military cars from Tientsin, having been sent by Minister Cane to find out the Chihli end of the situation. As Governor Ts'ao had no proper place to entertain a foreign guest, he asked me to take care of the Major, which of course I was delighted to do. Gen. Wu promised that he could go to the front as soon as the fighting commenced.

After several days wait, on Thursday, July 15, Gen. Wu sent word that he was going to attack that afternoon and that the Major and his interpreter should come on the first train. Major Philoon had brought with him from Peking a foreign educated Chinese to act as interpreter, but when the word came to go to the front he was suddenly taken ill and decided that he would not be able to go. The Major does not speak Chinese, so had to have an interpreter, and I was very much delighted to accept his invitation to go with him in that capacity.

We left Paotingfu at midnight and arrived at Gen. Wu's headquarters on his special train at Sung Tien Railway station just before daybreak. The Chihli front line was about two miles north of the station. Fighting had been going on continuously since the day before. When the battle started the Anfu troops held positions enveloping both of Gen. Wu's flanks. He placed his youngest and least experienced troops in the centre, with his two brigades of veterans, the best troops in the Chinese Army, one on each flank.

On the other hand, the Anfu commander, Gen. Ch'ü T'ung Feng (an old friend of mine, as he was for some time the head of the National Military Academy at Paotingfu) had placed his best troops, the Anfu First Division, in the centre, while his less reliable troops were on his flanks. His own headquarters were at Chochou, and the reserves there were under the command of Tuan Chih Kuei, the nephew of Tuan Ch'i Jui. Gen. Wu, staking all on the result of the first battle, had no reserves, all troops being thrown into action as soon as they could be brought up the railway.

The battle started Thursday noon with attacks by Gen. Wu. He drove straight out on both flanks against the encircling Anfu wings, and after desperate fighting, especially on the left, succeeded in driving the enemy back from their commanding position, until by evening the line had been practically straightened out. I saw a number of dead brought in, riddled with bullets and their faces and clothing burned by powder, where they had literally thrown themselves on the Anfu machine guns, hindering the working of them long enough to give their comrades a chance to overpower the gunners and take the guns. Against the bravery of such men, fighting for a real cause, the Japanese paid Anfu troops were powerless and had to retreat.

It was at this juncture that the Major and I arrived on the scene. Gen. Wu was out inspecting the positions on the right flank when we arrived, but had left orders that we were to be made as comfortable as possible and that we were to be allowed to go wherever and see whatever we pleased. The battle had been kept up all night, and the roar of the Anfu artillery, mixed with the rattle of machine guns and rifles was continuing without let up. Gen. Wu was short of artillery ammunition, so his field guns were using very little, but as he had given instructions to fire only when the enemy troops could be clearly seen, when they were used it was with a telling effect, so that the Anfu losses from artillery fire were actually much greater than those of the Chihli troops, at a cost of hardly one percent the amount of ammunition. Both sides were using only shrapnel.

As soon as we had breakfasted Major Philoon expressed a desire to see the trenches, so Major Fan, of Gen. Wu's staff, was detailed to take us out. By keeping under cover of a village we managed to get up safely to the centre of the battle line, which was in command of an old friend of mine, Gen. Wang, one of the largest contributors to our Paotingfu Association. He detailed one of his aides to lead us out to the most advanced post, which was only a short distance from the Anfu trenches. Here there were a couple of small field guns hidden behind a clump of bushes and supported by a squad of infantry. They had no connected trench system, but each man had scooped out a shallow ditch for himself, which protected him from rifle fire as long as he lay down.

Luckily for us we had arrived during a lull so there was only desultory rifle fire going on right there. However stray bullets kept whining overhead, and I must confess that my 250 pounds never seemed to fill up quite as much space before. A couple of Anfu guns were still keeping at it in that sector, and the shells were exploding at intervals of about a minute about a quarter of a mile to the left and rear of us. It was the first time I had heard the shriek of a shell, and I cannot say that I find it at all a musical sound. I was very much relieved when the Major decided he had seen enough and we started back.

Gen. Wu continued to drive back the Anfu flanks all that day, Friday during the night, and by Saturday morning his men were in touch with the extreme outposts of the Anfu reserves on both sides of Liu Li Ho, ten miles to the rear of their front line. Friday afternoon Gen. Ch'ü made a desperate attempt to break the Chihli centre, but in spite of their heavy losses the green troops, (many of whom were merchant and student volunteers serving without pay in order to drive out the Anfu Club) held like veterans. The Major and I crept up the railway as far as the shrapnel would allow us to watch this attack, but owing to the flatness of the country we could not see much. We could, however, get some idea of the desperate character of the fighting from the large number of wounded brought in. Some of the walking wounded stopped to rest as they came in, and we had a number of interesting conversations with them. The impressive thing about these men was their understanding of the issues involved in the battle, their spirit of patriotism (a new thing in China), and their intense loyalty to Gen. Wu. It gave me a feeling of optimism for the political future of China as I never felt before.

Just at this juncture a brigade of Fengtien (Manchurian) troops arrived from the south to reinforce the Chihli troops and were immediately thrown to the line. Shortly afterwards the troops opposing them, a brigade of the Anfu division, realizing that their case was hopeless, deserted and came over to the Chihli side, making victory absolutely certain.

Saturday

Just before noon a French flag was waved from a point on the Anfu centre, and as firing ceased a Chinese Catholic priest came forward with a letter for Gen. Wu from Gen. Ch'ü T'ung Feng. Luckily the Major and I had just gone forward on our second visit to the front lines, and we arrived there just as the priest came in. As he was waiting for Gen. Wu to reply to the letter, he came to us and asked if we spoke French. Happily Major Philoon had been in France during the War and had picked up quite a bit of French, so the priest talked to us very freely and we were able to get a lot of inside information from him as to conditions in the Anfu camp. Gen. Ch'ü had offered to withdraw his forces and retreat if Gen. Wu would not press the attack. In reply Gen. Wu agreed to grant an armistice of 24 hours in the centre, but not on the flanks, and he gave Gen. Ch'ü until noon the next day for his troops to lay down their arms, while he was to come and give himself up in person. So the priest was sent back with this message.

This armistice gave us a good chance to get out and estimate losses. As near as we could find out Gen. Wu had lost about 100 killed and 250 wounded, while the Anfu losses had been more than double that number. (We have since learned that owing to losses in the panic at Liu Li Ho and to heavier proportionate losses on the flanks and in the centre, the total Anfu loss must have been at least 2500 killed and wounded.)

Meanwhile on the flanks Chihli troops had driven up behind the Anfuites as far as Liu Li Ho, though still a number of miles from the railway on both sides. Gen. Tuan Chih Kuei, nephew of Tuan Ch'i Jui, was in command of the Anfu reserves there and had his headquarters at the railway station. Hearing the sound of firing out on their flanks, his troops seem to have been suddenly seized with panic, and leaving guns, munitions, and stores partly loaded in cars and scattered all over the railway yards, they fled across the long, high railway bridge just north of the station toward Peking. Gen. Tuan himself jumped into a locomotive, cut it loose from the train to which it had been attached, and running through his own troops on the bridge, did not stop until he was safe within the walls of Peking. The bridge here is about a quarter of a mile long and perhaps forty feet above the river, and was apparently crowded with fugitives. Some were actually run down and killed by the engine, but many more were crowded off the bridge and drowned in the river below. Our Chihli troops arriving the next evening reported pulling seventy bodies from the river below the bridge, and as the river was swollen with heavy rains in the hills, it is possible that at least as many more were swept farther on down the river.

This took away their last chance of the front line troops at Chochou extricating themselves, and shortly before noon Sunday an engine pulling a box car came down the track, and Gen. Ch'ü himself got off and came in to give himself up, announcing that his troops had stacked their arms and equipment on the railway platform at Chochou and had surrendered. About the middle of the afternoon Gen. Wu gave the command to advance, and taking Gen. Ch'ü and his officers along as surety against treachery, we went forward on the special train to receive the surrender. The Anfu troops were not kept as prisoners, but after giving up their arms, were given transportation and sent home.

We found the platform at Chochou piled high with equipment as Gen. Ch'ü had said. This was turned over to the Chihli troops and they were allowed to help themselves. The Chihli troops had been purposely kept poorly equipped by the Anfu government in Peking, while their own Frontier Defense troops had been given everything Japanese money could buy, and it was a sight to see those poor fellows load themselves down. Most of them had had no blankets, no mess kits, no trenching tools, and only cloth shoes, while now each had two blankets, two mess kits, leather shoes, and all the trenching tools he could carry. A large supply of ammunition, a lot of rifles, and a number of big guns were also taken and sent back to the arsenal at Paotingfu.

After receiving the surrender of the front line of Anfu troops Gen. Wu started to get in touch again with his flanks, which according to schedule should now be in Liu Li Ho. As he thought that all the reserve Anfu troops had fled north, he took no precautions about sending cavalry ahead of the train, but taking only his small body guard on board, started up the railroad to Liu Li Ho. As we approached the station just at dusk, Anfu troops dashed out. Immediately the train came to a stop, and Wu's body guard piled off and rushed out to meet them. Gen. Wu called to them to hold their fire, and just as the two bodies came together and it looked as if there would be a big fight, the Anfu troops all dropped on their knees and held their guns up over their heads in token of surrender. On inquiry it was found that they had been left behind after the panic the night before, and had stuck to their post, though without food for over 24 hours. Hearing this, Gen. Wu ordered a lot of boxes of hard tack rolled off the train and broken open, and after they had given up their arms they were all fed. Then calling them around him in a circle, Gen. Wu made them a speech, telling them clearly just what the issues of the war were. He said that he knew they had not understood but had been deceived by their officers, and so to give them a chance to show that they were really patriotic, he would return their arms to them, give them one of his own most trusted staff officers as commander, and enroll them in his own army. And several days later when we finally left the army, they were contentedly guarding the Liu Li Ho Bridge, as loyal as any troops in the Chihli army.

It was now fully dark, so we went on to the station, finding it entirely deserted, everything showing clearly the absolute panic in which the Anfu troops had left the night before. There the advanced Chihli troops joined us about midnight, having been delayed by the rains.

I found out later from the Standard Oil comprador at Liu Li Ho village, two miles from the station, that there had been a large body of Anfu troops posted in the village who had not been infected by the panic of Saturday night. However, Sunday night when they heard our train come in from the south and stop just outside the station, they supposed that we were detraining troops there to make an attack on them, and though they had us badly outnumbered, they threw away arms, equipment, and even clothes and fled toward Peking, the last of the Anfu army. I saw later where one had fallen into a large mudhole and lost his cap and one shoe. He did not even stop to retrieve them but scrambled out on the other side and ran on. The marks of his hands and feet, one shod and one bare, were still plainly visible in the mud.

As soon as the troops we were waiting for came in, Gen. Wu ordered his train to return to Paotingfu that he might deliver Gen. Ch'ü over as a prisoner and consult with Gen. Ts'ao K'un as to his future course. We arrived there the next morning and found the whole city had turned out to welcome back the conqueror. The students were especially hilarious as Gen. Wu has expressed himself very strongly in favor of the broadly liberal policies advocated by the Student Unions. Gen. Wu informed us that he considered the fighting to be all over, but that he would like very much for us to return with him to the front that evening, as he would like us to carry a letter for him to the Diplomatic Corps in Peking. So we went home for an all day sleep as we had spent the last four nights in a railway compartment too crowded to admit of any sleep.

We left Paotingfu again with Gen. Wu that evening, but before getting to Chochou ran into a trainload of Fengien troops, which has stopped for the night out between stations without putting up any lights as a warning. Our engine was very badly smashed up, and two cars overturned, killing one man, seriously injuring another, and smashing up all the glass and crockery on the train. We walked on to Chochou where Gen. Wu succeeded in getting another train and went on to Liu Li Ho to establish his headquarters there, while he cleaned up the remnants of the Anfu army between there and Peking. His idea was that with the Anfuites defeated the liberal elements in Peking would take control of the affairs so that it would not be necessary for him to attack the city and thus endanger the legations and other foreign residents of Peking.

Meanwhile there had been a little fighting on the eastern front along the railway between Peking and Tientsin. Owing to the interference of the Japanese troops sent out to keep the railway open between Peking and the coast for the benefit of the foreign legations, the Chihli troops were obliged to retreat almost to Tientsin, but they were there reinforced by two divisions of Chang Tso Lin's Fengtien troops, and the Anfu troops retreated. Then, hearing of the annihilation of their western army and that Gen. Wu was sending troops across the country to catch them in the rear, they fled around Peking and tried to get back through Mongolia. But they were turned back at Nankow Pass by a division of Chihli troops stationed there, and dispersed, and are now wandering around the country north of Peking in small groups, their organization being entirely broken up. They will be disarmed and sent home as fast as they can be rounded up. There are still several provincial Anfu governors, with their own troops, at large, but it is not expected that they will give any serious trouble.

We stayed at Liu Li Ho two days, until Wu's cavalry had advanced to within a few miles of the Peking walls. Then the general gave us a letter to the legations and gave us a special engine and car to take us to Peking, and we went through, the first through after the fighting. We found the Peking gates closed and fortified to keep out the dispersed Anfu troops, as it was feared they would try to get in and loot the city. After some delay we succeeded in proving to the guards that we were not Anfuites in disguise, and were allowed to go in and deliver our letter to Mr. Crane, the American Minister. As Gen. Wu had predicted we found that the liberal elements had taken control of the city, the President had been restored to power, and the Anfu leaders had taken refuge in the Japanese legation, where they are still being protected from the punishment they deserve both legally and morally.

No regular trains were running to Tientsin, but I was able to get in next day as interpreter on the "Legation Special", a military train kept running back and forth by the diplomatic corps in order to keep the legations in communication with the coast. From Tientsin I had no trouble in getting a train to Peitaiho, and was finally able to rejoin my family, from whom I had not been able to get word for almost three weeks.

Just what the result of this struggle will be it is hard to predict, but without question Gen. Wu's victory takes the country a big step forward. China still has a long way to go to get a real democratic government, but the defeat of the Anfu Club has taken away one great obstacle to the reunion of the north and the south and is a marked triumph for the liberals.

As for my work in Paotingfu, I feel that this has been the most valuable fortnight I have yet spent in China. It has given me a chance to become well acquainted with the majority of the Chihli army officers (Paotingfu is essentially a military centre, you know) and I was actually under fire with some of them. I am sure that hereafter I will always be able to get the friendship of Gen. Wu P'ei-fu, who is undoubtedly the greatest man in China today, and if he lives out his allotted three score and ten, will probably go down as one of the greatest men of history.

Major General Wu P'ei-fu (later Field Marshal)
"The Greatest Military Strategist of Modern Times"
(caption by R.W. Clack; photo 1920)

A Unit of Wu's Field Artillery
(caption by R.W. Clack; photo 1920)

Gen. Wu's Headquarters at the Sunglintien Railway Station
(caption by R.W. Clack; photo 1920)

Gen. Ch'ü T'ung Feng Comes in to Surrender
(caption by R.W. Clack; photo 1920)

Gen. Ch'ü and Staff Being Greeted by Gen. Wu and His Staff
(caption by R.W. Clack; photo 1920)

Gen. Chang, Wu's Chief of Staff and Brother-in-law; Maj. Niu, Liaison Officer; with the "Author" on the Station Platform at Sunglintien
(caption by R.W. Clack; photo 1920)

[Editor's note–the "Author" is Robert W. Clack who wrote a manuscript about this experience.]

The Author [sixth from left] **with a Group of the Staff. The Judge Advocate is in Black**
(caption by R.W. Clack; photo 1920)

**The Author Negotiating for Entrance to the Capital
at the Railway Gate through the West Wall of the "Chinese City"**
(caption by R.W. Clack; photo 1920)

Later . . . in the words of journalist Upton Close
A brief portrayal of R.W. Clack in Paotingfu in the early 1920s can be found in the pages of "In the Land of the Laughing Buddha", a 1924 book by journalist, adventurer, and lecturer Upton Close, in which he recounted his experiences in China during the previous eight years. Close had become friends with Rob during the 1920 events described in this book; which were part of the warlord era that Close referred to as "the Anfu campaign".

    Close wrote: "We rickshawed through Paotingfu's muddy streets. Muck from madly-rushing military Fords deluged us. Finally we reached the house of Mr. Robert W. Clack, popular Y.M.C.A. man, introducer of athletics, and expert on local Chinese affairs, who had been through the Anfu campaign. The tree-shaded, grass-covered yard, the huge wisteria arbor in full bloom, seemed to promise a haven. Mr. Clack and his charming wife soon appeared and within a short time we were washed, fed and rested. Many times, in the nightmare weeks to follow, was their hospitality a life-saver."

    When Clack tried to help Close get an interview with a Chinese general, Close noted, "There was hardly an officer, non-com or private in the region who did not know Clack and proudly claim him as a personal friend." A few days later, Close wrote that he was able "to get some good goat's-milk ice cream" and some Western-style food "at the kindly Clack's".

    (pages 287, 288, 301) [12]

23 North China Famines and National Athletic Competitions

The Great Famine of 1920-21 in China

As the result of a year-long lack of rainfall in northern China before the fall crop of 1920, there was a major famine in five provinces (including Chihli) in 1920-1921. Of the roughly 50 million people in those provinces, about 20 million were estimated to be completely destitute. The Chinese government, provincial and local Chinese groups, foreign missionaries, foreign famine relief funds, and other organizations all engaged in relief efforts. International famine relief committees were formed in Peking, Tientsin, Shanghai, and other cities to coordinate Chinese and foreign relief efforts. Rob was chosen as executive secretary of the Paotingfu Branch (one of six major branches) of the Peking United International Famine Relief Committee. The Paotingfu Branch, made up of foreign missionary organizations and Chinese charitable groups, fed about 950,000 people and engaged in other activities to help famine victims. The funds came largely from America.

Highlights: September 1920 - June 1921

- Edith is home-schooling Gordon (age 7) and Constance (age 5) based on the Calvert Course of study received from America.

- In late 1920 Rob travelled to Mukden (now Shenyang) about 600 miles northeast of Paotingfu for his Y.M.C.A. duties, to help them organize their committee to manage the North China Athletic Meet scheduled for the following spring. From Mukden he went 270 miles further north to Kirin (now Jilin) to help them run off their big provincial field meet.

- Famine relief: "We have already organized a Paotingfu Christian Union Famine Relief Committee, of which I am chairman, and have started to work. Our district covers 34 counties with a population of probably 7,000,000 or 8,000,000 people of whom 2/3 have not enough food in sight to carry them through, and perhaps half a million are already driven to leaves and bark in order to supplement the little grain they can get."

- Money is being collected from people in the U.S. for famine relief efforts, including from Rob's hometown of Clear Lake, Iowa (this comes to Rob via his father). So far "America has given $6 million in gold and 10,000,000 bushels of corn."

- The Clack's fourth child, Hugh Llywelyn "Lee" Clack, was born on April 22, 1921.

- Letter of April 23, 1921 – "Our total [Y.M.C.A. membership] is now 1085. … When we got back from furlough a little over three years ago the membership was 48. Last year it was just under 800."

- Rob is planning to assist with (and participate in) the Far Eastern Games in Shanghai from May 30 to June 4, 1921.

THE LETTERS

Letter written by Rob to his mother

Paotingfu, North China / Oct. 19, 1920

Five international Y.M.C.A. secretaries came down with me to Paofu on the train yesterday morning and stayed till midnight last night, so I put in a full day. Edith and the children are well. She has been so busy helping Constance Hubbard get settled that she has not written.

Letter written by Rob to his father

Paotingfu, North China / Oct. 25, 1920

It is a long time since I wrote home, but I have been so busy that correspondence has just piled up on me. I just got back last week from a two-week trip up into Manchuria. I first went to Mukden, which is about 600 miles from here, where I helped them organize their committee to manage the North China Athletic Meet there next spring. I also went after the Commissioner of Education for a permanent athletic field for the city, and he got from the government a tract of about 7 acres in the south suburb, and he and several other officials subscribed enough money to build a quarter mile cinder track with a 220 yd straightaway and to make the field the best so far in China. I also did a lot of work on famine relief, as Manchuria has bumper crops this year. The People's Union of Mukden have promised to take over several counties of our Paotingfu field and be responsible for the relief work. They have sent delegates down for investigation, who are here now. Since we announced this plan a lot of other communities outside the famine area are copying it and taking for themselves definite areas for relief work.

From Mukden I went 270 miles further north to Kirin to help them run off their big provincial field meet. They had a very successful meet and broke one national high school record. I acted as starter and referee. The Association secretary there is a new man, Verink, formerly of Coe College, who was the biggest point winner in the Iowa State Meet in 1913 and 1914. He had not been acquainted at all in the city, but as the confidential secretary of the Governor of Kirin is an old friend of mine, I was able to get him in with a lot of the official class. Kirin has 130% crops this year, and is going about relief contributions in a very business-like way.

I was invited to attend and address the provincial assembly (corresponding to our state legislatures) and was honored by having all my suggestions passed unanimously by the assembly. They have put what practically amounts to a 10% income tax on everyone for three months of relief work. I was able to head off a suggestion that this money be turned over to the officials of the provinces (who would squeeze a large share of it) and got them to vote to turn it all over to our International Relief Committee in Peking.

The country between Mukden and Kirin looks more like Iowa than any place I have seen in China. Near Kirin, however, the hills get a little higher, and Kirin itself is set down in a bowl surrounded by wooded hills with the Sungari River sweeping along the base, a very picturesque location. The amount of wood around the city is very noticeable compared with the rest of China. They have wooden sidewalks and most of the yards have high board fences around them instead of brick walls. The climate is colder than here, as they were already, the first part of October, having very heavy frosts.

The great drawback to the country, however, is the number of Japs. They have their noses and fingers into everything to the great detriment generally of whatever that thing is. I put one over on them, however, on the railroad. They insist on examining passports at Changchun, a thing which of course they have absolutely no legal right to do, as that is only in the power of the Chinese authorities. I had forgotten to bring my passport, but I had along my International Committee identification certificate and succeeded in inducing them to believe that was an American Passport. As the ordinary Japanese official's knowledge of English if very superficial, I succeeded quite easily as he dared not question me for fear of exposing his ignorance of English, in which he is supposed to be proficient in order to get his job.

Famine Relief

I expect that the greater part of our efforts the next eight months will be famine relief. It is going to be so much worse than it was three years ago, that that will almost seem like luxury. We have already organized a Paotingfu Christian Union Famine Relief Committee, of which I am chairman, and have started to work. We have put out so far about $30,000 in relief, of which about $18,000 went into seed wheat to insure a crop next spring.

Our district covers 34 counties with a population of probably 7,000,000 or 8,000,000 people of whom 2/3 have not enough food in sight to carry them through, and perhaps half a million are already driven to leaves and bark in order to supplement the little grain they can get. After the New Year it is going to be awful.

Letter written by Rob to his family

Paotingfu, North China / Nov. 17, 1920

It has been at least two weeks since we wrote home, but we have been so busy that it just seems impossible to get around to writing. Being the only foreign secretary at the Y.M.C.A. now gives me a lot of extra responsibility and though I am generally at home in the evening, I am usually too tired to write. We have five Chinese secretaries now, and they are taking most of the details, but with the growing influence and field of the Association, I have so many other things to do that I am really very much busier than when I had to do everything myself. Then we had only about 50 members, and now we have almost 900 which accounts for some of the difference. Also then we had relationships only with churches, but now we are tied up in various ways with practically every important organization in the city.

Famine conditions are gradually getting worse. We now have all our local benevolent societies affiliated for the sake of efficiency and are doing all we can, but it is very little compared with the awful need. We are opening soup kitchens as fast as we can get funds and also have started a lot of workshops for the women and girls to support themselves in.

What we need is enormous pieces of public work where all the able bodied men could be put to work, but that is too big for anyone but the government to handle, and the government is inefficient and has no funds. We have a number of schemes we are trying to put through which will help some, but will still be woefully inadequate. At the very best we can do there will literally be millions starve to death this winter. Even the worst regions in Europe will be small compared with it.

PAOTINGFU YOUNG MEN'S CHRISTIAN ASSOCIATION

保定基督教青年會

OFFICERS
- WANG TZU YU — PRESIDENT
- WANG TZU MING — VICE PRESIDENT
- HU CHEN SHENG — SECRETARY
- LIU AN KUO — TREASURER
- ROBT. W. CLACK — GENERAL SECRETARY

DIRECTORS
- LI CHUNG YIN
- PAN WU LOU
- JEN SHOU PENG
- JEN CHUNG LU
- YANG WEI MIN

Letter written by Rob to his family in Iowa

Paotingfu, North China / Jan. 3, 1921

We asked Moore [Edith's brother] to come down and take general charge of all the famine relief work in the Paotingfu district and the University has consented to release him till summer, so that now it is up to Moore himself. They will have the Hubbard's house on the American Board Compound just next to us.

I am acting as secretary of the Paotingfu Relief Committee now, and it takes a lot of time so I'll be glad to have Moore take most of it off my hands. We have a big Union Committee comprising Catholics, Protestants, Buddhists, Confucianists, and all else. Our field comprised 12 counties with a population of 2 ½ million (about the same as Iowa) of whom 1,000,000 are now starving. And we are only one of over a dozen committees, some of whom have larger and more badly hit fields than we have. We have gotten our skeleton (this is not a pun) organization set up now with about 150 distribution points and are just beginning to get down to real relief.

We expect about 600 tons of grain in this week and hope to keep it coming in an increasing stream after that. But even the best we can do we are too short of funds and workers to keep thousands from dying. And warm clothing is another problem. Luckily, the weather has been warm until day before yesterday, but we had six inches of snow last week (which is a heavy snow here) and now it has got suddenly colder. It was 4° below zero this morning, and practically none of the famine sufferers have any way of getting to a fire! And that is bad enough when one's belly is full. We have given out several thousand suits of wadded clothing, but they are a mere drop in the bucket.

I suppose you folks all got shaken up by the earthquake [*] Dec. 15, '20. It seems to have been felt pretty generally all over the world. We had quite a severe shock lasting for about two minutes. It made a slight crack in the plaster in our living room and rattled the windows and made everyone feel seasick, but did no real damage. Over in Kansu it caused landslides and knocked down houses and quite a number were killed.

I got a present today from Ts'ao K'un [Governor-General], a 44-piece Chinese dining set. Beautiful porcelain, though strictly Chinese pattern and style. I don't know just why he gave it to me, but I suppose he wants me to do something for him. Well, I will if it is anything I can, as I want to go after him for a several thousand dollar subscription next week. [*Editor's note – Ts'ao K'un, former Chinese warlord and politician who served as President of the Republic of China from 1923 to 1924, as well as the military leader of the Zhili clique in the Beiyang Army.* [13]]

* The earthquake hit at 19:05:53 Gansu-Sichuan time reportedly 7.8 on the Richter magnitude scale. Total casualties were reported as about 235,000. [14]

Letter written by Edith to Rob's sister

Paotingfu, N. China / Jan. 23, 1921

    This famine is awful. Keep out of it as much as you can, you can't entirely avoid it, and altho' we have so much coming in, in money, still there is unthinkable suffering all around us. So many froze to death during the coldest weather, but taken all together this winter has been very mild. We are having our second snow of the year today, but it is so warm that it is melting all day today. What with famines and sickness (small-pox has broken out in several places) and soldiers running amok and looting, I must say we don't lack for excitement. The soldiers have settled down now (at least I hope so) and we are getting in weekly about 1/10 as much grain as we need to relieve the misery around us so we are hoping for a little more quiet.

    But I must say most of us are going to need a "rest-cure" after this year is over. The snow we have had already assures a spring wheat crop, at least around here. And I assure you that means an awful lot this year.

Letter written by Edith to her mother (with note by Rob)

Paotingfu, N. China / Feb. 25, 1921

    This year we have decided not to give birthday presents, but to use the same amount of money for the Famine Relief that we would spend for a present. So you will be credited with two dollars. I am going to give it to Dr. Mackey to use in the relief of expectant mothers. All the extra money we get hold of goes that way. She has such a good chance of knowing of such cases in the work she is in. Do you like that kind of a birthday present?

    Constance Foster Hubbard is leaving in a few days with her little trio for Shanghai. I shall miss her so very, very much. She has been such a good neighbor and has helped so much in making the winter pleasant for us all. Our children have enjoyed hers so much. Her parents return to China the first part of May. She doesn't know yet whether they are to be located in Shanghai or are coming to North China. She hopes for the latter, as they all like N. China the best.

    Rob wants to add a few lines to this.

Dear Mother; – You asked about giving your house money to the famine relief.

    The first obligation we foreigners have is to keep ourselves efficient for our real work of bringing the Gospel to the Chinese. Of course famine relief is a very important work, and the part the Christians are taking in it will probably open up China to evangelistic work more than years of preaching, but if Christian workers are not in proper physical and mental condition to push their work after the famine is over the great opportunity will be lost. Therefore none of us are justified in giving past the point where it interferes with our keeping up our own efficiency for work.

    As an example take the Hughes, of the Anglican Mission, brother-in-law to P.M. Scott, who had charge of the relief work in Anping during the flood three years ago. He thought he was not justified in living on a better scale than the Chinese workers with whom he was associated. He died last summer after a year and a half in an insane asylum in England.

    At present there are big drives going on in all the cities of China which should net several million dollars from the Chinese themselves. America has also given $6,000,000 gold and

10,000,000 bushels of corn which is being rushed to China as fast as possible. While this will not be more than enough to relieve the situation, it is really going to be more than the workers can handle properly, and I do not feel that missionaries should endanger their future usefulness to give any more at present.

Letter written by Edith to Rob's sister Nan

Paotingfu, N. China / March 22, 1921

    We have been made very proud and grateful with the wonderful way that America has responded with her help to our pleas. Other nations may call us a nation of money grabbers, etc., but I guess by this time they are glad someone had the sense to grab the money. I sometimes wonder if there is no limit to what America will give. She certainly has showed that her heart is in the right place all right. We have been very pleased, too, with the wonderful way the Chinese have given too. They have responded most remarkably well in the big drive for funds. But enough of Famine. I'll let Rob tell that.

    Poor Rob, like all the rest of the men, and lots of the women too, is being driven pretty hard, but he not only is giving all his time to the Famine Relief but is also trying to keep his Y.M.C.A. work going as well. I do hope and pray that he won't break under the strain. It looks now as if the work would have to be carried on most or all of the summer. In that case it will mean little or no vacation for our men.

Letter written by Rob to his father

Paotingfu, North China / March 23, 1921

    Many thanks for the cheques for famine relief which came through O.K. I got $85.00 Mex for the $40.00 Gold. That ought to carry more than a dozen families through to wheat harvest. When we get what we have on hand now distributed we will be feeding about half a million people. It's quite a job, I tell you. While the wheat harvest in June will take care of the majority we will have to keep on our relief work well into the fall, I guess. The wheat in T'ang Hsien, the worst hit county in China, was winter killed, and in our own local county, unless we get rain within two weeks the crop will fail again. That is where the American corn will come in handy, as none of it will probably get here till summer. I enclose a bunch of photographs that give the situation more graphically than I can write it.

    I don't know whether I wrote you or not about the earthquake last December. We felt the shock very distinctly and it now develops that the centre was out in Kansu Province, and it is estimated that there were 40,000 people killed or injured. At exactly the same time there was also a severe earthquake in the Argentine Republic which is exactly opposite on the earth's surface. There have been a number of shocks out there since, but we have felt no more here. It is reported that the Mohammedans out there were planning a big uprising against the government, but felt that all their leaders were killed by the earthquake, and considering it a direct sign from Allah the rest have returned to their allegiance.

    Plans are going ahead rapidly for the Far Eastern Games in Shanghai May 30 to June 4. I expect to go down with the North China Team if I can possibly get away from here. I will take the family to Peitaiho first and go from there direct.

After nibbling for a year or more Ts'ao K'un (the Governor) has at least promised definitely to give the Y.M.C.A. a piece of land of 2 ½ acres in the south part of the city. We haven't got the deed yet, but he sent a representative around yesterday to get a copy of the form in which we wanted the deed, and said he would have it fixed up right away. It really seems too good to be true. That will mean we can get to work right away on our big building.

Letter written by Rob to Mr. West (probably of the Y.M.C.A. home office)

April, 2, 1921

My dear Mr. West; –

Dust! dust! dust! A yellowish gray coating over everything. Even inside the house with the windows sealed up, in a few minutes time a coat will gather on the furniture thick enough to write in. And out-of-doors one must breathe it, eat it, and even the eyes get caked up with mud in the corners.

Year before last the rainfall was far below normal; last year there was almost none; and now for three months only a flurry of snow which was absorbed by the dust without even making it muddy. All of the roads are ankle deep in dust, making travel almost as difficult as if they were running with mud. Unless we get a good rain around Paotingfu within ten days, all our wheat will be dead and we are in for another famine. Fortunately in most of the sections outside of the Paotingfu Territory there has been rain, so that the distress will be confined to a relatively small area.

The central distributing dump of the American Board is in the yard just across the street from our house, directly adjoining the churchyard where Horace Tracy Pitkin and Miss Gould and Miss Merrill, Portland's gift to the Boxer Uprising, are taking their last sleep. It is poetic justice that they should thus look upon the saving of thousands of lives of the relatives of those who put them to death. And it is not at all improbable that many of those we are now feeding were actually members of the mob which attacked them.

We are getting in grain shipments almost every day now, and there is a continuous procession of carts and wheelbarrows through the dust, either bringing in grain from the railway, or taking it out to the substations in the counties southeast of this. Then every day or two the people from one or another of the country sections of this county come in for their month's supply of grain. They come on foot from as far as 15 miles and carry the grain home on their backs. Yesterday I saw one poor old woman of 70 just starting out on her little bound feet with 40 pounds of grain for a twelve mile trip home. She had left home at midnight in order to get here in time, and would not get back till after dark that evening as her poor crippled feet and the abominable roads made speed impossible. The greater part of those who come are children or old people, as the able-bodied are busy carrying water to try to save their wheat, or else getting the ground ready to try to start a new crop.

This famine relief is now, of course, our greatest responsibility. We were disappointed in our hope to get someone else to take the executive responsibility in our Union Committee, and so I have had to shoulder it as best as I could. Luckily, we have Mr. Galt of the American Board as treasurer, and Mr. Leavens, of the Changsha Yale Mission, has come to take charge of the accounts for several months so that the hardest part is being very efficiently handled. We now have our organization all set up and this last month fed almost half a million people (467,757). This is only a little over half those needing help, but we can quite easily feed the rest if we can get the funds.

Our Association Secretaries are now taking the entire responsibility for receiving the grain as it comes in, assigning the proper amounts to the various counties, and unloading it and delivering it to the missions and other agencies who do the actual distributing to the people. Wang Ching Hsiu, the youngest member of our staff, takes the main responsibility for this and is handling it in a very efficient manner. He gives his whole time to the work and the other secretaries take turns helping to superintend the actual unloading of the grain.

Owing to so many students dropping out of our day school because of the famine, we have been obliged to discontinue it temporarily since the winter vacation. But we have reorganized our night school so that some of the students who have been able to find work to do during the day may still continue their studies in the evening. We hope to reopen the day school again after the famine is over.

But as most of our members are of the city rather than the country they are only indirectly affected by the famine, and we have to do our best to keep up the work for them. The Youth's Department is trying a new method in student Bible classes which so far promises to be very successful. They have organized a Special Bible Study Committee of three students from each high school or college (except one whose director is violently anti-Christian) and these students are themselves organizing the classes in schools. We only furnish the teachers. Each school has from one to three classes. These classes are to run for ten weeks and then prizes will be given to the schools having the largest total attendance and the largest percentage of attendance.

The physical Department, under the leadership of Mr. Liu, entered teams in both Senior and Junior divisions of the International Hexathlon in February. We got third place among the Chinese Associations in the Senior division, and second in the Junior. One of our Juniors, Ma Hsiang P'o, competed in both divisions and won the highest individual total of points not only in the Junior division, but in the Senior as well.

Our annual membership campaign starts tonight. We have set our goal at 500 members and have the best set up we have had yet, but with the famine conditions it is rather a problem to know what the result will be. Last year we set 400 as our goal and got almost 600, and I hope we can do at least as well this year. I will report what success we have in my next letter.

Yours very sincerely, Robert W. Clack

Letter written by Edith to Rob's family

Paotingfu, N. China / April 18, 1921

Please tell Mother not to worry about our not getting enough to eat. This famine is really not so much a food famine as a money famine. We have all we want to eat the same as usual and so do all the Chinese who have the money to pay for it. That just goes to show how very, very poor the majority of the Chinese are. We cannot but admire the wonderful patience and endurance of these poor people. Almost any other people would have had continuous uprisings under these conditions rather than the few we have had. Those few have not been by the people, but by the soldiers.

Letter written by Rob to his mother

Paotingfu / April 23, 1921

Well, your fourth grandson [counting Gordon and Douglas Clack and Melville Hughes] arrived on the scene at 8:15 last evening. He and Edith are both getting along fine. His name is Hugh Llywelyn; Hugh for Hugh Hubbard and Llywelyn for the original Prince of Wales who temporarily threw a monkey wrench into the first British attempts to absorb Wales about 700 years ago. We will call him Llywelyn.

We will probably go up to Peitaiho about May 16 or 17. Then I will go on up to Mukden from there for the North China Meet May 20 and 21, and from there will accompany the North China athletes to Shanghai for the Far Eastern Games May 30 to June 4. Then I expect to come back here for most of the summer, as with the almost certain failure of 80% of our wheat, it looks like we shall have to keep up relief work in our area through the summer. Luckily, outside of our Paotingfu area, most places have had good rains so the affected area will be cut to only a small fraction of its original size. We are now feeding about 600,000, about three-quarters of those who need help, so we feel that we are really beginning to meet the need.

Our annual Y.M.C.A. membership campaign just ended this week. We started out for 500 members and got 986. There were 99 unexpired memberships so our total is now 1085, and there will be enough belated ones come in this next week to carry it over 1100. We have certainly made a lot of progress. When we got back from furlough a little over three years ago the membership was 48. Last year it was just under 800.

Letter written by Edith to Rob's sister Ida

Peitaiho, May 31, 1921

I think I have written you once since coming up here. We came up two weeks ago last Monday. We had a very nice trip up until we arrived at the station. It was raining and blowing a gale. We could only get three rickshas to bring us over 2 ½ miles, so we had to come in relays. Rob and Douglas and the sewing girl and Llywelyn and I came over first, leaving Gordon and Constance and the Amah to await the second trip. We had two men to each ricksha, but when we came to the tops of the hills it was all they could do to budge a step. The road is very good until we get about two blocks from here. Then Rob and his rickshaw men had to get out and push the other rickshas. My! but I was frightened for fear we would be tipped over. They held us up by main force. And Oh! it was so cold, but the boy we had sent on ahead had a fire in the grate and steaming cups of cocoa ready for us, so we were soon dry and warm.

June 1st

Just received Dad's letter of Apr. 23 & 24 containing the check for $350.00. I think it is simply wonderful the way the American people still keep giving and giving and giving. Hoover says we have given over 2 ½ billion dollars to relief in Europe alone since the war began and still we go on giving. It certainly makes one very proud to be an American.

Letter written by Rob to his father

Paotingfu, North China / June 24, 1921

    Edith has just forwarded a bunch of letters which were sent to Peitaiho by mistake and which included several cheques from you. I am glad you finally decided to send the money that way as it is much the best. We can always deposit drafts and cheques directly in the bank and get the very best rate on them, while any other method entails a great deal of red tape and expense before we can get the cash. The total amount you have sent to date is $522.00, coming from the Rotary Club, the Progress Club, and 22 individuals. As it is costing us now about $1.25 a month to feed the average family, you can easily figure how many lives you have saved. We are now feeding 700,000 but will begin now to taper off, and hope that by the middle of September everybody will be on his own. I wish I had time to write each one of you a personal thank you letter, but instead I'll have to ask you to pass this around. I am enclosing tag receipts for everyone, which we used in campaigning for funds locally. The characters on them read "Famine Relief. Paotingfu Campaign for Funds".

    I have turned part of the money into the regular fund, part into a special fund for buying new seed for an area just North of here where a terrific hail storm last week beat the new grain into the ground. It was so bad that three men are reported killed by the hail, though I am inclined personally to believe it was lightning. But anyway the grain was literally beaten down to the roots, as I saw with my own eyes a day or two later. I am also holding a small share for emergencies which are always coming up, for which we have no funds provided. Generally we have to make sums for such emergencies up out of our own pockets, and I tell you for most of us the pockets are getting pretty shallow.

    America has certainly done herself proud on the relief contributions. At least two thirds of all we have had has come from good old Uncle Sam. And the Chinese appreciate it too, and while I know none was given with the purpose in view, I think Uncle Sam will get it back in the long run. It certainly has been an object lesson to the Chinese as to what real Christianity is.

    We hope to get all the grain out in July which is needed to keep the people until they can harvest their own, but can't tell yet if we will succeed. I certainly hope so, as it is getting pretty hot.

Crowd waiting grain distribution (photo March 1921)

Famine Relief unloading grain, American Board Church (photo March 1921)

Famine Relief, giving out grain (photo March 1921)

24 Famine Relief Work, 1921

Highlights: July-December 1921

- "We are just getting our last famine relief accounts checked up. We handled about 17,000 tons of grain and $900,000 in addition, and fed in all just under 1,000,000 different people. In all we had 44 foreign and 370 Chinese workers, besides the coolies, carters, etc." (from a letter written on October 14)
- Automobiles are starting to make an appearance in this area of China.
- An Aviation School has been established in Paotingfu and mail delivery to Peitaiho is by airplane.

Y.M.C.A. ANNUAL REPORT, PAOTINGFU
Two years ended September 30, 1921
Written by Robert Wood Clack, General Secretary

Dear Mr. Herschleb;
Your letter and questionnaire on the work of the past year came only a few days ago, and I hasten to reply.

1. One very favorable aspect of our work is the beautiful harmony existing between the missions and Associations. Practically all the city work of the missions is now done as union work, or at least in close co-operation, and is under the control of union committees, of which an Association representative generally acts as chairman. Examples of this are the Student Work and the Prison Evangelistic work. Steps have also been taken leading to organize a union of the two churches.

   The famine relief work done chiefly by the Christian forces has almost entirely overcome the prejudice against Christianity on the part of the ordinary people. In this connection it is interesting that the Protestant churches have made the greater gain owing to their much more just and impartial attitude in distributing relief. Another advantage has been the much larger field of personal acquaintance we have gained from pooling our interests in this work with the local Chinese secular organizations made up of the influential people of the city.

   Paotingfu is becoming increasingly important as a Military centre. Of the three great military men of the country, Ts'ao K'un has made this his permanent capital, while Wu P'ei Fu, the most able of all, has his home here. The National Military Academy is also located here. We can work with these students only on Sunday, but we have a small Student Association among them; one of the half dozen student Associations in the Government schools of China. We have neither the staff nor the equipment to do very much for the regular soldiers though there are from 15,000 to 20,000 of them here all the time.

We are covering the student field better all the time, having now at least one-sixth of all those in middle or higher schools (except Military) enrolled in Bible classes. Of these schools, the authorities of all but one are very friendly. Of the grammar and primary schools, on the other hand, the authorities are not so friendly. This seems to be because the majority of the teachers are graduates of the one Normal School whose Director is anti-Christian.

2. During the past year I have attempted to act as General Secretary [of the Y.M.C.A.] and as Executive Secretary of the Famine Relief Committee at the same time, and both jobs have had to suffer in consequence. The National Committee, however, would give no assistance. I have taken my recreation chiefly in helping out with the North China Athletic Federation and the Far Eastern Games.

3. One of the encouraging results of the past year has been the starting of Free Schools for Poor Children all over the city patterned after those started last year by the Association. The largest of these, run by the students of the largest middle school of the city, is affiliated with our own school, but most of the other higher schools have them, as do the police. This is a direct result of Association example. We also took the initiative in forming the union of all charitable institutions of the city for famine relief, and had a large share in organizing the work of relief, though the actual distributions was done by the Catholic and Protestant missions.

4. As to my own contribution, I feel that outside of training Chinese workers and acting as a go-between between the Christian forces of the city and the officials and non-Christian leaders, I do not do much.

5. The main criticism I have of the International Committee is that they seem to pay so little attention to problems raised in letters similar to this. For example, two years ago I brought up the question of our residence here, which has been condemned by the doctor as unsanitary, and have written since both to New York direct and to Harvey to pass on, but received no reply until two or three weeks ago when I got a letter from Jenkins passing the buck to Harvey. Last year I asked certain questions about the fund which Eddy raised a number of years ago for a [Y.M.C.A.] building here, but the letter has not even been acknowledged.

6. As to personal relations with men, it is very hard to judge what influence one is having. I can only state that a few of the men with whom I am in contact each year join the Church, though I would not say that it is entirely due to my own influence. I have also been able to lead several students to decide for Christian work as a life work.

7. I enclose on a separate sheet a list of books read during the past year. Of these I think I would consider the most stimulating to be "The Theology of an Evolutionist", "The Executive and His Control of Men", "Practical Christianity", "John Woolman's Journal", "The Making of an American", and "A Man for the Ages". I would recommend that men coming to China should be thoroughly grounded in modern religious thought and

especially should know their Bible from cover to cover. A good knowledge of history will also help one to be more sympathetic in China's problems.

8. There is very little Association literature which applies to such a field as Paotingfu, or at least I have seen very little of that sort. Super's new book, however, which I am now studying, is exactly what we need. Most books have only the American secretary or the American constituency in mind. There is very little worthwhile available for the Chinese secretary who does not read much English.

9. My greatest personal hindrance at present is lack of a decent place to live. In addition to its un-healthfulness which I will touch upon under the next question, there is only one bedroom available for the whole family, which is rather inconvenient for a family of six, especially as the two oldest are eight and seven, a boy and a girl, respectively. In addition to this, the only place I have for a study is the main living room of the house, and it is rather hard to do any work requiring close application with four children under foot. It is also rather embarrassing at times to have to receive Chinese callers in such cramped quarters, as Chinese are not used to being received in the bosom of the family. With no adequate quarters for the Association it is also impossible for me to have a study in the city.

10. The family has been only fairly well the past year. The chief trouble with all of us, however, is the colds which come on in the fall and seem impossible to break up entirely until we leave for Peitaiho in the summer. Douglas has had bronchitis every winter since he was born [1918]. Dr. Mackey says that this is mostly due to the house. I have written this in before, but this time to emphasize it I enclose a copy of a signed statement the doctor wrote out for Mr. Harvey. Personally I have kept fairly well, though the strain of the last year has left me quite tired out nervously. Besides the sights and sound of famine, we have had four mutinies of troops with the accompanying riots in Paotingfu the past year which has probably contributed somewhat to the jumpy feeling. I also failed to get much real vacation last summer as the only time I could get away from the work here was while Mrs. Clack was so bad off during the summer and that was not exactly a restful time.

11. Financially, we manage to keep going by strict economy, though obligations we had to assume because of the famine have temporarily run us into debt. By making the old clothes do a little longer we ought to be able to get out [of debt] again in a year or two.

12. The greatest source of inspiration I have in times of discouragement is looking over the growth of our work here in spite of the exceedingly inadequate way in which we can handle our responsibilities. It is a sure proof that God is backing us up and no matter how unpromising the outlook may seem at any time, He will always bring us through into a much stronger position to help those around us than before. [15]

THE LETTERS

Letter written by Rob to his mother in Iowa

PAOTINGFU YOUNG MEN'S CHRISTIAN ASSOCIATION

保定基督教青年會

OFFICERS
- Wang Tzu Yu - President
- Wang Tzu Ming - Vice President
- Hu Chen Sheng - Secretary
- Liu An Kuo - Treasurer
- Robt. W. Clack - General Secretary

DIRECTORS
- Li Chung Yin
- Jen Shou Peng
- Pan Wu Lou
- Jen Chung Lu
- Yang Wei Min

Paotingfu, North China, ... July 23, 1921
Peitaiho

    We have had a number of home letters since we wrote last. Drafts for $11.00, $10.00 and $112.16 came in them. I enclose little tag receipts for the people there. I sent letters and receipts direct to Nan's friends. It certainly is fine to have the home church come across so generously. We have had great backing from America this year. The famine is practically over now. We are still having to carry a number of people over on part rations till harvest, but we have the money and grain already out at the distribution centres for them. It is an awful job to know how to withdraw relief in such a way as to force them back to work where there is no work available, without making those unable to work suffer. While not being so obvious, the reconstruction work will be as hard a job as the relief, as so many people have of necessity been partly pauperized.

    I think the money which just came I will hold to help out worthy students from the country, who were obliged to drop out of school last year because of the failure of the family crops. In most cases it will be several years before the families will be back to where they can send them to school again without help. I am enclosing some pictures of the relief distribution.

Letter written by Rob to his sister Ida

Peitaiho, North China / August 8, 1921

    Dad's plans for the new house sound very fine. We won't know whether we can go on furlough next year or not until late in the fall, probably.

    We are having a very wet season now to make up for the dryness of the last two years. It has rained practically every day for the last two weeks. Luckily the soil here is so sandy that the mud dries up within an hour or two after the rain stops, so it doesn't keep people shut in except while it is actually raining. It has rained a lot down country, too, and there will be exceptionally good crops except where they are flooded out. This is happening in a number of places, though there is no general flood yet.

    We tried our best to get the General Relief Committee to use a lot of their relief funds in building dykes, but they wouldn't consent. The American Red Cross built a lot of roads, which are now practically all washed out and they have no permanent good to show for their money. I suppose this cycle of floods and famines will keep on; until we get a responsible government in China who will put through a gigantic scheme of afforestation and of building big reservoirs in the mountains to hold the flood waters to be used for irrigation during times of drought.

Letter written by Rob to his sister Nan   **Peitaiho / Sept. 2, 1921**

Moore [Edith's brother] has left the University and will take charge of an Industrial School for famine orphans in the hills just west of Peking. Will have 1000 of the orphans. They will be in the old Imperial Deer Park very near Wo-Fo-Ssŭ, where we have our Y.M.C.A. conferences. I think it is the most beautiful place I have seen in China. It is on the side of a hill about 1000 ft. high and is almost a forest there are so many trees with dozens of old ruined temples and lodges hid among the trees. There are also a number of springs and a small waterfall.

We have an aeroplane mail now from Peking every week. The plane lands very near us and the children are always on hand for the arrival and start. We were all over in the plane the other day. It carries eight passengers.

I suppose you have noticed in the paper that my friend, Wu P'ei Fu, is again coming to the front. He has been made Super Tuchun of the whole Yangtze Valley which makes him the most powerful man in China. He now has the job of uniting all the warring elements, and will certainly show himself a super-man if he succeeds. No one else can do it, that is certain. The new Governor of Hupei, Gen. Hsiao is also a friend of mine, while Feng Yü Hsiang, who has just been made Governor of Shensi, is more than a friend. He is "the Christian General" you know.

Letter written by Edith to Rob's sister Celia   **Paotingfu / Sept. 15, 1921**

We left Peitaiho last Wednesday (this is Thursday) and arrived home Saturday. We stopped two days in Peking and had a nice time. We stopped at Moore's house while in Peking.

One night we went to the movies with Verna [Foulke Johnson] and her husband. I only wish you could have been with us. Not that the movies were anything exceptional, altho' they were a treat to me, but the setting was most extraordinary. It was in the old palace grounds and in one of the old palace buildings. It was a huge long building, very high, brick floors, many huge pillars all red lacquer and all the beams etc. in the ceiling were red lacquer and painted in gold and greens, blues, etc. It was so incongruous, such a mixture of the old and the new, electric lights and phonographs fastened up all around in the most unlikely places. One was away up at the top of the building at the top of the screen! The phonographs are all on one line. It sounds so weird having this squeaky sound coming down out of the dust and cob-webs, and dark, because in spite of all the lights the ceiling is so high it is quite dark. There was one thing there that we enjoyed greatly, and that was the music. There was a dandy violinist and the man who accompanied him was very good too, but the piano wasn't as good an instrument as the violin. During the interlude they played a most beautiful selection from *Thaïs* and played it beautifully too. We (three couples) gave him a good hand when he finished. My! but he seemed so pleased! No one else in the place seemed to realize they had heard anything unusual.

Letter written by Rob to his father

Paotingfu, North China / October 14, 1921

We are just getting our last famine relief accounts checked up. We handled about 17,000 tons of grain and $900,000 in addition, and fed in all just under 1,000,000 different people. In all we had 44 foreign and 370 Chinese workers, besides the coolies, carters, etc. It really makes a pretty big piece of work. The fall crops were above normal so it makes it quite easy now to get out from under. The immediate vicinity about Paotingfu has been too dry to get in the normal amount of wheat for next spring, but that will not be serious as it is only a very small section affected near the city, and all the rest of our district has good prospects. That means that there will be plenty of work in the city so that those affected can get jobs to tide them over.

The Governor has been making a lot of improvements in and around the city which have taken care of a lot of laborers. He has widened the principal streets in the South Suburb and the Southern part of the city, and rebuilt a number of public buildings which had not been repaired for several hundred years. He has also cleared out about a hundred acres of old graves just south of the city between the city and the river, and built a fine amusement park. So you see we are getting quite up to date. It will be a good financial investment for him, too, as they charge 24 coppers admission to the park and there are crowds in there all the time. The children are very much taken with the park as they have a lot of monkeys, parrots, deer, etc. The whole place is a mass of bright colored flowers, and there are a lot of little artificial hills and lagoons, so that it is quite attractive. They have movies every night, free, and they have a foreign restaurant where one can get a seven-course meal for $1!

We have been awfully busy at the Y.M.C.A. this fall, taking care of our Bible classes. We have from one to five now in every one of the Government schools, and it is quite a job to get teachers. Several of us are teaching five apiece. There are about five hundred enrolled, which means almost 20% of all students. The military college has not started in yet or we would be swamped. They have about 1500 students and if the same proportion there want classes we will sure be up against it. We are planning a big lecture campaign the last of the month. "The Wireless Telephone". Prof. Robertson [Mr. C. H. Robertson, travelling lecturer for the Y.M.C.A. in China] will be up from Shanghai with his apparatus. We will have three lectures a day for five days, so that everybody in the city who wants to hear it will have a chance.

Letter written by Edith to Rob's family

Paotingfu, N. China / Nov. 20th, 1921

We have just had Mr. and Mrs. Murray of the International Com. of the Y.M.C.A. and Mr. Harvey of the National Committee here. The latter was supposed to tell us if we were to go home this year, but we didn't get time to talk it over with him. I am so disappointed I could just cry. Maybe he will write about it later. If we don't get to go home next spring we are certainly going the *next* spring. But I do so hope we can get away this coming spring. China is getting on our nerves again so badly. Last year was so perfectly horrid that all of us who had to live thru' it are so very anxious for a change.

Mr. and Mrs. Murray who were here with Mr. Harvey are the dearest old couple you would ever want to know. He is a regular Santa Claus sort of man and is so extremely fond of children. He is especially interested in residences for the Y.M.C.A. people, so we are in hope that we may get a home. This Chinese house is just getting entirely too small for us and is so very inconvenient.

Since coming home from Peitaiho this fall we have had lots of autos going by our place and just this last week they have started an aviation school for the Army in the East Suburb so we have had airplanes flying over us a few hours each day.

Letter written by Edith to Rob's sister Ida　　　　　　　　　　　**Paofu / Dec. 31st, 1921**

The children love the "Bubble Books". They would very much appreciate having more. The first two books as well as others.

Editor's note – Billed as the "book that sings", the "Bubble Book" was the creation of Harper Collins publishers and was the first product believed to combine the world of book publishing with the then emerging recording industry. ... The "Bubble Book" series got its name from the cartoony "bubbles" that the first book's unnamed lead, a little blue-clad boy, blows from a magical pipe he has been given. Soon after, the bubbles ... become the little boy's entertaining window, a looking glass of sorts, a possessor of various characters who come suddenly alive to entertain him with rhymes and music. From a 2003 essay by Cary O'Dell. [16]

Thanksgiving Party, November 20, 1921
(L-R) Constance Clack, Harold Robinson, Ralph Galt (chair in foreground), Beltram Hubbard, Gordon Clack, Edith Galt (back of head), Marjorie Hubbard, Edith (standing), Douglas Clack

This is Mother's Peitaiho house called "Friends' Rest" [Elma on porch]
built just back of the McCann's house across that little road.

(Elma Gordon, Edith's mother, was a mission worker in China.)

25   Under Martial Law and Return to the United States in 1923

Highlights: 1922

- Letter of March 24 regarding the Y.M.C.A. building project: "I got a $1000 subscription for our Y.M.C.A. building site from the president the other day. I guess I already bought part of the land and have enough left to get what is necessary, but not quite enough to get all we want. … We can start work on our building next spring, and by the time we get back from furlough in 1924 it should be all ready for occupancy."

- April 19: "Paotingfu, of course, is the headquarters of the Chihli Party so we are under martial law at present, and practically all business has stopped except that of preparing for the conflict. Even the schools have all closed. We are getting things ready for Red Cross work, especially to take care of the women and children of the city in case Wu should be defeated and the army driven back in disorder past here."

Highlights: 1923 and 1924

- Early 1923 finds Edith and five-year-old Douglas quarantined due to illness.

- In May 1923, the family left Paotingfu for what they thought was a short-term sabbatical to the United States; however, they did not return to China.

- The family arrived in the U.S. and settled in Clear Lake, Iowa. While living in Clear Lake, Iowa, from mid-1923 to mid-1924 Rob continued to work for the Y.M.C.A. and traveled throughout Iowa, Minnesota, Illinois, and South Dakota speaking and helping to raise money for Y.M.C.A. foreign work.

- Their fifth child, Roderick Whittier Clack, was born in Iowa on February 13, 1924.

- On April 22, 1924, Rob was ordained as a Congregational minister (Clear Lake, Iowa).

- Rob accepted a teaching position with Alma College in Alma, Michigan, and the family moved to Alma prior to the beginning of the 1924 fall semester at the college.

THE LETTERS

Letter written by Edith to her mother

Paofu. / Feb. 14, 1922

    Almost everyone over at the big Compound have been having the flu. All the Hubbard children, Mrs. Galt and her three, and Mr. and Mrs. Price and Abbie have all had it. The Robinsons just got over it before the others came down.

    We are wondering how you are. We do so hope you are keeping well. We at last got word that we are <u>not</u> to go home on furlough. We are so relieved. I just didn't see how I could get ready. I am sorry for Rob's people tho'. They wanted us to come home so badly. We are planning to go to Peitaiho June 1. Rob hopes to stay up two weeks then.

Letter written by Rob to his father

Paotingfu, North China / March 24, 1922

    Yes, it is true that the bodies of most of the Chinese who die in America are shipped back here for burial. If a man is not buried in the ancestral cemetery his spirit will get no share of the offerings made by the living members of the family, and I understand that it is pretty poor pickings in the hereafter living on what the other shades leave over. The only recourse would be to haunt the person who was responsible for his non-removal to the sacred family lot, and no Chinaman takes a chance on a ghost, especially an ancestral one.

    Your account of the bootlegging news was very interesting. There are such diverse accounts of the effect of prohibition in the papers that it is hard to tell what is happening. It seems to me, however, that it cannot be such an awful failure as some try to make out or the liquor interests would not fight it so hard. Of course, I know that their real reason for fighting the law is that it is creating such a lack of respect for all law, and they have always worked so hard to have all respected. It is so pathetic it moves one to something akin to tears. And then these poor fellows who get wood alcohol by mistake. They are such a loss to the community.

    I got a $1000 subscription for our Y.M.C.A. building site from the president the other day. I guess I already bought part of the land and have enough left to get what is necessary, but not quite enough to get all we want. That will not be very hard to raise, now that we have the back of the thing broken. We can start work on our building next spring, and by the time we get back from furlough in 1924 it should be all ready for occupancy.

Letter written by Rob to his father

Paotingfu / Apl. 19, 1922

    We are having another illustration of the fact that whatever life in China may be it is never dull. I suppose you have seen accounts of the threatened trouble in the papers, and probably by the time you get this it will all be fought out and finished.

    Chang Tso Lin (pronounced jŏng zō´a lĭn), "the uncrowned king of Manchuria," ex-robber, etc., has succeeded in uniting most of the corrupt military leaders in China with the purpose of suppressing Wu P´ei-fu and has advanced a lot of his troops into Chihli Province in the neighborhood of Tientsin and Peking. Wu is now calling up his troops from Central China and is concentrating them north and east of here in order to resist any further advance. Undoubtedly unless Chang withdraws within a few days Wu will attack him in order to prevent his juncture with his Southern sympathizers. Sun Yat Sen has at last thrown off his disguise by allying himself with Chang, who is notorious as the most corrupt (and probably the most able) of the politicians of China.

Under Martial Law

Paotingfu, of course, is the headquarters of the Chihli Party so we are under martial law at present, and practically all business has stopped except that of preparing for the conflict. Even the schools have all closed. We are getting things ready for Red Cross work, especially to take care of the women and children of the city in case Wu should be defeated and the army driven back in disorder past here. However, though Wu is outnumbered as usual, he is so much better a strategist and the morale of his troops is so much better that I haven't the slightest doubt but what he will win out. He always seems to have the knack of unerringly picking the enemy's weakest point and concentrating on it and smashing through before they have a chance to bolster the place up. Furthermore, he has a lot of very able leaders under him, while Chang himself is the only really able man in the other crowd.

Meanwhile, all the leaders not definitely lined up with one of the parties are doing their best to bring about a compromise. That, however, will only postpone the conflict, as Wu and Chang are so extremely opposite in ideals and methods that one or the other has to get out ultimately. Personally, I think the sooner they have it out the better. Even for Chang to win would probably be better than the present situation, as it would at least unite the country and put a responsible (even though corrupt) head of the government at Peking. If Wu wins, he will probably attempt to get some sort of really representative Parliament together and cut down the power of the practically independent military leaders.

Letter written by Edith to her mother   Paofu, April 30, 1922

There is hope at last of being able to get letters thru' soon. The Chinese in the city have been very anxious over the situation, but outside of that there has been no undue excitement here. They have feared that if Wu's troops were defeated that there would be looting, but as there seems to be no danger of that their fears are diminishing somewhat.

Journalist "Upton Close"

We have had two newspaper correspondents here most of the time since last Sunday. Joseph [Josef] W. Hall [pen name "Upton Close"] and a Miss Edna Lee Booker. It has been very fine for us as General Wu has been giving them the straight of events as they happened. Mr. Hall has been stopping with us, and until last evening Miss Booker was staying in the city at General Wu's residence. But yesterday she said she couldn't stand it any longer, so Mrs. Robinson has taken her in. She said they were extremely kind to her in fact they nearly killed her with attention. She said she didn't have a second alone. At night an Amah slept in her room with her and a guard was outside each window and two outside her door. And as soon as she opened her door in the morning until she went to bed at night the whole family just camped in her room. She is a lovely Southern girl. She is certainly getting some experiences.

Letter written by Edith to her mother

Paofu, May 12, 1922

General Wu returned yesterday and our newspaper man, Mr. Josef Hall [penname "Upton Close"], returned with him. It's fine to be getting first hand news again. The railroad south of us near Kaifeng is broken so now all our news is coming around via Tientsin and Peking again.

Letter written by Rob to his father

Paotingfu / May 16, 1922

The fighting seems to have stopped. Wu has come back to Paotingfu and is waiting here to take up the reorganization problem. He drove back Chang Tso Lin to Lanchou, just this side of Peitaiho. He is allowing him to reform what is left of his army there to take back to Manchuria with him. He lost about 40,000 of his original 80,000 men, besides all his artillery and most of his munitions. Wu seems to be afraid if he crushes him completely Manchuria will fall into anarchy and the Japanese will use that as an excuse to annex it, as they did Korea. The plan now seems to be to recall the Parliament which was disbanded at the time of Chang Hsün's attempt to restore the monarchy in 1917, to put Li Yüan Hung back as President and let them work out a new constitution. This ought to bring the Southern Provinces back into the fold.

We have several correspondents here with us. Josef Hall [aka Upton Close] of the *China Press, Millard's Review* and several other papers, who is acting unofficially as Wu's publicity agent is living at our house, while Miss Booker, of the International News Service [Hearst's combine] and Dailey, of the Chicago Tribune, are at the Robinsons. I help them prepare their dope [information], so if you see any of their stuff in the papers, I probably had a hand in it.

Major Horsfull, of the American Legation was here the other day. He is a son of Dave Horsfull, of Prairie du Chien [Wisconsin] and vicinity, and was brought up there. He knew Robert Collier, Grant Ballantyne and most of the Grant Co. people that I knew.

Moore's family [Edith's brother] stuck by their home during the fighting. They were only four or five miles from it and up on the hill where they could look down and watch it at Changhsintien, the crucial point. Margaret, Jessie's sister, has been down here helping out in the hospital. There are about 1500 wounded in town, and they have been sending the worst cases to the Presbyterian hospital.

Letter written by Rob to his mother

Paotingfu / June 1, 1922

Day before yesterday was Decoration Day. We had a picnic over at the West Suburb in the afternoon. Decorated the American graves here in the morning. Here in the South Suburb there are the martyr's graves and that of the first Mrs. Price. At the picnic we had some sports for the children.

We are still unable to get to Peitaiho as Chang Tso Lin is still at Shanhaikwan and has practically all the rolling stock of the Peking-Moukden Railway. After he was driven out of Peking and Tientsin he retired to Lanchow about half way up the line. He was driven out there by a flank attack by Josef Hall of the *China Press* and myself. That is one of the jokes of the campaign. We were in at headquarters talking with Gen. Wu's Chief of Staff and I suggested that they ought to send a division across country from Tungchow and catch him on the front. He thought a minute and then said that was exactly what they had done. Hall immediately began to scent a big scoop and asked if he might send the news in.

The Chief of Staff (whose name also is Chang) said that he might, as Chang Tso Lin could not get it in time to do him any good. So Hall immediately telegraphed it in. The next day Chang Tso Lin pulled out suddenly back to Shanhaikwan giving out that he did so to avoid being outflanked. The Chief of Staff then informed us that there had been no force sent across country at all, but that he had been trying to figure out a scheme of getting Chang out of Lanchow (which was a very easily defended position, a deep river with high hills on the other side) without a great sacrifice of life, and that my suggestion had given him the idea of scaring him out through the newspapers and it had worked.

The position at Shanhaikwan is not very strong and I do not think Chang will try to hold it. His troops are very badly demoralized by their defeat and he lost most of his artillery, so I expect him to pull back into Manchuria as soon as the Chihli troops get in a position to attack him there. That ought to happen within a couple of days now as their advance is up to within five miles of Chang's outposts now. Then we will be able to get to Peitaiho.

A News Reel on the War

The *Pathe News* is going to have a reel on the war. They sent a camera man down here last week to get some films. Hall and I set it up for him. I took him over to the hospital and he got some of the wounded soldiers. They were just operating on an emergency case, an infected bullet wound in the breast. One of the big arteries had been cut and when pus and clotted blood were removed the blood spouted up like a fountain and they had three doctors working as fast as they could to get it stopped. The camera got the whole thing. In spite of all they could do the soldier died later in the day. He also took a lot of pictures of Wu P'ei Fu and Ts'ao K'un and their staff in at Ts'ao's Residence. Ts'ao insisted on having a close up taken of him and me together, as "Ts'ao K'un and his American Friend". I felt quite honored as it is the first time he has ever had his picture taken with a foreigner. Gordon and Constance were along and also appear in a number of the pictures. If the theatre at home carries the "Pathe" stuff you want to be on the lookout for it.

We will probably go up to Peking next week and spend a few days out at the hills with Moore and Jessie before we go on to Peitaiho. We want to wait until we are sure we can get through to Peitaiho as we don't want to have to stay there indefinitely.

Letter written by Rob to his sister Nan   **Peitaiho, North China / June 26, 1922**

Well, here we are at Peitaiho at last. Got here last Thursday after the easiest and cheapest trip we ever had while everyone else is having the hardest and most expensive.

The railroad has been all balled up with military trains, so that they are only just getting passenger trains started (three a week now) and they are having an awful time getting any baggage through at all because of the shortage, so we went to the military authorities at Paotingfu and got permission to come on a military train. They gave us a big 40 ton steel freight car for our own use, and the Hubbards another, and even shifted them onto the branch line to the arsenal back of our house for us to get on. So we took goats, baggage, servants and family altogether. We had cots so that we had a very comfortable night and we did not have to get off the car till we got to the Beach Station at Peitaiho, so we avoided all the usual bother of baggage transfers. It took us just 24 hours to come through, and as we got here in the early morning we were all settled down by night. And we only had to pay third class fare and brought all our fifty-odd pieces of baggage and boxes of stores through free.

It certainly is a comfort to be cool again. We had been having it from 100° to 110° in the shade at Paotingfu for over two weeks and so hot in the sun that it blistered right through one's clothes, but here it is cool enough to wear a sweater. The sea is quite warm, however, so I have been going swimming. I am not planning to go back to Paotingfu until September unless they send for me, so I hope I get a good vacation.

We were almost the first ones up here, but the two trains in since and one boat have been just jammed. The have had some awful experiences. No food or water on the trains arriving here in the middle of the night, finding their baggage has been left behind, etc. We have been quite famous with our "side-door Pullman" because of the easy time we had.

Letter written by Edith to her mother (in China)

Paofu / April 25, 1923

I don't believe I have written you since Rob decided that we wouldn't go home [U.S.A.] by way of Japan. It has been such a great relief to us both. I think Rob was dreading it worse than I was. It meant such a lot of extra work for Rob. So now we don't have to leave here until three weeks from Saturday, May 19th. We have taken passage from Shanghai, so you see we will have a much easier trip. I have been taking things easy the last week and can have another week's rest before the general break-up.

The American Minister is to visit Ts'ao K'un [President of the Republic of China] next Monday. All the American men are to dine with them at noon at the Governor's and in the evening at 6 o'clock we are all to dine with him at the West Suburb. The Minister and his party are coming down on a Special Train and start back about 8 o'clock P.M. Rob and Gordon are going on the same train on their way to the Meet in Tientsin. When Mr. Long and Joan visited us several weeks ago they invited Rob to stop with them and to take Gordon with him. Gordon is so pleased over the prospect. They will be gone a whole week, stopping at Moore's on their way back. As soon as they get back we will start the final packing up. I am so glad for this rest. It was what I needed so badly.

Letter written by Edith to her brother Karl (in China)

Paotingfu / May 10, 1923

I am just nearly ill with anxiety over this bandit outrage at Linch'eng. It's just about the time they set for looting your Compound, and I am extremely anxious to hear from you. The papers don't mention anything about you and I hope and pray that silence means there is nothing unusual to write about, but I assure you I will certainly be one relieved sister when I do hear that you are alright.

I don't know as I am very keen on taking that trip thru' Shantung after all. I do wish we could visit you in some more peaceful place. No wonder Mabel's nerves are upset. I should be perfectly wild under such circumstances, not so much for myself as for my children. It un-nerves me so to even think of them being frightened and hurt.

We are all well and getting packed up nicely without any undue hurry and rush. It will be such a relief to get out of China for a while. I can stand it just about so long, when I feel I simply have to have a change.

Letter written by Edith to her brother Moore and his wife Jessie (in China)
Shanghai / May 31, 1923

We arrived yesterday morning at 7 A.M. It was misting a little then but rained harder all day long. Is cloudy now, but the streets are all drying up. Evan's man met us and we arrived here in good time for breakfast. We have a very nice big room with balcony and bath-room. No sign of rats. If fact, there is nothing at all to complain of. A Mr. and Mrs. Beeman have charge and are extremely kind and thoughtful. Mrs. Beeman has told me several times that if I want anything at all for the baby to be sure and ask for it. The meals are very well-balanced, well-cooked and served. The downstairs rooms are full of beautiful flowers, white and yellow daisies, great bowls of sweet-peas, etc. The children have found nice play-mates here and are having a good time. We have the same room and the same room boy that we had the last time we stopped here. It feels very much like getting home, only I miss Mrs. Evans.

I haven't been out at all yet, so haven't seen anyone. Rob has been out most of the time tending to business. Mr. and Mrs. Cole and family and Mr. & Mrs. Geldart and family of the Y.M.C.A. are going on our boat. Also the MacRays; Canadians. We have known them at Peitaiho.

Letter written by Edith to her mother
Letterhead – Canadian Pacific Steamships, Limited

Yokohama (Japan) / June 8, 1923

If your plans carried out I suppose you and Mabel and the children are going to Peitaiho today. I sincerely hope you are having nicer weather than we are. It wasn't raining when we got here but it began about four o'clock and is raining hard now at 8:30. We docked at eleven o'clock and Rob took the three children ashore. I am so glad they got in their jaunt right away, because later they couldn't have gone.

After they got back I went shopping with Mrs. Stanley, who came from Tokyo to see us. They used to be in the Y.M.C.A. in Kaifeng and for the last three years have been in the student work here for the Chinese. She just took me all around and I got everything I started out for. It was such a pleasure to be taken around by someone who knew all the ropes. It was so kind of her to take all that trouble for me. I did appreciate it so much.

We have had a beautiful trip so far; the sea has been so very smooth. It is said that we are planning to make a record trip, getting to Vancouver in eight days instead of nine. I fear we are going to have rough weather when we leave here. It feels like it.

Letter written by Edith to her mother

On board "Empress of Canada"
Saturday - June 16, 1923

    The children have been having a lovely time. There are 35 children on board. Gordon has made quite a hit with the Captain. He is a handsome, hale old fellow of about seventy. He told Gordon to call him Capt. Jim. I never was on a boat before where everyone is so exceptionally kind. We are all allowed so much freedom and everything we could ask for. The food is so good and so well served.

    We have a good chance of breaking the record from Yokohama to the sound. It is held now by the "Russia" for 8 days and 18 hours and 24 min. We hope to make it in 8½ days. (8 days, 10 hours, 53 minutes). We land in Vancouver sometime tomorrow and hope to take the evening train right out. That will get us home by Thursday noon.

Y.M.C.A. 1923 REPORT WRITTEN BY ROBERT W. CLACK (March 1924)

Editor's note: This is an excerpt from his final report for the Y.M.C.A.

Clear Lake, Iowa, March 31, 1924

ADMINISTRATIVE REPORT FOR 1923 (an Attachment) – R. W. Clack

We left Paotingfu the last of May for furlough. The Association there was left in good condition, with money enough on hand to run them until after the fall membership campaign. The Presbyterian Mission had agreed to allow Mr. Stevenson to give half time to the Association for a year, or until the National Committee found it possible to assign an International Committee secretary. We finally got our building site completed and all deeds turned over to the National Committee. Two new secretaries were just being added to the staff, and we had a larger membership, and Bible and educational enrollment than ever before. The later part of the year was spent in financial work in the Central Region [of the U.S.]. [17]

Highlights of Professional Accomplishments
Robert Wood Clack – China from 1910 to 1923

- Taught for three years at Chihli Provincial Collee in Paotingfu before it closed in June 1913.

- Organized Government School athletics in the capitals of four North China Provinces: Paotingfu, Taiyuanfu, Mukden, and Kirin.

- Served for two years as the first President of the Chinese Amateur Athletic Union.

- Assisted in establishing the Y.M.C.A. in Paotingfu in 1913.

- Became the first General Secretary of the Y.M.C.A. in Paotingfu after his teaching contract expired in June 1913.

- Took a team of 200 Chinese athletes to Manila to compete in the 1919 Far Eastern Championship Games.

- Acted as personal advisor in affairs involving foreigners to the Warlord Dictator of North China, Ts'ao K'un, including traveling as an interpreter for one week in July 1920.

- Acted as the Executive Secretary of the International Famine Relief Committee of Chihli during the Great Famine of 1920-21, supervising the feeding of nearly a million people.

- Served as Chinese representative to the International Olympic Federation from 1920 to 1923.

- Trained a Chinese staff for the Paotingfu Y.M.C.A., raised funds for building and operating, increased the number of members which grew to over 1,200 members by 1923 (his final year as General Secretary).

- Authored nine Y.M.C.A. Reports that are filed in the Kautz Family YMCA Archives at the University of Minnesota.

**Robert Clack's name
in Chinese characters**
(more information on page 310)

The Robert Wood Clack family in 1923 before leaving China.

L-R: Douglas (age 4), Edith, Constance (8), Gordon (10), Lee (2), and Robert

PART THREE: LIFE AFTER CHINA

IOWA – 1923-1924

In June 1923, Rob and Edith returned to the United States with their four children, aged 2 to 9 – Llywelyn, Douglas, Constance, and Gordon. The family lived near his parents in Clear Lake, Iowa, for one year. Rob continued to carry out work for the YMCA and traveled throughout Iowa, Minnesota, Illinois, and South Dakota speaking for and helping to raise money for YMCA foreign work. Their fifth child, Roderick Whittier Clack, was born in Mason City, Iowa, on February 13, 1924. The following year the family moved to Alma, Michigan.

In addition, in 1924 he completed the requirements to become ordained as a Congregational Church gospel minister. "Although never a parish minister, for he was a teacher at heart, he wore the mantle of ordination with dignity and grace and discharged his ministerial vow in winsome words and gracious service." (from his funeral service in 1964) [1] He occasionally officiated at wedding ceremonies for members of his family.

Clear Lake, Iowa, Summer 1923
The William Rollinson Clack family (Robert's parents and sisters)
(L-R): Celia, Adda (mother), Nan, William (father), Robert, Ida

MICHIGAN – 1924-1954: Alma College

Beginning a New Career in Michigan
In 1924, while living temporarily in Clear Lake, Iowa, Rob secured a position as a professor of mathematics at Alma College, a small Presbyterian-based school in Alma, Michigan. In addition to mathematics and astronomy, he also taught Chinese history, culture, and language. They bought a house across from the city park and a few blocks from Alma College. The family lived in this home for 34 years.

Their sixth child, Wynne Rollinson Clack, was born in Alma on June 2, 1925.

In addition to his classroom responsibilities, in 1928 Rob was appointed Registrar of Alma College – a position that he held until 1943. He also continued his studies of Chinese and Japanese languages and began work on interpreting and translating into English notable historic Chinese and Japanese poems from the 11th Century B.C. through the "Modern" time.

A Final Visit to the Orient
During the summer of 1929, Rob assisted his long-time friend "Upton Close" (Josef W. Hall) in taking an expedition – a study group of almost 120 students and teachers – through Japan and China. Close was a "Far East" journalist and author and would become a noted radio commentator following World War II.

Receives Significant Poetry Award
In 1934 Rob submitted a manuscript of his translations of Chinese poetry for a publication award sponsored by *Verse-Craft Magazine* and Emory University. He received the Verse-Craft Poetry Manuscript Award for this collection. The prize was the publication of a limited edition of a small, hard-cover book titled *From Bamboo Glade and Lotus Pool (translations of Chinese Classical Poetry in English Verse)* published by The Banner Press at Emory University. The book included 104 poems, grouped chronologically by eras and dynasties, from about 2,000 B.C. to the present, in addition to explanatory introductions and footnotes. Following the book's publication, reviews were published in at least seven newspapers. He had speaking engagements in several Michigan cities about this book and his thirteen years in China.

The *Detroit News* published an article about this book in November 1934 under the headline "Chinese Poetry and English Words" by Clyde Beck.
The Chinese have had poets for about 4,000 years; they sang long before the days of Homer and Vergil [sic]; but the western world knows little about them. In the last decade I have seen two anthologies of Chinese verse in translation. The latest one is the work of Prof. Robert Wood Clack, of Alma College, Alma, Mich., and it particularly deserves the notice of those who would get the spirit of Chinese poetry. Prof. Clack translates directly from the Chinese; and since he has a nice sense of rhyme and rhythm the result is probably as accurate a reproduction of the Chinese intention as is possible in English. ... [2]

Journalist Upton Close wrote the following about the book in its Foreword:
Robert Wood Clack is the first to rewrite this Beauty that was Cathay for the man, woman and child who never reads poetry as such. His translations are accurate, with the precision he brings

to them as a mathematician. They are poetical—he is a poet. They are appealingly human. Now and then one takes wings and soars; now and then one glows like a red ruby or a pale star sapphire in a jewel casket. This makes a tremendously worthwhile book. [3]

One of these translated poems was included in the national poetry magazine, *Kaleidograph* (Dallas, Texas), in October 1936 and is transcribed here:

The Old Trysting Place, by LI PO (705-762), Tang Dynasty.
(Translated from the Chinese by Robert Wood Clack)

The last farewell is over on the hill;
My eyes are dimmed by years—the wind is chill.
No friendly face remains but the pale moon;
No voice is heard except the mocking rill.

In sunny spring sweet lotus filled the lake;
But autumn now makes sere the bamboo brake.
To bring the past and present into tune,
I linger here and sing for old time's sake. [4]

Additional Studies and Associations
In December 1934 Rob read a paper before the Mathematics Association in Lansing, Michigan, which presented "a mathematical treatment of the old Chinese musical scale described in the Book of Rites, and showed that it is even closer to our modern equally toned scale than the equally tempered is to the diatonic." This paper would become a part of his book *Celestial Symphonies: A Study of Chinese Music*.

During his 30-year tenure at Alma College, he was a member of several professional associations, including
- *Who's Who in Michigan (1936)* as Registrar and Professor of Mathematics & Astronomy at Alma College
- Mathematical Association of America (past president, 1933)
- Association of Collegiate Registrars (president, Michigan Registrars Association, 1932)
- Michigan Poetry Society (one of its founders; served as secretary and vice president for a number of years, and had a lifetime membership)
- Alma Representative of the Michigan Intercollegiate Athletic Association (since 1927)
- *Who's Who in America* – 1937, 1938, and 1939 editions (also in the 1950-1954 editions)
- *Who's Who in the Central States, Vol. 1 (1947)*

In the summers of 1937 through 1939, Rob took intensive classes in Japanese language and others in Chinese and Japanese politics, history, and culture at the Far Eastern Institute at the University of Michigan. While there he also taught a second-year Mandarin class.

1938 through 1958 – Translations and Writings
Encouraged by the 1934 poetry award and aided with further scholarly studies in Chinese and Japanese, Rob spent about two decades "in his leisure time" working on poetry translations,

interpretations, and explanatory writings in preparation for publication. He translated both Chinese and Japanese poems – about 1,200 Chinese and 1,500 Japanese – written by some 500 poets. In addition, he expanded his previously written paper that analyzed Chinese music.

Through the years many of these translated poems were published in journals such as *Verse-Craft, Avon, Kaleidograph, Westminster Magazine, Florida Magazine of Verse, The Lantern, American Bard, Step Ladder, Down, Flame, Caravan, La Petite, Poet Love, Peninsular Poets, Poetry Digest, The Detroit News,* and the *New York Herald-Tribune*.[5] His entire body of work eventually was published in four books (seven volumes) about a decade after his death. [see the Epilogue for further information]

The World War II Years (1943-1946)
In addition to teaching, Rob served as Coordinator of Studies for the V12 Navy Program at Alma College. Three of the Clack's sons served in the U.S. Navy during World War II. Lee enlisted in July 1942 and he was a Lieutenant junior grade while serving as a Radar Naval Technician in the South Pacific. Roderick joined the Navy in March 1943 and worked in the States. Wynne enlisted in the Navy in May 1943 and served aboard a Landing Craft Tank (LCT) in the South Pacific until the end of the War.

Clack Family Reunion, 1950, Alma, Michigan (photo in backyard of their home)
(L-R) Robert, Edith; (in birth order) Gordon, Constance, Douglas, Lee, Roderick, Wynne

Honorary Degree
In April 1952 "Prof" Clack was awarded an honorary doctorate degree (Hon. D.Sc.) from Alma College.

Family Tragedy
On May 27, 1952, their son Roderick died in an automobile accident in California. He left his wife and two young daughters.

"Prof Clack Day"
Alma College's Homecoming Day, October 17, 1953, was dedicated as "Prof. Clack Day" and there was a parade float decorated and named in his honor. The following tribute was read: "During the pageantry of our Homecoming, we pause to pay tribute to you for your long and fruitful life of service here at Alma. Through the years you have inspired us and given us a clearer vision as we have associated with you in the class room, in the area of sports, and in your home. We want to say to you and your gracious wife that your contributions will live in our memories and hearts as we face life more confidently and courageously from knowing you. We feel that Shakespeare coined these words especially for you:

> 'His life was gentle, and the elements so mix'd in him
> That nature might stand up and say to all the world this was a man!' "

RETIREMENT YEARS – 1954 to 1964

Retirement
Rob retired in June 1954 at the age of 67, after teaching at Alma College for 30 years. He was given the honor of being designated "Professor Emeritus".

In their centennial history book, *Within Our Bounds*, Alma College identified "Prof" Clack as one of the "Giants of the Middle Years (1920-1940)". His "… outpouring of literary and poetic creativity, as well as interpretive historical and cultural analysis, will long be recognized by Alma College and by Far Eastern literary scholars as a monumental scholarly achievement by a dedicated and imaginative mathematics professor and registrar."[6]

During retirement, Rob continued his writings and poetry study and translations. He also kept up on local community issues, both in Alma and nearby St. Louis, Michigan.

"Michigan on a Chopstick"
In 1955 the town of Coleman, Michigan, tried to capture the claim of being the "Middle of the Mitten" from St. Louis, Michigan (a town close to Alma). Rob decided to use the principles of physics to determine the geographical center of Michigan's Lower Peninsula. He proved that the center of gravity for the State of Michigan is a point near St. Louis by balancing a cutout highway map of the state on the point of a chop stick. His notable accomplishment was covered in local newspapers. Rob and family members attended a re-dedication ceremony in St. Louis, Michigan, on December 17, 1955.[7]

1955 – "Michigan on a Chopstick" / Robert W. Clack
(proving the center of Michigan's Lower Peninsula
by balancing a cutout of a map on a chopstick)

Second Family Tragedy
On November 8, 1957, their son Lee and his family – wife, Ann; children Bruce, Scott, Kimi, and Mariko, died in the crash of a Pan American Boeing 377 Stratocruiser in the Pacific Ocean. They were on the way back to Japan (Lee was Manager of Dow Chemical International-Tokyo) after a family leave in the U.S.

Rob and Edith Relocate to Midland, Michigan
After living in Alma, Michigan, for 34 years, in 1958 Rob and Edith moved into a house in Midland, Michigan, to be near their eldest son Gordon and his family.

March 21, 1961 – Celebrated 50th Wedding Anniversary
(*Midland Daily News* / Michigan)

"Dr. and Mrs. Robert Clack, 310 Harrison, will celebrate their 50th wedding anniversary, Tuesday. During this time and before, they have seen a lot of the world with its adventures and tragedies. …

[While in China], Mrs. Clack took advantage of reasonable prices and the wide selection while she was there to acquire a collection of 50 pieces which includes a low table with a circular engraved brass top and scalloped edges and supported by three wooden legs. Another interesting piece in her collection is an original painting by the Dowager Empress, Tzu Hsi of the Manshu [sic] line, whose rule ended in 1910, shortly after Clack's arrival in China. …"[8]

Alumni Award from Grinnell College
On June 2, 1962, Rob received the Grinnell College Alumni Award. Unfortunately, he was not able to attend the ceremony due to being hospitalized. He was mailed the formal certificate and a copy of the Citation which had been read to the assembled multitude at the college.

Funeral Service - December 1964
Rob passed away in Midland, Michigan, on Tuesday, December 15, 1964, at the age of 78. Funeral services were held Thursday in the Midland Presbyterian Church. The eulogy was led by The Rev. Dr. T.M. Greenhoe. In addition to several Biblical readings and stories about his life, six of Rob's own poems were read. In the minister's words, "Not everyone has poetic skills to record one's faith and hope and love, but Dr. Clack was so endowed and has left for all of us a testimony of his life in verse."[9] This is one of his poems that was read during the service:

BOUQUETS

I might have sent you orchids, fresh with the morning dew –
But they seemed too inadequate to bare my heart to you!
Such blossoms quickly wither as soon as dew has dried –
And withered, might betoken that love and faith had died!

And so I send you memories, still fragrant of a day
We can't forget: sweet moments that never fade away –
Bouquets of poignant memories, watered with unshed tears,
That keep them still unwithered through long and empty years!

by Robert Wood Clack

* * * * *

Following Rob's death, Edith remained where they both had been living with the Kindy family at the Kindy Nursing Home (their Amish farmhouse) in Midland County, Michigan. Several years later she moved in with daughter Connie's family in Riva, Maryland. She passed away in 1972, at the age of 83.

Rob and Edith are buried in the Midland City Cemetery, along with other family members, in Midland, Michigan.

LIFE IN HAIKU (Immortality)

Bright beams through the pane –
But when the glass is shattered
Stars shine still more.

by Robert Wood Clack

Robert W. Clack as *Lao Yeh "Grandfather"* (photo ca. 1960)

Edith Clack as *Lao T'ai T'ai "respected Elderly Lady"* (photo ca. 1960)

EPILOGUE

⌘ Robert Wood Clack: His Published Work
⌘ Selected Poems Composed by R.W. Clack: Reflections on his Experiences in China
⌘ Clack Art Center, Alma College, Alma, Michigan: Inaugurated in 1971

Despite the occasional perils that the Clack family experienced during the years they lived in early twentieth-century China; the essence of China continued to have a positive influence on their lives when they came back to the States. In college classrooms Rob taught students about the history of the Chinese people, their culture, and language. Their home was filled with cherished objects from their years in China and they enjoyed showing these to acquaintances and colleagues and sharing their stories of that time. Both Rob and Edith gave community presentations about their experiences. Furthermore, throughout his years in Alma, Rob dedicated a good amount of his free time to analyzing and translating the poetry of ancient China and Japan. The unique experiences of the years they lived in China would have a lasting impact on their lives – and beyond.

ROBERT WOOD CLACK: HIS PUBLISHED WORK

Robert Clack's first published book was *From Bamboo Glade and Lotus Pool: Translations of Chinese Classical Poetry in English Verse*, by Banner Press in 1934. The volume is divided into six parts and includes 125 poems grouped by eras and dynasties encompassing 4,000 years. A book review was written by Prof. Arnold Mulder of Kalamazoo College and published in several newspapers in Michigan in 1934. He wrote:

> *... That a professor of mathematics in Michigan should become the translator of the classical poetry of China into English is astonishing enough; that he should win high praise from an authority like Upton Close for the accuracy of the translation and for the fidelity to the spirit of the original but heightens the happy surprise.* [1]

During his years at Alma College, Rob continued to work on translations of additional poetry, and he prepared manuscripts which were published posthumously. This body of work was printed in seven volumes – four on interpretations and translations of classical Chinese poetry, two on Japanese poetry, and one on Chinese music. Each volume contains a comprehensive introductory explanation of its subject. Published in the mid-1970s by Gordon Press, the translations and writings were done over a 20-year period from about 1938 to 1958. The editing and publication were coordinated later by Douglas Clack, Robert and Edith's son.

- *The Herd Boy and the Weaver Maid: A Collection of Chinese Love Songs Translated into English Verse*, Gordon Press, 1977 (224 pages)

  > "The oldest Chinese poems we still possess are found in the *Shih Ching* (Poetry Classic), generally referred to in English as the *Book of Poetry* or the *Book of Odes*. This is a selection of just over three hundred poems probably written in the latter half of the Second Millennium B.C. and the early part of the First Millennium. ..." [page 1]

"Li Po (705-762 A.D.) is generally considered by the Chinese as the greatest poet of all time ... in matters of pure technique and subtle beauty of expression he is unsurpassed by any poet of any age or nation. ... When the [drawn] characters are analyzed into their component parts they may suggest rich connotations, so that a clever skillful poet like Li Po expresses much more than the mere surface meanings of the words he uses. ... each lyric is really a kind of scroll painting, unrolling to give us a series of bewitchingly drawn vistas of beauty, subtly suggested." [page 134]

TWO FLUTES (by Li Po)

One evening as I lingered by the stream
To breathe the twilight's delicate perfume,
There faintly came an essence still more sweet:
Wind-wafted echoes from a far-off flute!

To answer it I cut a willow plume –
A poor response to music so sublime –
And when at last all other sounds grew mute,
Trilled back a tune upon the enchanted night!

Since then at dusk when day's harsh din grows still,
The birds hear two mysterious songsters call.
They do not recognize what creatures sing –
But none-the-less they understand the song! [2]

- *Millenniums of Moonbeams: An Historical Anthology of Chinese Classical Poetry, 3 volumes*, Gordon Press, 1978 (995 pages) ("dedicated to Ch'ang-o, the Moon Goddess")

His most ambitious undertaking – the three volumes of *Millenniums of Moonbeams* – covers a period of almost four thousand years and contains translations into classic English verse forms of nine hundred poems by some four hundred different poets. He chose not to "translate" the poetry literally, or freely, as is the case "when dealing with languages of similar structure and related in their origin". Instead, he chose to "saturate himself with the spirit and the essence of the original poetry, and then rewrite it in the verse forms of his own language ...". He used this method – called "recreation" [re-creation] – to "produce in the mind and heart of the Occidental reader an effect comparable with that produced upon the Chinese reader by the original verse."

In the introduction to *Millenniums of Moonbeams* he wrote:

> ... my purpose is not at all to add any great contribution to the scholarship of the world; but rather it is to give to Western readers some slight appreciation of the poetic genius of the Chinese and a realization that, when we find a common medium of communication, *people of all races and ages are essentially the same at heart!* ... and if I have caught enough of the spirit and the music of the Chinese verses so that you desire to read more, I shall have accomplished my purpose. Especially have I tried to keep them musical; for it has often been said: "All Chinese poetry is song!".

He did much more than simply translate, or re-create, these poems. He also wrote thought-provoking descriptions of the dynastic writing periods and noteworthy biographies of the poets. An example of this approach is about Wang Po from the early T'ang Dynasty (7th and Early 8th Centuries A.D.):

Introduction to Wang Po
"Wang Po is sometimes called the 'First of the T'angs'. He was a precocious lad who wrote verses at six, took his Chin Shih Degree at sixteen, and died at twenty-eight. … At nine Wang Po knew his history so well that he was able to correct errors in a *History of the Han Dynasty* written by the Imperial Librarian! After taking his degree he was employed for a time at editing the current dynastic records. He angered the Emperor by his criticism, and fled to Szechuan, where most of his poetry was written. He was finally condemned to death for killing an escaped criminal whom he had harbored for a time; but powerful friends succeeded in getting the sentence commuted, and he was allowed to join his father in exile in Annam. But his ship was wrecked enroute and he drowned. He was especially noted for his ability to dash off impromptu verses so well done that not a single character needed revising. He received so many presents of rolls of silk in return for such poems that it was said that 'he spun with his mind'." [pp.235-6]

LONESOME (by Wang Po)

Above the green pagoda tiles the listless mists hang low;
In southern skies the waxing moon augments the twilight glow.
I leave my tower to shiver through the chilly silent air –
River and night and solitude are more than I can bear! [3]

- *The Soul of Yamato: An Historical Anthology of Japanese Poetry, 2 volumes*, Gordon Press, 1978 (582 pages)

    "In preparing this book of my own translations, my aim has been to give a larger sample of the material and its backgrounds, and a better appreciation of the charm of the original Japanese verse. I have tried to keep all translations in the original syllabic metrical patterns, the only element of the Japanese verse form that can be carried over into English."

    Poem from the Manyoshu (Seventh Century, Anonymous)

Loosed from Winter's bonds,
At last Spring has come forth.
At dawn of morning
The white dewdrops now gather;
In the evening dusk

The mists trail over the hills;
And in the valley,
Beneath his screen of green trees
A nightingale is singing! [4]

- *Celestial Symphonies: A Study of Chinese Music*, Gordon Press, 1976 (92 pages)

Chapter I – "History and Theory of Chinese Music"

"China does have a great body of music of rare beauty, even to the cultivated Occidental ear, in her old temple and court ritualistic chants and in some of her old folk songs; but unfortunately most of the former have been locked away from the general public by ritualistic taboos and ceremonial laws, while the latter have been largely unavailable because of a dearth of artists trained to make the most of them." [page 1]

"As with all early nations the beginnings of Chinese music are lost in the dim vistas of prehistory. Its invention is credited in some legends to supernatural beings, in others to mythical Emperors. One story says that a ruler who lived in the time when spirits dominated the earth invented the rules of pronunciation, the written characters for the language, and finally music." [page 4] [5]

Chapter II – "The Ancient Chinese Scale and the Equally Tempered Scale"

Chapter III – "Chinese Musical Instruments"

Chapter IV – "Music as a Theme in Chinese Poetry"

Chapter V – "Some Examples of Chinese Melodies"

Image of cover of book (red with gold lettering)

SELECTED POEMS COMPOSED BY R.W. CLACK

Reflections on his Experiences in China

In his later years, not only did he work on his translations of oriental poetry, but he also wrote some of his own poems about China.

THE GREAT WALL SPEAKS

From dunes far out on Gobi's dusty wastes,
Past ancient cities lost in drifting sand,
O'er desert vast I stretch on mountain tops
Against the storms my tower-crowned bulwarks stand.

I climb to rocky heights among the clouds;
Great gorges out by cataracts I span:
Headlong I plunge down terrifying steeps,
To reach the sea at last at Shan-hai-kwan.

The mighty Chin Shih Huang erected me
To guard his realms against the Tartar horde:
In vain – for twenty centuries I've stood
While over me barbarians have poured.

Fierce Khitans, Mongols, Manchus, and the Huns,
Whose horses' hoofs the Chinese fields have spurned,
I've watched their millions flow in from the North –
Yet of those conquering hosts none have returned.

I've failed to keep these warlike raiders out,
But seem to keep them in with utmost ease:
And yet within these regions to the South,
One finds no race, no culture, but Chinese.

And shall these puny dwarfs who now invade
Fare better than that virile Tartar strain?
Their aping of barbaric Western ways,
Their haughty boastings, likewise, will be vain.

For China lasts, unconquered and unchanged,
Though other empires rise, expand, and fall:
A hundred generations more may pass,
Yet I shall still remain the CHINESE Wall.

The following original poem was dedicated to his friend – explorer, adventurer, journalist, author, and radio commentator Upton Close – about Close's Sixth Oriental Adventure in 1930.

THE CALL OF THE EAST

I am tired of dusty blackboards, and teaching that's never done;
And I want to leave it and travel out toward the setting sun.

For the charm of dainty Nippon, her manners and her grace,
And the lures of Cathay, mysterious, are drawing me apace.

I want to feel the salt spray, as it stings and cools my brow;
And hear the wash of the billows against the staunch ship's prow.

As refreshed by a fortnight's journey, across the Pacific's breast,
I want to learn the secrets that the East keeps from the West.

I want to learn from the Orient that placid serenity,
That seems to come from contented heart, and assured eternity.

I want to see Dai Butsu, mid Kamakura's shrines,
And the tombs of the sleeping Shoguns, 'neath Nikko's towering pines.

I want to see old Fuji, and Asama's smoking cone,
And feed the deer at Nara, to the temple bell's sweet tone.

I want to see Nagoya, with its castle old and grand,
And the Inland Sea by moonlight, that magic fairyland.

Then on through the Hermit Kingdom, with customs quaint and queer;
And still on into China, till Peking's walls appear.

I want to see the yellow roofs of the Son of Heaven's home,
And Heaven's marble altar, with its gold and purple dome.

I want to scale those Western Hills, and feel their breezes cool;
And sleep by the Sleeping Buddha, and bathe in Black Dragon Pool.

I want to climb old Tai Shan, Confucius' sacred mount,
And Nanking's Purple Mountain; and drink at West Lake's fount.

I want to know the history and the poetry of the East;
And see the geishas dancing, and eat at a Chinese feast.

I want to gain perspective, and a truer culture fine,
And sympathy with others whose ways are not like mine.

But best of all the profits when my summer's venture ends,
Will be the love and loyalty of a host of new found friends.

CLACK ART CENTER, ALMA COLLEGE
ALMA, MICHIGAN (Inaugurated in 1971)

The following description is from the Alma College website (2020).

"The Clack Art Center is named in honor of Dr. and Mrs. Robert Clack, and in memory of Mr. and Mrs. Hugh "Lee" Clack and their four children, who died in a plane crash in 1957. Robert Clack, registrar and professor at Alma from 1924 to 1954, was Lee's father, and Lee and his wife, the former Ann Carter, were Alma College alumni. An estate contingency clause in the will of Lee and Ann Clack provided nearly a quarter of the funds needed for the project.

The building that is now the Clack Art Center was originally constructed as a Memorial Gymnasium in 1922-1923 in memory of World War I veterans from the College and from Gratiot County [Michigan]. After completion of the new Physical Education Center in 1968, it was completely renovated for use as an art center.

The innovative 1970-1971 renovation converted the building into an exceptionally fine facility for the instruction of art. The Clack Art Center provides excellent studios and classrooms for undergraduate art students. Excellent digital facilities, individual artist's studios, gallery, lecture hall and studios for each area. There have been more than 400 art majors who graduated since 1970. This building has had a lot of impact over the generations!" [6]

Clack Hallway of Chinese Artifacts

In a hallway of the Clack Art Center at Alma College there is a wall of floor-to-ceiling wooden cabinets with protective glass doors. More than 50 items are displayed in these 30-or-so linear feet of cabinets. Among the items nestled within these cabinets are three colorful embroidered robes, brass candleholders and plates, ceramic vases and bowls, a watercolor scroll, and dozens of smaller items. These items were brought back from China by Robert and Edith Clack in 1923.

The Clack's youngest son, Wynne, was the one who – a number of years after the opening of Alma College's Clack Art Center – had a vision that the family's Chinese objects be donated to Alma College for display and education. Over the years many of these artifacts had been distributed throughout the family. Wynne packed up most of his own inherited items and persuaded other family members to also contribute. He then made an inventory of the items and donated them to Alma College.

These artifacts were in storage for several years until an appropriate area could be provided for their display. Finally, the cabinets were ready and a student who was an Art History minor researched, organized, and labeled the collection for her Senior Practicum. This handsomely displayed collection offers a glimpse into a uniquely historic period in Chinese history.

The following four photographs were taken by Norma Geraldine Clack in 2019.

A section of the display case in the Clack Art Center hallway

Brass bell hanging on original stand (see letter of August 1, 1912)

Beijing porcelain bowl and matching top made for Imperial use
(see letter of January 3, 1921)

Chinese robe, embroidered silk
(dark royal blue background, gold and white embroidery)

APPENDIX

CONTENTS

Name Conversions (Wade-Giles and Pinyin)	294
Selected Major Political Events in China, 1911-1921	295
Glossary 1 – Descriptions of Selected Places and Organizations	296
Glossary 2 – List of Individuals Mentioned in the Letters	298
Glossary 3 – Annotations for Family Members in the Clack Letters	309
Information from Yiding Gao, A Current Resident of China	312
Endnotes	317
Additional Bibliography	320
Copyright Permission	320
Photography Credits	321
Creator and Editor, Norma Geraldine Clack	322

Name Conversions

Since the time of the Clack letters, the Pinyin system of romanization was adopted by the People's Republic of China and is now in common use. The following list of Chinese names and places used in the text is shown here for both Wade-Giles and the Pinyin systems (if the names differ).

Wade-Giles	*Pinyin*
Anhwei	Anhui
Chefoo	Zhifu
Chihli (province)	Zhili
Ch'ing (dynasty)	Qing
Dairen	Dalian
Fenchow	Fenzhou
Foochow	Fuzhou
Han-k'ou	Hankou
Harbin	Ha-er-bin
Honan (province)	Henan
Hsiku	Xi Gu
Hwang Ho River	Huanghe
Kaifeng	Kaifeng
Kalgan	Zhang Jiakou
Kiangsi (province)	Jiangxi
Kuomintang (party)	Guomindang
Li Hung-chang	Li Hongzhang
Paoting(fu)	Baoding
Pechihli (Gulf)	Beizhili
Pei Ho River	Beihe
Peitaiho	Beidaihe
Pei-yang (government)	Beiyang
Peking	Beijing
Shanhaikwan	Shanhaiguan
Shantung (province)	Shandong
Shensi (province)	Shaanxi
T'ien-chin (Tientsin)	Tianjin
Tuan (prince)	Duan
T'ung-chou	Tongzhou
Yangtze River	Yangzijiang

Selected Highlights of Major Political Events in China, 1911–1922

BACKGROUND:
"As traders, diplomats, and military representatives of expanding European powers began to intrude into the Chinese Empire during the 19th and early 20th centuries, different segments of the Imperial Chinese government and Chinese society reacted in different ways. The Boxer Rebellion (1899-1901) was one reaction. Some other people responded by trying to reform traditional Chinese institutions in order to meet the challenges posed by the West. Many ethnic Chinese became dissatisfied that China was being ruled by foreigners (the Manchu Dynasty) and organized secret societies and revolutionary organizations in hopes of ending Manchu rule. Between 1895 and 1910, there were over a dozen small, unsuccessful uprisings against the Manchu Dynasty. A specific Imperial Government action that added to the general resentment against it was a 1911 effort to nationalize several provincial railway development projects. An uprising in Wuchang on October 10 ("Double Ten" day--the 10th day of the 10th month), 1911, triggered uprisings in most other provinces in what became known as the Revolution of 1911." [1]
[Gordon M. Fisher, editor, 2020]

Selections below are from *A Short History of Chinese Civilization*, by Tsui Chi, published by G.P. Putnam's Sons, N.Y., 1943 – Appendix II, Great Events of the Last 100 Years (pp.353-356). These were the major political events that occurred during the time Robert and Edith Clack lived in China.

1911 – Outbreak of revolution at Wuch'ang, October 10, soon followed by many other provinces.
1912 – Sun Yat-sen installed as Provisional President of Republican [*sic*] China. Abdication of the Manchu Emperor, P'u Yi, February 12. Yüan Shih-k'ai installed as Provisional President, March 10.
1913 – Formal recognition of the Chinese Republic by the U.S.A., May 2.
1914 – Yüan Shih-k'ai dissolved Parliament, January.
1915 – Yüan Shih-k'ai declared himself Emperor; General Ts'ai O declared the independence of Yünnan Province, December 25. Troops were sent to fight Yüan.
1916 – Yüan Shih-k'ai renounced his imperial position, March 25. Yüan Shih-k'ai died June 6. Li Yüan-hung, the Vice-President, succeeded him as president.
1917 – China broke off relations with Germany, March 14 … declared war on Germany, August 14. Dr. Sun Yat-sen was elected by the Extraordinary Parliament in Canton as Commander-in-Chief of the Chinese Navy and Army and declared his wish to protect the Constitutional Law.
The military leaders broke into two groups under Tuan Ch'i-jui and Wu P'ei-fu: [the] Anfu and Chihli schools.
1918 – Tuan Ch'i-jui became Prime Minister of the Peking Government, March. Secret Agreement between Peking Government and Japan re Shantung signed September 24-28. Tuan Ch'i-jui resigned his post as Prime Minister. Hsü Shih-ch'ang became President of China, October.
1919 – Peace negotiated in Shanghai between the Canton Revolutionary and Peking Governments, February. Great Demonstration of students in Peking, May 4.
1920 – China formally accepted as a member of the League of Nations, June. Forces of Tuan Ch'i-jui were defeated by those of Wu P'ei-fu in July.
1921 – Dr. Sun Yat-sen was elected President of the Republic by the Extraordinary Parliament Assembly in Canton, May 5. Liang Shih-i ("the Mammon") became Prime Minister of the warlords' regime in Peking.
1922 – War broke out between the military leaders Wu P'ei-fu and Chang Tso-lin, heads of Chihli and Fêngt'ien warlords; the latter defeated, May. Dr. Sun Yat-sen's Northern Expeditionary Army entered Kiangsi Province, May 6. Ch'ên Chiung-ming, Dr. Sun's general, revolted in Canton and the Northern Expeditionary Army was recalled engaging the rebels, June.

GLOSSARY 1

Selected Places and Organizations in China in the Early 20th Century

Ch'ing (now Qing) Dynasty
The Ch'ing (now Qing) dynasty was the last imperial dynasty of China. It was officially established in Manchuria in 1636, and ruled China from 1644 to 1912. It was preceded by the Ming dynasty and succeeded by the Republic of China. It was a multi-cultural empire and the fifth largest in world history. [2]

Republic of China
The Republic of China (ROC) controlled the Chinese mainland between 1912 and 1949. It was established in January 1912 after the Chinese Revolution of 1911, which overthrew the Ch'ing (now Qing) dynasty, the last imperial dynasty of China. [3]

Paotingfu (now Baoding), China
In 1910, Paotingfu was a walled city, with a population of approximately one hundred thousand. The city is about ninety miles southwest of Peking (now Beijing), and about one hundred miles west of Tientsin (now Tianjin), so that the three cities form an equilateral triangle. Baoding dates back to the Western Han Dynasty (206 BC–220 AD). The name "Baoding", acquired during the Yuan dynasty (1271–1368 AD), is roughly interpreted as "protecting the capital", referring to the city's proximity to Peking. Baoding served for many years as the capital of Chihli (now Zhili) Province and was a significant center of culture in the Ming Dynasty and early Ch'ing (now Qing) Dynasty. [4] (The syllable fu was suffixed to the names of provincial capitals during the Manchu and early Republican periods.)

Chihli Provincial College in Paotingfu, Chihli (now Zhili) Province, China
This school was established in 1902 and began to offer some western courses, such as English and physical chemistry. In 1913, the college was merged into another school, but the land and school buildings were still used. Later, it was used by a succession of universities. [5]

Military College in Paotingfu, China
In 1902, Yuan Shikai, the Viceroy of Chihli (now Zhili) Province and the Minister of Beijing, founded an officer academy in Paotingfu (now Baoding), the capital of Chihli Province. From 1902 to 1912, this officer academy in Paotingfu took on a number of different names, including the Peking (now Beijing) Army Expedited Martial Studies Academy. The academy trained officers for the New Army, which was a significant factor in Yüan Shi Kai's rise to power at the end of the Qing dynasty and the pivotal role he played in the Chinese Revolution of 1911. In 1912, after Yüan became the provisional president of the Republic of China, the academy was briefly moved to Peking and became the Army Academy. In October 1912, the academy was relocated back to Paotingfu and formally became the Paotingfu Military Academy. [6]

American Board of Commissioners for Foreign Missions (ABCFM)
The ABCFM was among the first American Christian missionary organizations. It was created in 1810 by recent graduates of Williams College. In the 19th century it was the largest and most important of American missionary organizations and consisted of participants from Reformed traditions such as Presbyterians, Congregationalists, and German Reformed churches. [7]

Young Men's Christian Association in China

Although the YMCA movement had been active in China as early as the 1870s, the first North American YMCA work in China dates from 1889. Part of the appeal of the YMCA was the International Committee's policy of stressing indigenous leadership, support, and control, which appealed to the burgeoning nationalism of the Chinese. While the YMCA's foreign work was rooted in the missionary movement and Bible classes were among the first activities offered by the fledgling association, the program included a variety of other educational programs, including English classes, lectures, and vocational training. Physical training, public health education and other fields of work were soon added as the YMCA responded to local needs. The YMCA introduced many Western-style sports competitions, organized the **Far Eastern Games** (the first international competitions in the far east), and was instrumental in the early organization of the Olympic movement in China. [8]

Wo Fo Ssŭ (Sleeping Buddha Temple)

The Sleeping Buddha Temple is in the foothills at the base of Longevity Hill on Beijing's western fringes. Sleeping Buddha Temple owes its unofficial name to the presence of a sculpture in the form of a reclining figure of Sakyamuni Buddha, the founder of Buddhism. During the Yuan Dynasty (1271-1638 A.D.) restoration and enlargement of the temple, a new reclining figure was cast in bronze and made larger than the original sandalwood figure. [9]

North China Athletic Federation Meet (Y.M.C.A. Report) – After the New Year (1919), as the only member of the Games Committee of the North China Athletic Federation who had had previous experience in running off a big meet, Robert Clack was obliged to spend a good deal of time in preparations for the North China meet, which was held in Taiyuanfu, Shansi, in April 1919. He was also secretary of the committee which had charge of rewriting the constitution of the Federation. [10]

Far Eastern Athletic Association / The Far Eastern Games (1919) – When Mr. Swan, head of the Physical Department of the National Committee, left for America on furlough in April, Rob went to Shanghai to take his place as executive secretary of the Committee for China of the Far Eastern Athletic Association. [They] took advantage of having representatives from all parts of the country together at Manila to initiate a **National Athletic Union**, something which had never before been attempted. Rob was appointed head of a committee to draw up a constitution and rules. *From a letter written by Robert Clack April 12, 1919* – "… the Committee consists chiefly of Tang Shao I, the southern delegate to the Peace Conference in Shanghai; Chu, the northern delegate; Dr. Tsui, former president of Tsing Hua College, and secretary of the Peace Conference, and C.C. Heih, head of the Shanghai Chamber of Commerce."

Chinese Amateur Athletic Union (1922-1924)

In the spring of 1919 the representatives of North, South and East China appointed a committee to draft a provisional constitution for a national athletic organization. The result was the formation of the **Chinese Amateur Athletic Union**, formally founded on April 3, 1922, in Peking. There were nine members on the executive committee, and three of them were foreigners (YMCA physical directors), who played an active role in promoting modern sport in China. In 1924, in an anti-imperialist atmosphere, the China Amateur Athletic Union was abolished. [11]

GLOSSARY 2

Individuals Mentioned in the Clack Letters

NOTE: The dates in parenthesis indicate the first mention of the person in the Clack correspondence. These descriptions are drawn primarily from the Clack letters with occasional clarifying information from other sources.

Chihli Provincial College, Paotingfu – Teachers and Staff (1910-1913)

- Mr. Ch'i Hao **Fei**, a graduate of Oberlin College in Ohio. was secretary in the Tientsin Y.M.C.A. and also president of the Chihli Provincial College in R.W. Clack's first year teaching. (5/1/1910)
- Mr. S.B. **Harvey**, "our new man" in 1910 (8/7/1910 / photo 1913)
- Mr. James A. Russell **Henderson**, science teacher from Scotland; leaving in 1910. (5/8/1910 / photo 1913) Captain **Henderson**, father of J.A.R. Henderson; "a delightful old sea captain". (9/11/1910 / photo 1913)
- David **Lattimore**, American Board Mission; a language teacher from America. His wife was Margaret (Barnes). The Lattimore family came to China in 1901, following China's Boxer Rebellion, which saw many foreigners killed over increased political and commercial presence in Northern China. The family returned to the United States in 1920 when David took a position at Dartmouth College. Children: Owen, Richmond, Katherine, Isabel, Eleanor, and Dixie – see descriptions of three below. (5/8/1910 / photos 1913) Information on Lattimore family from en.wikipedia.org.
    - Owen **Lattimore**, born 1900 (d.1989), became an American educator and author. He was one of the most distinguished Sinologists of the 20th century, director of The Johns Hopkins University's Page School of International Relations and became a target of Sen. Joseph McCarthy.
    - Richmond **Lattimore**, born 1906 (d.1984), became an American poet and translator of the "Iliad" and "Odyssey".
    - Eleanor **Lattimore**, born 1904 (d.1986), became an American author and illustrator of about 60 children's books over a forty-five-year period. Her best-known take place in China, such as *"Little Pear: The Story of a Little Chinese Boy"*. She drew on her upbringing in China and sought to make multiracial understanding a goal in her writing. (photo June 1912)
- Edward R. **Long**, a French and drawing teacher from England. Rob shared a house with him in 1910. He attended the Clack-Gordon wedding in 1911. (5/1/1910 / photo)
- Norman Hinsdale **Pitman**, an English and history teacher from Tennessee; his parents were missionaries. (5/8/1910 / group photo, 1913) His wife was Lucy (Ayers) Pitman. They had three children born in China (one died in infancy). He became a well-known author of children's books (*The Chinese Wonder Book* and *Fairy Tales and Legends of China*) and died in China in 1925.
- Mr. **Porter**, athletic director of the college (6/19/1910)
- Mr. L. Roy **Woodward**, from Iowa, hired as a teacher. (6/9/1912) According to an Iowa newspaper story, Woodward and Robert W. Clack had been classmates and roommates at Iowa (now Grinnell) College; Woodward married Lynne Webster in Iowa in 1911 before they left for China.

American, British, Canadian, and other non-Chinese

[A]
- Dr. Henry Carter **Adams**, advisor to the Board of Communications; attended the 1913 annual dinner in Peking of the American College Club. He was a "Grinnell man", Class of 1874. An economist, promoter of the American Economic Association; led movement to regulate "natural monopolies" in economic life. (b.1851-d.1921) (12/1/1913)
- Dr. George L. and Mrs. E.E. **Aiken**, Congregationalists of the American Board Mission (Paotingfu). He was supported by the Grinnell [Iowa] church. (5/8/1910)
- Miss **Anderson**, 1916 Grinnell College graduate; attended Grinnell picnic in Peitaiho in August 1918. (8/2/1918)
- Susan **Arvis**, 1902 Grinnell College graduate; attended Grinnell picnic in Peitaiho in August 1918. "She was a missionary in Turkey, but a large party of them were driven across into Russia last year and so came out thru Siberia. A lot of them are staying here to help the American Board, several permanently probably." (8/2/1918)

[B]
- Frank P. **Beal**, of the Tientsin Y.M.C.A. – at the Clack-Gordon wedding (3/21/1911 / photo)
- Mr. Fletcher S. **Brockman**, Senior Secretary of the National Committee of the Y.M.C.A., "who has just returned from a six month's campaign in America, came and stayed until Thursday afternoon". (12/1/1913) Written in a letter by Edith: "Mr. Mott's right-hand man ... Oh! He is the nicest man." (3/24/20)
- Mr. (John) Stewart and Mrs. Stella (Fisher) **Burgess** were with the Y.M.C.A. in Peking. Stewart Burgess first served as a missionary (teacher and Y.M.C.A. volunteer) in Japan. Stella Fisher was born in the U.S., but her parents soon went to Japan as Baptist missionaries. After she graduated from college, she worked for the Y.W.C.A. in Japan, where she met Stewart. After their marriage, they went to China. (7/15/1912)

[C]
- Lyman **Cady**, 1910 Grinnell College (Iowa) graduate; attended Grinnell picnic in Peitaiho in August 1918. (8/2/1918)
- Mr. **Carr**, a young Siamese who studied in Paotingfu. (5/8/1910)
- Mr. Harry W. **Carritt**, a teacher in the Tientsin Anglo-Chinese College and one of Moore Gordon's colleagues; attended the Clack-Gordon wedding. (3/21/1911 / photo)
- Whit **Chambers**, Peking Y.M.C.A. staff; Princeton graduate. (8/7/1910)
- Miss Abbie Goodrich **Chapin**, in charge of the girls' school at the American Board Mission in Paotingfu, went through the siege at Peking in 1900. She was the only Paotingfu missionary who escaped, as she happened to be in Peking on a visit when the missionaries were massacred (5/8/1910); she is the only American woman to receive the Victoria Cross for women (which she received for services rendered at Peking's International Hospital during the Boxer Rebellion). (12/1/1918) She was born in T'ungchou and her parents were American missionaries in China for three decades during the late 19th century.
- Upton **Close** (penname; born Josef Washington Hall), American explorer, adventurer, journalist, author; also radio commentator in the 1940s. (4/30/1922) He stayed at the Clack's home in May

1922. (also see page 244) Close conducted a number of expeditions to the Orient and Robert went with him on his tour in the summer of 1929.
- Mr. and Mrs. George **Collingwood**, an American from New Orleans, "who has been out here for nineteen years". Manager of the Tientsin "Press". Also Mrs. Collingwood's sister, Lady Betty. Rob met them on board the ship from Hawaii to Japan. (3/19/1910 / photo)
- Rev. A.M. and Mrs. Beth (Neely) **Cunningham**, of the Presbyterian Mission. Mr. Cunningham was Vice President of 1913 Y.M.C.A. Board. Lived in the Presbyterian West Suburb. (11/13/1911 / photo in group 1912)

[D]
- Miss Edith **Davis**, of Tientsin, "… the new young lady who just came to the mission; formerly Y.W.C.A. secretary in Des Moines, Iowa" – attended the Clack-Gordon wedding. (3/21/1911 / photo)
- Dr. and Mrs. **Davis**, of the Methodist Mission in Paotingfu; the Clacks attended their retirement farewell tea. (8/3/1913)
- Mr. A.B. (Bennie) and Mrs. Sarah (Seymour) **DeHaan**, Bennie was a college friend of R.W. Clack and "helps out with sports". By September 1912, the DeHaans were stationed in Pangkiachuang, Shantung Province. (6/19/1910)
- Captain Robert **Dollar**, a Scots-American industrialist, lumber baron, shipping magnate, and philanthropist born in Bainsford, Scotland in 1844. The title "Captain" was honorary. (8/12/1912)

[E]
- Mr. George Sherwood and Mrs. Alice Maud Harriet (Arden) **Eddy** – Mr. Eddy was Y.M.C.A. Associate General Secretary (New York); Secretary of International Committee. (1914 – raised funds for new building by way of speaking to groups about the Y.M.C.A.) (6/10/1911)
- Dr. Charles W. **Eliot**, former president of Harvard College (youngest president; served 1869-1909), came to Paotingfu to speak to 2,000 college students at the Li Hung Chang Hall about their duty to the new Republic. (4/22/1912) (photos p.85)
- The Rev. Emery Ward **Ellis**, was brother of Mrs. Hugh (Mabel) Hubbard of the American Board Mission in China. Rev. Ellis, born in 1876 in Iowa, was an A.B.C.F.M. missionary in Tehchow, Shantung, from 1904-1927. (3/14/1915)
- Mr. Charles E. and Mrs. Bessie (Smith) **Ewing**, missionary and head of the Tientsin American Board Mission – attended the Clack-Gordon wedding. (3/21/1911 / photo) Their daughter formerly lived with the Gordons (Elma and Edith) in Tientsin so that she could go to the English School (12/25/1913) [see *Death Throes of a Dynasty: Letters and Diaries of Charles and Bessie Ewing, Missionaries to China*, ed. E.G. Ruoff, published 1990 Kent State University Press]

[F]
- Verna **Foulke** Johnson, a young woman who frequently assisted and stayed with Edith when Rob was away (1919-1920). Her wedding (to an American Marine, surname Johnson) was held at the Clack home in November 1920. Verna's mother, Mrs. Foulke, was a missionary friend of Edith's mother, Elma Gordon. (9/15/1921)
- Mr. and Mrs. Thomas **Foster**, parents of Constance Foster Hubbard. (3/24/1920)
- Marion **Frank**, 1910 graduate of Grinnell College (Iowa), was in the Methodist Mission at Nanking, but spent the summer in Peitaiho with her uncle, Bishop Bashford. (6/23/1913)

[G]
- Rev. R.R. (Robert) **Gailey**, International Committee, Tientsin – performed Clack-Gordon marriage ceremony at the Methodist Mission, Hsiku, in Tientsin. (3/21/1911 / photo)
- Rev. Elmer W. and Mrs. Altie (Cumings) **Galt**, American Mission Board/South Suburb, from Tabor, Iowa. (6/19/1910)
- Rev. Francis **Gamewell**, Secretary of Education, Methodist Church, Peking. (8/3/1913)
- Mrs. Mary **Gaunt**, "an Australian authoress who has been staying at the Lewis's this winter. She set off today on a trip overland to Kashgar, the farthest western city of China. She will be the first white woman who has made the trip. One of my former students is going as interpreter, and our best mason is to act as guide." (4/6/1914) [In 1914 she wrote *A Woman in China*.]
- William **Gleysteen**, Grinnell College graduate; attended Grinnell picnic in Peitaiho in August 1918. (letter 8/2/1918)
- Rev. Jonathan **Goforth**, of the Canadian Presbyterians in Hunan. (8/3/1913)
- Dr. Chauncey and Mrs. Sara B. (Clapp) **Goodrich**, Peking. Missionary of the American Board of Commissioners for Foreign Missions. R.W. Clack's letter, December 1912: "Dr. Goodrich is 76. He has been in China 47 years. He is the author of a little Chinese dictionary which is probably the most used of any in North China. [*A Pocket Dictionary (Chinese-English) and Pekingese Syllabary*] He is now working on the revision of the Old Testament in Chinese. Mrs. Sarah Boardman (Clapp) Goodrich is General Secretary for China for the Woman's Christian Temperance Union." (12/22/1912) Sarah B. Clapp was a missionary in China in 1879-1880 before she and Chauncey Goodrich were married.
- Miss Edith E. **Gumbrell**, in China studying the language; resided in Presbyterian West Suburb of Paotingfu. (5/8/1910)
- Mr. Arthur M. and Mrs. Myrtle (Chaney) **Guttery**, Language School; stationed in Peking. (4/6/1914)

[H]
- Josef Washington **Hall** (b.1894-d.1960) [see Upton Close]
- Mr. Raymond S. and Mrs. Margaret **Hall**, of Tientsin, attended the Clack-Gordon wedding. (3/21/1911 / photo)
- Dr. and Mrs. **Hart**, founders of the Anglo-Chinese College in Tientsin about 1902; left China in 1912 due to health concerns. (3/12/1912)
- Mr. and Mrs. Charles Way **Harvey**, National Secretary for North China (Y.M.C.A., Tientsin). Had to go home in March 1914 because of their health. (4/10/1910)
- Frances **Harvey** (child), of Tientsin (possibly a daughter of Charles W. Harvey of the Tientsin Y.M.C.A.) – attended the Clack-Gordon wedding. (3/21/1911 / photo)
- Mr. L. Newton **Hayes**, of Tientsin – attended the Clack-Gordon wedding. (3/21/1911 / photo)
- Mr. **Herman**, business manager of the hospital. He was a Hungarian citizen. (7/9/1918)
- Mr. Roscoe M. and Mrs. Grace (Baird) **Hersey**, of Tientsin – one of the Y.M.C.A. secretaries (from Syracuse University); attended the Clack-Gordon wedding. (5/1/1910 / photo) Their son, John Hersey, born 1914 in Tientsin, became a famous American author.
- Major **Horsfull**, the American Legation, from Grant County, Wisconsin. (5/16/1922)

- Rev. and Mrs. Horace W. **Houlding**, Congregational clergyman and founders of the South Chihli Mission, a nondenominational mission founded in 1896 in Chihli (now Hebei) Province. (11/22/1918) Elma Gordon and daughter Edith had known them in San Francisco, California.
- Mr. Beltran C. and Mrs. Constance (Foster) **Hubbard**. Two of their children (Beltran Jr. and Marjorie) are in the Thanksgiving party photograph on page 263. (3/24/20)
- Mr. Hugh W. and Mrs. Mabel (Ellis) **Hubbard** (American Board Mission/South Suburb); formerly P.E. director of Tientsin Y.M.C.A. (going home in 1910 for three years to take a seminary course) – Congregational Church members; married in 1912. (8/7/1910) Hugh W. Hubbard was a second-generation missionary; he was born in Sivas in what is now Turkey, where his father, Albert W. Hubbard, was a missionary for the American Board of Commissioners for Foreign Missions during the late 19th century. Mabel Ellis was a missionary in China for several years before she and Hugh Hubbard were married.

[J]

- Ernest **Jaqua**, born in 1882, was a graduate of Iowa College; he and Rob would have known one another there. He was the person who recommended that Rob investigate the teaching position in China. (2/5/1910) Jaqua went on to Columbia University and then received a Ph.D. from Harvard. In 1926 he was appointed first president of Scripps College (California); served until 1942.
- Dr. **Jee**, of Tientsin, "an American born and trained Chinese", one of two physicians with the athlete group at the Far Eastern Olympian Championship Games in Manila. (5/7/1919)
- Mr. Edward C. **Jenkins**, business manager of the International Y.M.C.A. office in New York City, visited Y.M.C.A. stations in China to review how things could be improved. (5/17/1914)

[K]

- Miss Lillian H. **Keyes**, a Presbyterian in Paotingfu studying Chinese language. (5/8/1910)
- Rev. Charles A. and Mrs. Louise (Scott) **Killie**, missionaries from the American Presbyterian Mission (Paotingfu via Tientsin). Sent home in April 1912 due to ill health [Charles died in America in 1916]. He took photographs in 1900 of the Boxer siege in Peking. (4/14/1912) He was "one of the 'Six Fighting Parsons' of the Peking Siege in 1900" (keeping fortifications built up). (8/17/1913) His photographs can be viewed at "hpcbristol.net" (search: Killie), the University of Bristol, England.
- Mr. Samuel S. **Knabenshue** (the American General Consul in Tientsin) – official witness for the Clack-Gordon wedding per Certificate of Marriage. (3/21/1911 / photos 1911 and 1912)
- Mr. W. Percy **Knight** from Pingyangfu in Shansi, "a great friend of both Karl and Moore Gordon (Edith's brothers). He is an Englishman, belongs to the China Inland Mission, but spends all his time traveling around and training Bible teachers. He was pastor of a church in New York for four or five years and married a Canadian woman." (6/1/1913)

[L]

- Mrs. (nee Bonsquet) **LaForce**, 1916 Grinnell College graduate; attended Grinnell picnic in Peitaiho in August 1918. (8/2/1918)
- Dr. and Mrs. Charles **Lewis**, (A.M., M.D.) Dr. Lewis was a medical missionary from the American Presbyterian Mission (Paotingfu via Tientsin). He established a hospital in Paotingfu and was Superintendent and General Surgeon at the hospital. His wife, Mrs. Cora "Carrie" (Savage) Lewis was Superintendent of Nurses and spent a total of 32 years in missionary work

in China. They and their children, John and Anne, lived in the Presbyterian West Suburb. (5/8/1910 / photo in group 1912)
- Ida **Lewis**, of the Methodist mission of Tientsin. She was the daughter of Bishop Lewis. (8/13/1913)
- Bishop Wilson S. **Lewis** "preached here (Peitaiho) September 7, 1913. He was the founder of Morningside College (Methodist; Sioux City, Iowa) and is now Bishop of Foochow." (9/8/1913)
- John B. **Lord**, "the man who pays my [Y.M.C.A.] salary"; chairman of the board of the Ayer & Lord Railroad Tie Company, was a member of the board of the Presbyterian Hospital, the Chicago Orphan Asylum, the Sunday Evening Club, and the central committee of the Y.M.C.A. (2/15/1914)
- Reverend Dr. James W. **Lowrie**, D.D., head of the Presbyterian Mission; born in China, educated at Princeton College and Seminary, and in 1894 went to serve in Paotingfu. He was the bachelor son of Mrs. Amelia Lowrie; both were buried in Baoding Martyrs' Cemetery. (5/8/1910)
- Mrs. Amelia (Tuttle) **Lowrie** (1833-1907) – widow of Rev. Reuben Lowrie, missionary in Shanghai; mother of Dr. James Lowrie. (4/24/1911)
- Reverend Henry W. **Luce** was a Presbyterian missionary who was stationed at Tengchow, Weihsien, and several other places in North China. (6/18/1911) He was the father of Henry R. Luce (born in Tengchow), the co-founder of *Time* magazine and head of the Time/Life/Fortune publishing empire.
- D. Willard **Lyon**, secretary of the Peking Y.M.C.A. (4/10/1910)

[M]

- Mr. Paul and Mrs. Helen **MacEachion**, 1909 Grinnell College graduate; attended Grinnell picnic in Peitaiho in August 1918. (8/2/1918)
- Miss Marian G. **MacGown**, of Tientsin, – "she is to live with Mrs. Gordon" – attended the Clack-Gordon wedding. (3/21/1911 / photo)
- Dr. Maud A. **Mackey**, living in the Presbyterian or West Suburb; a single woman at the head of the women's hospital in Paotingfu. (5/8/1910)
- Miss Drusie Rubelt **Malott**, "who belongs to a mission in southern Honan (Pi Yang Hsien) has been in Tientsin all fall and winter, but is just returning to her station, and being an old friend of Edith's, stopped off over Sunday with us." (2/15/1914). "She came to China in the same party that Karl [Edith's brother] came in in 1904. She came as a stenographer to Mr. Houlding … ." (11/22/1918)
- Dr. W.A.P. **Martin**, "who has been in China longer than any other foreigner now out here and a number of others"; attended the American College Club banquet in Peking. (4/22/1912)
- Rev. Wm. Arnot and Mrs. Grace (Burroughs) **Mather**, missionaries, their son Brewster, and Mrs. Mather's mother (Mrs. Catherine E.L. Burroughs), all live in the Presbyterian West Suburb in 1910. (5/8/1910 and 10/6/1913) In a visitors book on October 1913, Mrs. Burroughs indicated her address was Brooklyn, N.Y.
- Mr. and Mrs. C.H. **McCoy**, of the Standard Oil Company, moved into the house in the American Board Compound that the Clack family had lived in previously. (7/9/1918)
- Dr. Josiah Calvin **McCracken**, a medical missionary and educator in China from 1906 to 1942; was chief surgeon of St. Luke's Hospital in Shanghai. Involved in athletics, he was an All-

- American guard (football), and one-time holder of World's record in the hammer throw. (5/7/1919) According to R.W. Clack's letter of 4/14/20 – He "is a special pal of mine".
- Mr. **Messer**, of the Chicago Association; led the Y.M.C.A. Conference in Peking, 1914. (3/30/1914)
- Rev. James Albert and Mrs. Mary Agnes (McGaw) **Miller**, American Presbyterian Mission in Shuntehfu, Chihli Province. (4/22/1911)
- Thornton **Mills**, American soldier, 15th Infantry, Co. D., stationed in Tientsin, early 1912; became a close friend of the Clacks. (2/18/1912 / photo)
- John R. **Mott** (born 1865) was an evangelist and long-serving leader of the Y.M.C.A. and the World Student Christian Federation (WSCF). (1/14/1913) He received the Nobel Peace Prize in 1946 for his work in establishing and strengthening international Protestant Christian student organizations that worked to promote peace.
- Mr. and Mrs. **Murray** of the International Committee of the Y.M.C.A. (11/20/1921)

[N]

- Mr. and Mrs. (Katherine) **Nowack**, residents of Pi Yang Hsien, Honan. (11/26/1913)

[P]

- Mr. **Palmer**, "… formerly in the Normal College; now one of the Salt Commissioners." (11/17/1914)
- Miss Martha (Moffett) **Paxton**, Presbyterian missionary to China about 1916 to 1932. (6/2/1914)
- Major W.C. **Philoon**, U.S. Army military attaché of the American Legation in Peking. He took the photographs during the Tuchuns' War in July 1920. (8/1/1920)
- Rev. Francis M. and Mrs. Sarah Jane **Price**, missionaries, "are to be in the American Board/South Suburb this winter [1912-13]. We are so glad as we like them so much." (9/16/1912) Sarah died in 1916. Rev. Price married Mrs. Jennie E. Reeves in 1919; they left China in 1926 (he was 74).
- Fredrick **Pyke**, Tientsin Methodist Mission, married Frances L. **Taft** of the Y.W.C.A. (8/10/1914)

[R]

- Alice **Reed**, Peking Presbyterian Mission (1/3/1916) and 1913 Grinnell College graduate; attended Grinnell picnic in Peitaiho in August 1918. (8/2/1918)
- Dr. Paul S. **Reinsch**, American Ambassador to China; guest of honor in 1913 American College banquet. (11/17/1913) Dedicated the new Y.M.C.A. building location. (Y.M.C.A. Report 1917)
- Miss **Reyes**, Presbyterian Mission in Paotingfu. (8/7/1910)
- Mr. C. H. **Robertson**, travelling lecturer for the Y.M.C.A. in China. (Y.M.C.A. Report 1914)
- Mr. H.W. and Mrs. Mary S. **Robinson** – "new people to live in Galt's house" in the South Suburb of Paotingfu. (9/26/1917)

[S]

- Mr. and Mrs. Rubert H. **Stanley** of the Y.M.C.A. in Tsinan, Shantung Province, East China. Edith helped nurse their sickly newborn baby in December 1913. (12/22/1913)
- Emma Florence **Steel**, teacher in Tientsin, from England; (per Rob, "lived with the Gordons at Peitaiho last summer"); at the Clack-Gordon wedding. (3/21/1911 / photo) A good friend of Edith's mother, after moving back to England she corresponded with Edith Clack for decades.
- Mr. Alfred H. **Swan**, Y.M.C.A. National Physical Director in Shanghai 1913-17. (4/12/1919)

[T]
- Rev. Edward W. **Thwing**, head of the Chinese Reform League (the International Reform Bureau at Peking). (8/7/1910)

[V]
- Mr. **Verink**, Y.M.C.A. secretary in Kirin, North China. (10/25/1920)

[W]
- Dr. Frederick J. and Mrs. Rebecca (Skeggs) **Wampler** "…are Virginians and he just graduated from Rush last spring and has been appointed doctor for the Dunkard Mission at Pingtingchou over in Shansi. Doing an internship with Dr. Lewis in Paotingfu". (11/17/1914)
- Dr. W.D. **Weatherford**, of Nashville, Tennessee, "formerly of Vanderbilt University but now traveling secretary for the South for the Y.M.C.A. was in Paotingfu [on November 18, 1912], on a trip around the world he is making". (11/24/1912)
- Mr. Albert K. and Mrs. Marion D. (Oskamp) **Whallon**, joined the College, fall 1911. He was a Rhodes Scholar, and played on the Oxford tennis team. They lived in the house Mr. Killie used to have in the Presbyterian West Suburb. (9/8/1912)
- Mr. Hollis A. **Wilbur** of the Shanghai Y.M.C.A. accompanied Mr. Jenkins of the International Y.M.C.A. of New York City during a visit to Paotingfu. (5/17/1914)
- Mr. Amos Parker **Wilder**, American Consul-General, ABCFM of Peking, spoke to student gathering at Chihli Provincial College, June 15, 1912, regarding "good government". He also spoke in November about Bible study. (6/16/1912 / photo July 1912)
- Miss Kate B. **Winterbotham**, of Tientsin, – "a very sweet old lady who has a little school next door to where the Gordons lived" – attended the Clack-Gordon wedding. (3/21/1911 / photo)

Chinese with the Y.M.C.A. in Paotingfu

April 28, 1913 letter:
"Yesterday the '**Chihli Provincial Capitol Y.M.C.A.**' was organized with 23 charter members, 4 Americans and 19 Chinese. There are about ten more who want to join immediately but were unable to attend yesterday. **Dr. Chêng**, the head of the Paotingfu Military Hospital is president; **Mr. Cunningham** is vice-president; **Mr. Sun**, the Chinese pastor of the Congregational church is recording secretary; I am corresponding secretary, **Mr. Hu**, the district Postal Inspector is treasurer; and **Mr. Ting**, formerly head of the American Board Boys School, has been asked to become regular secretary giving all his time to the work."

- **H. L. Sun** (Paotingfu, local), Chinese pastor of Congregational Church; recording secretary of first Y.M.C.A. Board in 1913. (3/30/1914)
- **Dr. T.K. Fu**, member of Y.M.C.A. (Y.M.C.A. Report 1919)
- **Dr. and Mrs. Chêng**, head of Paotingfu Military Hospital; president of first Y.M.C.A. Board in 1913. (4/28/1913)
- **Mr. Ch'eng Hu and Mrs. Hu**, District Postal Inspector; treasurer of first Paotingfu Y.M.C.A. Board in 1913. Mr. Hu was educated at Boone College, Wuch'ang. He was up at Ch'engtu in Ssǔch'uan for several years and there was treasurer of the Ch'engtu Y.M.C.A., the strongest in China. (2/16/1913 / photo) [departed in 1913 for Shuntêfu]

- **Mr. Ting**, formerly head of American Board Boys School; regular secretary of first Y.M.C.A. board in 1913. (1/14/1913)
- **Chang P'ei Chih**, "Chinese secretary of the Peking Y.M.C.A. was here over Sunday to give a lecture and stayed with us. … speaks the purest kind of Pekingese." (11/17/1913)

Y.M.C.A. Staff 1915-17
- **Mr. Shih Ch'ing**, first trained Chinese secretary at Paotingfu. (Y.M.C.A. Report 1915)
- **Mr. Huang**, added as educational director in 1917. (Y.M.C.A. Report 1917)

Chinese – Y.M.C.A. Paotingfu Board of Directors, 1919 (beginning on page 212)
- **Mr. Wang Tzu Yu**, President – Superintendent of language study of the American Board Missionaries.
- **Dr. Wang Tzu Ming**, Vice President – Head of Chinese staff in the Presbyterian Hospital.
- **Dr. Hu Chen Sheng**, Secretary – Doctor and proprietor of one of the leading drug stores in Paotingfu.
- **Mr. Jen Shou Peng**, Director – Principal of American Board boys' school.
- **Mr. Yang Wei Min**, Director – Teacher at the American Board boys' school.
- **Dr. Pan Wu Liu**, Director – prominent physician
- **Mr. Liu Kuo Chu**, Staff –American Board Mission, in charge of the new Y.M.C.A. Boys' Department.
- **Major Li**, teacher in the Military College; elected to Y.M.C.A. Board.

Chinese – not Y.M.C.A. affiliated (listed by date they were mentioned in the Clack letters)
- **Lao Tsung**, servant in Long and Clack house. (5/1/1910)
- **Li Chên**, table-boy in Long and Clack house. (5/8/1910)
- **Li Chang**, brother to Li Chen; was table-boy for Clacks. (5/8/1910)
- **Chang Po Lin**, a Christian, the head of the Private Middle School in Tientsin, "… was forced to head the student movement" on behalf of the students, to call Parliament to meet and resolve encroachments of Japan and Russia in Manchuria. (12/25/1910)
- **T'ang Shao I**, the Premier, "had just come back from Shanghai that day, so was unable to attend the April 1912 banquet in Peking". (1/9/1912) Later he was forced to resign his position.
- **Mr. Li**, new President of Chihli Provincial College in 1911; in mid-1912, he became President and director of the Paotingfu Normal School. (3/31/1912)
- **S.K. Alfred Sze**, the Chinese Minister of Communications, attended the American College Club banquet in Peking. (4/22/1912)
- **W.W. Yen**, the Chinese Minister of Justice, attended the American College Club banquet in Peking. (4/22/1912)
- **Dr. Wu Lien Lê**, "who has just returned from the Hague where he was the Chinese representative at the Opium Congress" attended the American College Club banquet. (4/22/1912)

- **General and Mrs. Chang** "came to visit with us over Sat. night (Nov. 1, 1913). He is the President of the National Anti-Opium Society. He came down [from Peking] to lecture for the Y.M.C.A. so of course they stopped here." (11/3/1913)
- **Mr. Kwong**, Edith's mother, Elma Gordon, chaperoned his children to the U.S. (3/14/1915)
- **Mr. Yung T'ao**, famous merchant and philanthropist in Peking, and former Confucianist who purchased and oversaw the distribution of 5,000 Bibles. (Y.M.C.A. Report 1916)
- **Mr. C.T. Wang** (teaching Chinese language to the Clacks), one of the College secretaries; "a close personal friend. He was in the Y.M.C.A. for a long time …". (2/22/1919)
- **Chu En Tê**, a student at the Peking Normal School, went with the athlete group and participated in the Far Eastern Olympic Championship Games in Manila. He won and set records in both the pentathlon and decathlon (5/24/1919)
- **Ts'ou Hsi**, athlete who converted to Christianity (Y.M.C.A. Report 1919)

Nurses who assisted with birth of Douglas Clack (see Edith's letter 11/22/1918)
- **Miss Sun** – will graduate from Peking Medical School.
- **Miss Lee** – maternity nurse; married pastor of one of the Presbyterian Mission churches.
- **Miss Lin** – Dr. Mackey's right-hand medical assistant.
- **Miss Chang** – nurse

Chinese Military Leaders and Politicians
- **T'ang Shaoyi**, first "Premier" of Republic of China for three months (1/9/1912)
- **Dr. Sun Yat Sen**, born 1866; appointed Provisional President of the newly established Republic of China in 1912; "Last Tuesday … passed through Paotingfu". (9/22/1912 / photo)
- **Huang Hsing**, a Chinese revolutionary leader; first commander-in-chief of the Republic of China under Sun Yat Sen. (8/17/1913)
- **Yüan Shih K'ai**, born 1859 (also referred to as Yüan Kung Pao; "Kung Pao" is an honorary title given him by the old Empress Dowager meaning "Guardian of the Palace"); established an efficient army and provincial government in North China before 1911, became first president of the Republic of China in 1912. (2/15/1914)
- **Chang Hsǔn**, Manchu military general. (2/15/1914)
- **Hsü Shih Ch'ang**, inaugurated as the new president of the Republic of China on the seventh anniversary of the beginning of the Revolution. (10/10/1918)
- **Governor-General Ts'ao K'un** – warlord, politician, and military leader of the Zhili Clique; also President of the Republic of China 1923-24. (10/10/1918)
- **Bai Lang ("White Wolf")**, bandit during the rebellion from mid-1913 to late 1914. (2/15/1914)
- **General Wu P'ei-fu**, military leader (Y.M.C.A. Report 1919)
  Wu Peifu or Wu P'ei-fu (1874-1939), was a major figure in the struggles among the warlords who dominated Republican China from 1916-27.
- **General Ch'ü T'ung-Feng**, stationed in Hunan; "started an evangelistic campaign among his men". (8/1/1920)

- **General Feng Yü Hsiang** (Yuxiang), new Governor in 1921 of Shensi (Shaanxi), referred to as the "Christian General" – a friend of R.W. Clack. (Y.M.C.A. Report 1919)
- **General Hsiao**, new governor of Hupei (in 1921) "is a friend of mine". (9/2/1921)
- **Chang Tso Lin**, the "uncrowned king of Manchuria", "has advanced a lot of his troops into Chihli Province" causing residents to be under martial law. (4/19/1922)
- **Li Yüan Hung**, born 1864; military governor of Hubei province after 1911 revolution; President of the Republic of China 1916-17; restored to presidency 1922. (5/16/1922)
- **Empress Dowager Longyu**, born in 1868, her personal name was Jingfen. She was a member of the Manchu Yehe Nara clan. In 1889, she was chosen as the Empress Consort because her aunt, the (old) Empress Dowager Cixi (who subsequently died in 1908), wanted to strengthen the power of the Yehe Nara clan within the imperial family. Jingfen married the Guangxu Emperor on February 26, 1889, and became his Empress directly after the wedding ceremony. She became Empress Dowager and was de facto regent of China from her husband's death in 1908, when her adopted son, the child Puyi (1906-1967) (known as the Last Emperor of China) was emperor until the office of emperor was officially abolished in 1911. However, the imperial family continued to enjoy their titles, to reside in the Forbidden City, and run it as if they still held power. Empress Dowager Longyu was 45 years old when she died on February 22, 1913. (funeral matshed photo – page 135)

GLOSSARY 3

Annotations for Family Members in the Clack Letters

Robert Wood Clack (1886-1964)

Father –	Dr. William Rollinson Clack (1852-1932)
Mother –	Sarah Adda "Addie" (Wood) Clack (1854-1942)
Sisters –	Ida (1884-1974)
	Edna Ann "Nan" (1888-1981)
	Celia (1891-1961) – married Melville P. Hughes

Edith (Gordon) Clack (1888-1972)

Father –	William Gordon (1857-1947) – separated from family in 1891
Mother –	Elma (Butler) Gordon (1859-1938)
Brothers –	Karl (1882-1955)
	Clark (1884-1954)
	Moore (1887-1969)

Half-sister (father's second marriage) – Elizabeth (Gordon) Myers (1899-1968)

Clack family (Robert's parents and siblings), 1917
(L-R standing) Celia; Edna Ann "Nan"; Robert; Ida
(L-R seated) William R. (father); Adda (mother)

Edith's mother, 1915
Elma (Butler) Gordon
(born 1859, Iowa)

Edith's brothers
photo above – San Francisco, 1925

(left) **Karl M. Gordon**
(b. Missouri, 1882; married to Mabel)
In 1925 was returning to the U.S. after living in China for 15 years employed in a variety of work for Christian missions.

(middle) **W. Clark Gordon**
(b. Missouri, 1884; married to Ethel)
In 1925 was residing in San Francisco where he was self-employed as an optometrist.

(right) **S. Moore Gordon**
(b. Chicago, 1887; married to Jessie)
In 1925 was on his way back to China where he had been employed in teaching and Christian-related work for a total of 14 non-consecutive years

Asenath (Draper) Butler, 1920
Elma's mother / Edith's grandmother
(born 1836, Indiana)

FAMILY OF ROBERT AND EDITH CLACK

K.D. Gordon Clack (b. 1913 in China), wife Spray
    Children: Robert, Barbara
Constance Elizabeth (Clack) Fisher (b. 1915 in China), husband F. McCracken "Mac" Fisher
    Children: Gordon, Margaret, Lawrence
Robert William Douglas Clack (b. 1918 in China), wife LaNelle
    Daughter: Janet
Hugh Llywelyn "Lee" Clack (b. 1921 in China), wife Ann
    Children: Bruce, Scott, Kimi (adopted), Mariko (adopted)
Roderick Whittier Clack (b. 1924 in Iowa, USA), wife Marjorie
    Daughters: Katherine (Marjorie's daughter), Theresa
Wynne Rollinson Clack (b. 1925 in Michigan, USA), wife Barbara
    Children: Norma, David

Clack Family Reunion, 1950, Alma, Michigan
Back Row: Douglas, Ann (Lee's wife), Lee (son Bruce on his shoulders),
Gordon, Spray (Gordon's wife), Mac Fisher (Connie's husband), Rod
Middle row: Rob, Edith, Connie, Wynne, Barbara (Wynne's wife), Marjorie (Rod's wife)
Children in front: Norma Clack, Peggy Fisher, Gordon Fisher, Bob Clack, Barbara Clack

INFORMATION FROM YIDING GAO, A RESIDENT OF CHINA

Robert Clack written in Chinese (1910) – "A Gentleman from Afar"

This photo has your Grandfather's Chinese name written in it; I can now confirm that he used this kind of writing at that time "柯兰客（柯蘭客". The pronunciation of Chinese is "Ke Lan Ke".

At that time, there was no completely unified translation method, many foreigners would form their own Chinese names according to the pronunciation of their names and then find Chinese characters with similar pronunciations. These Chinese characters also generally have better meanings, not just simple similar pronunciations. Just like your grandfather's Chinese name, "柯(Ke)", it is a wooden name and also a surname of China. "蘭(Lan)" is the name of a flower.

In China, people think that this kind of remark symbolizes the moral character of a gentleman. And "客(Ke)", is the meaning of guests or people from afar. So put them together, the name means "a gentleman from afar".

Source: Yiding Gao, e-mail of July 14, 2018

On the following pages are photo images from Yiding Gao showing a comparison between R.W. Clack's early 20th Century snapshots and Yiding Gao's current day photographs of the same location.

Peking, Forbidden City. Photos 1912 and 2017.

The building is now the Chairman Mao Memorial Hall.

Summer Palace Central Tower, Peking.

Photos comparing 1914 and 2018.

First Gate in the San-yi Temple (photo 2018)

"Squadron of Wu's Cavalry Resting in a Temple just Back of the Lines"
(photo July 1920, taken by Major W.C. Philoon)

Second Gate in San-yi Temple (photo 2018)

"A Company from the Third Division – Wu's Personal Command"
(photo 1920, taken by Major W.C. Philoon)

ENDNOTES

Front Pages

p.xvi [1] Chinese Dragon (historical interpretation for photo image).
Chinese Dragon; en.wikipedia.org.

Part One (Chapters 1–12)

p.5 [1] Brief description of Paotingfu, North China.
Baoding; en.wikipedia.org.

p.31 [2] Explanation of the Boxer Rebellion.
Boxer Rebellion; en.wikipedia.org.

p.34 [3] Presbyterian Missionaries who died in Paotingfu during the Boxer Rebellion.
Presbyterian Heritage Center. 2007. Website: phcmontreat.org/BoxerRebellion.

p.36 [4] Mrs. Cora Savage (biographical summary).
Cora Estelle Savage Lewis. Website: findagrave.com/memorial.

p.55 [5] Empress Dowager Longyu (death and burial).
Empress Dowager Longyu; en.wikipedia.org.

p.76 [6] Gate of China (updated caption for photo image).
Gate of China, Beijing; en.wikipedia.org.

p.78 [7] Legation Quarter in Peking (brief explanation).
Beijing Legation Quarter; en.wikipedia.org.

p.83 [8] Dr. Charles W. Eliot (biographical summary).
Charles William Eliot; en.wikipedia.org.

p.113 [9] Dr. Sun Yat Sen (selected biographical details).
Sun Yat-sen; en.wikipedia.org.

p.125 [10] Temple of Heaven (brief explanation).
Temple of Heaven; en.wikipedia.org.

Part Two (Chapters 13–25)

p.143 [1] Y.M.C.A. History.
Kautz Family YMCA Archives – University of Minnesota

p.144 [2] Clack, Robert Wood, Secretary, YMCA, Paotingfu, China. Annual Report 1913.
YMCA Archives – U. of Minn.

p.163 [3] Clack, R.W., Secretary, YMCA, Paotingfu, China. Annual Report 1914.
YMCA Archives – U. of Minn.

p.173 [4] Clack, R.W., Secretary, YMCA, Paotingfu, China. Annual Report 1915.
YMCA Archives – U. of Minn.

p.187 [5] Clack, R.W., Secretary, YMCA, Paotingfu, China. Annual Report 1916.
YMCA Archives – U. of Minn.

p.191 [6] Clack, R.W., Secretary, YMCA, Paotingfu, China. Annual Report 1917.
YMCA Archives – U. of Minn.

p.198 [7] Clack, R.W., Secretary, YMCA, Paotingfu, China. Annual Report 1918.
YMCA Archives – U. of Minn.

p.213 [8] Olympic Games in China (early history).
Hong, Fan. 2005. Sports in Society, Vol.8, 2005–Issue 3, 392-403.

p.211 [9] Clack, R.W., Secretary, YMCA, Paotingfu, China. Annual Report 1919.
YMCA Archives – U. of Minn.

p.214 [10] Clack, R.W., Secretary, YMCA, Paotingfu, China. Annual Report (Vol. II).
YMCA Archives – U. of Minn.

p.218 [11] May Fourth Incident (student riots) in Peking.
May Fourth Movement; en.wikipedia.org.

p.244 [12] Description of friendship between R.W. Clack and Josef Washington Hall ("Upton Close").
Close, Upton. 1924. *In the Land of the Laughing Buddha*, G.P. Putnam's Sons, N.Y. and London, 287, 288, 301.

p.248 [13] Ts'ao K'un (selected biographical details)
General Cao Kun; en.wikipedia.org.

p.248 [14] Description of earthquake felt in Paotingfu on December 15, 1920
Earthquakes of the World; en.wikipedia.org.

p.257 [15] Clack, R.W., Secretary, YMCA, Paotingfu, China. Annual Report 1920-21.
YMCA Archives – U. of Minn.

p.263 [16] Bubble Books-Records for children.
O'Dell, Cary. *The First "Bubble Book" (1917) Essay.* National Registry, Library of Congress. 2003.

p.272 [17] Clack, R.W., Clear Lake, Iowa, March 31, 1924. Administrative Report 1923.
YMCA Archives – U. of Minn.

Part Three (Iowa and Michigan, 1924-1964)

p.275 [1] Robert Clack was a "teacher at heart".
Greenhoe, Rev. Dr. T.M. Funeral service. Dec. 17, 1964. Memorial Presbyterian Church. Midland, Michigan.

p.276 [2] Review of R.W. Clack's book of translated Chinese poetry.
Beck, Clyde. Nov. 10, 1934. Books and Authors, *Detroit News*.

p.276 [3] Review of R.W. Clack's book of translated Chinese poetry.
Close, Upton. 1934. *From Bamboo Glade and Lotus Pool*, by Robert Wood Clack. Banner Press at Emory University. Foreword, 6.

p.277 [4] "The Old Trysting Place by LI PO (705-762), Tang Dynasty", published translated poem.
Kaleidograph, Oct. 1936, Dallas, Texas.

p.278 [5] List of periodicals in which translated poems were published.
Within Our Bounds: A Centennial History of Alma College. 1986. Alma College, 85, 88.

p.279 [6] Prof. Clack, one of the "Giants of the Middle Years (1920-1940)".
Within Our Bounds: A Centennial History of Alma College. 1986. Alma College, 76, 88.

p.279 [7] "Michigan on a Chopstick" proving St. Louis, Michigan, is the "Middle of the Mitten".
Saginaw News. July 19, 1955. Saginaw, Michigan.

p.280 [8] Robert and Edith Clack 50th Wedding Anniversary article.
Midland Daily News. March 21, 1961. Midland, Michigan.

p.281 [9] Some of R.W. Clack's poems read at his funeral service.
Greenhoe, Rev. Dr. T.M. Dec. 17, 1964. Funeral service. Memorial Presbyterian Church. Midland, Michigan.

Epilogue

p.283   [1] Review of R.W. Clack's book of translated Chinese poetry.
         Mulder, Arnold. Dec. 17, 1934. Library Adventures. *Kalamazoo Gazette*. (Kalamazoo, Michigan)

p.284   [2] Text and poem "Two Flutes (by Li Po)".
         Clack, Robert W. 1977. *The Herd Boy and the Weaver Maid: A Collection of Chinese Love Songs Translated into English Verse*. Copyright Alma College. Gordon Press, 134.

p.285   [3] Text and poem "Lonesome (by Wang Po)".
         Clack, Robert W. 1978. *Millenniums of Moonbeams: An Historical Anthology of Chinese Classical Poetry, 3 volumes*. Copyright Alma College. Gordon Press, 235-6.

p.285   [4] Text and poem "Poem from the Manyoshu (Seventh Century, Anonymous)".
         Clack, Robert W. 1978. *The Soul of Yamato: An Historical Anthology of Japanese Poetry, 2 volumes*, Copyright Alma College. Gordon Press, iv and 37.

p.286   [5] Text from Chapter I, "History and Theory of Chinese Music".
         Clack, Robert W. 1976. *Celestial Symphonies: A Study of Chinese Music*, Copyright Alma College. Gordon Press, 1, 4.

p.289   [6] Description of the Clack Art Center on the campus of Alma College.
         From the Alma College official website. http://www.alma.edu.

Appendix

p.295   [1] Background of the Revolution of 1911.
         John K. Fairbank, Edwin O. Reischauer, and Albert M. Craig, *East Asia: The Modern Transformation*, Boston, Houghton Mifflin Company, 1965, chapters 5 and 8; *1911 Revolution* and *Railway Protection Movement*; en.wikipedia.org.

p.296   [2-7] Descriptions of selected places and organizations in China in the early 20th century:
         Ch'ing (now Qing) Dynasty
         Republic of China
         Paotingfu (now Baoding), China
         Chihli Provincial College in Paotingfu, Chihli Province, China
         Military College in Paotingfu, China
         American Board of Commissioners for Foreign Missions (A.B.C.F.M.)
             en.wikipedia.org.

p.297   [8] Description of the Y.M.C.A. in China.
         Kautz Family YMCA Archives – University of Minnesota

p.297   [9-11] Descriptions of selected places and organizations in China in the early 20th century:
         Wo Fo Ssŭ (Sleeping Buddha Temple)
         North China Athletic Federation Meet (Y.M.C.A. Report)
         Far Eastern Athletic Association/The Far Eastern Games (1919)
         Chinese Amateur Athletic Union (1922-1924)
             en.wikipedia.org.

BIBLIOGRAPHY

- Letters written by Robert W. and Edith Clack from China primarily to family members (1910-1924).

- Biographical sketch of Robert W. Clack in *Who's Who in Michigan* (1936 edition).

- Memoirs of Elma Butler Gordon, 1863-1928 (unpublished).

- Guest Book of Elma Butler Gordon, 1908-1920 (unpublished).

- Visitors Book of Robert W. and Edith Gordon Clack, 1910-1919 (unpublished).

- Boyd, Julia. *A Dance with the Dragon: The Vanished World of Peking's Foreign Colony,* I.B. Tauris & Co. Ltd., 2012.

- Chi, Tsui. *A Short History of Chinese Civilization.* G.P. Putnam's Sons, N.Y., 1943.

- Ebrey, Patricia Buckley. *The Cambridge Illustrated History of China*, Press Syndicate of the University of Cambridge, 1996.

- Ruoff, E.G. *Death Throes of a Dynasty: Letters and Diaries of Charles and Bessie Ewing, Missionaries to China*, the Kent State University Press, Kent, Ohio, 1990.

- Wright, Grace A. *Personal Letters from China 1919-1929 Hallie Cline (YMCA).* Self-published, 2011.

COPYRIGHT PERMISSION

Kautz Family YMCA Archives – University of Minnesota (obtained 2020)

Alma College Library (obtained 2020)

Yiding Gao (obtained 2020)

Smithsonian U.S. Copyright Office (obtained 2020)

PHOTOGRAPHY CREDITS

Reproduced in this book are 163 photographs taken by Robert W. Clack during his time in China (1910-1923). In addition, the following is a list of photographs from the Clack family personal albums that were taken by others as noted (if known). The captions (in bold type) that appear under each photograph are transcribed from R.W. Clack notes written on the back the photograph.

ii	Wedding of Robert Clack and Edith Gordon in Tientsin, China (1911)
iii	Camera, held by R.W. Clack at a track meet (1914)
v	Robert and Edith Clack in 1954 (family album)
v	Wynne Clack and "Prof" Clack in 1949 (family album)
xi	Memorial Hall in Paotingfu (2018 by Gao Yiding)
xvi	Image of one section of a four-dragon silk needlework (photo by Norma Clack, 2019)
3	On board ship (1910)
28	Clack-Gordon wedding party and guests (1911)
75	American College Club banquet / Paotingfu delegation, 1912 (family album)
92	R.W. Clack in Chinese robe, 1912 (probably taken by Edith Clack)
118	Chihli Provincial College faculty group (1912)
142	Non-Chinese teachers' group from Chihli Provincial College (1913)
169	White Marble Bridge in Peking / R.W. Clack in two photos, 1914 (Y.M.C.A. associate)
170	Y.M.C.A. Executive Committee / 2 group photos at conference (1914)
180	R.W. Clack and other Y.M.C.A. conference participants (1915)
182	Y.M.C.A. group at Shanghai conference (1915)
184	R.W. Clack and family photo for passport (1915)
189	Y.M.C.A. Secretaries and Board (2 photos, 1916)
190	Family photograph in California / Gordon-Clack families, August 1916 (family album)
195	Y.M.C.A. group photo of 27 individuals; Cleveland, Ohio office, 1916 or 1917 (family album)
196	William R. Clack family in Iowa, 1917 (family album)
226	R.W. Clack at Far Eastern Games, 1919 (family album)
240-4	8 photos "Tuchuns' War", 1920 (credit–Major W.C. Philoon, U.S. Army; prop. R.W. Clack)
274	Robert W. Clack family, 1923 (taken in China for passport)
275	William R. Clack family in Iowa, 1923 (family album)
278	R.W. Clack family reunion in Alma, Michigan, 1950 (family album)
280	Robert W. Clack "Michigan on a chopstick" (*Saginaw News* photo; July 17, 1955)
282	Robert Clack and Edith Clack in Chinese attire, about 1960 (studio photos)
286	Image of book cover (photo by Norma Clack, 2020)
290-2	Clack Chinese artifacts at Alma College (4 photos by Norma Clack, 2019)
309	William R. Clack family in Iowa, 1917 (family album)
310	E. Gordon (Cal., 1915), A. Butler (Cal., 1920), Gordon brothers (Cal., 1925) (family album)
311	Robert W. Clack family reunion in Alma, Michigan, 1950 (family album)
313-6	Current photos of China by Yiding Gao (2017-2018)
322	Norma Clack with grandfather, Robert Clack, 1957 (family album) and Norma Clack (First Presbyterian Church, Kalamazoo, Michigan, photographer, 2016)

Back Cover – Photographs taken in 2019 by Norma Clack of her collection
Top row (l–r):
  "Plum Blossom Chinese Lady" (element of 4-foot-high framed silk art work);
  Teacups from Qing Dynasty, porcelain (3.5" high); Brass bell (6.5" high) on wood stand (16" high).
Bottom row (l–r):
  Peacock feather and horsehair plume decoration for Court Hat, with jade holder (12");
  Ceramic glazed "Mud man" (10" high); Carved jade (3" high) on wood stand.

NORMA GERALDINE CLACK
Creator, Compiler, Editor

Norma is a native of Detroit, Michigan, and was raised in the Detroit metropolitan area. When she was a young girl, she always looked forward to her family's excursions to visit her Clack grandparents in Alma, Michigan. To her these visits were like taking an amazing trip to China, because their home was filled with countless artifacts which they had brought back from their years in China. Their visit always included homemade Chinese food, eaten with chopsticks. In between visits, Norma and her grandfather corresponded through letters – much the same as when he wrote from China to his family in Iowa.

During her college years, Norma moved to Saginaw, Michigan, where she married and gave birth to a daughter. While residing in Saginaw, she was employed for 30 years as an administrator in the Development Office at Saginaw Valley State University (SVSU). She earned a bachelor's degree in English from SVSU and a master's degree in educational administration from Central Michigan University.

During her career at SVSU, she gained experience in writing and designing of a variety of publications. In 2010 she moved across the state to Kalamazoo in order to live near her daughter's family. Post-retirement pursuits include oil painting, genealogy research, and writing essays about her ancestors. In 2018 she became a member of the Daughters of the American Revolution through her Clack lineage.

Norma with her grandfather, Robert Wood Clack (1957)

Made in the USA
Middletown, DE
13 November 2021